The Way of Torah

The Religious Life of Man Series
FREDERICK J. STRENG, *SERIES EDITOR*

Texts

Understanding Religious Life, Second Edition
    Frederick J. Streng

The House of Islam, Second Edition
    Kenneth Cragg

Japanese Religion: Unity and Diversity, Third Edition
    H. Byron Earhart

Chinese Religion: An Introduction, Third Edition
    Laurence G. Thompson

The Christian Religious Tradition
    Stephen Reynolds

The Buddhist Religion: A Historical Introduction, Third Edition
    Richard H. Robinson and Willard L. Johnson

The Way of Torah: An Introduction to Judaism, Third Edition
    Jacob Neusner

The Hindu Religious Tradition
    Thomas J. Hopkins

Native American Religions: An Introduction
    Sam D. Gill

Anthologies

The Chinese Way in Religion
    Laurence G. Thompson

Religion in the Japanese Experience: Sources and Interpretations
    H. Byron Earhart

The Buddhist Experience: Sources and Interpretations
    Stephan Beyer

The Life of Torah: Readings in the Jewish Religious Experience
    Jacob Neusner

Islam from Within: Anthology of a Religion
    Kenneth Cragg and R. Marston Speight

The Way of Torah
An Introduction to Judaism

THIRD EDITION

Jacob Neusner
Brown University

Wadsworth Publishing Company
Belmont, California
A Division of Wadsworth, Inc.

The Way of Torah: An Introduction to Judaism was edited
and prepared for composition by Kathleen J. Leahy.
Interior design was provided by Amato Prudente. The
cover was designed by Oliver Kline.

Library of Congress Cataloging in Publication Data

Neusner, Jacob, 1932–
    The way of Torah.

    (The Religious life of man)
    Bibliography: p.
    Includes index.
    1. Judaism.   I. Title.
BM580.N53   1979   296   78–31761

ISBN 0–87872–217–3

Printed in the United States of America
        3   4   5   6   7   8   9 — 83   82

For Ernest and Sarah Frerichs

Contents

Foreword   *ix*
Preface to the Third Edition   *xi*
Acknowledgments   *xvii*
Table of Dates   *xix*

PART ONE
The History and Definition of Judaism

1.   Prologue: In the Beginning   3
2.   The History of Judaism: The Three Periods   7
     The Biblical Period   7
     The Classical Period: Rabbinic Judaism   12
     The Modern Period   16
3.   Defining Judaism: The Jew and the Judaist   21

PART TWO
The Mythic Structure of Classical Judaism

4.   The Evidence   29
5.   Hear, O Israel   32
6.   Coming Together   37
7.   Going Forth   39
8.   The Only Kid and the Messiah   42
9.   The Land and Jerusalem   46

PART THREE
The Way of Torah: A Way of Living

10.   The Spirit of the Law   51
11.   Hear Our Prayer, Grant Us Peace   53

12. Sabbaths for Rest, Festivals for Rejoicing   58
13. Birth, Maturity, Death   64
14. The Center of Life: Study of Torah   66
15. The Rabbi and the School   70
16. The Philosopher   73
17. The Mystic   81
18. An Ordinary Man   87
19. Two Extraordinary Women   91

PART FOUR
Continuity and Change in Modern Times

20. The Historical Setting   99
21. For Some, the End of Traditional Society   104
22. Theology: Reform and Orthodoxy   110
23. Nationality and Peoplehood: Messianism and Zionism   116
24. Law and Ethics   120
25. Study of Torah and Modern Scholarship: *Yeshiva*,
    Seminary, and University   124
26. The Unbroken Myth   129

Notes   133
Glossary   140
Suggestions for Further Reading   146
Index   161

Foreword

The Religious Life of Man series is intended as an introduction to a large, complex field of inquiry—human religious experience. It seeks to present the depth and richness of religious concepts, forms of worship, spiritual practices, and social institutions found in the major religious traditions throughout the world.

As a specialist in the languages and cultures in which a religion is found, each author is able to illuminate the meanings of a religious perspective and practice in a community. To communicate this meaning to readers who have had no special training in these cultures and religions, the authors have attempted to provide clear, nontechnical descriptions and interpretations of religious life.

Different interpretive approaches have been used, depending upon the nature of the religious data; some religious expressions, for example, lend themselves more to developmental, others more to topical studies. But this lack of a single interpretation may itself be instructive, for the experiences and practices regarded as religious in one culture may not be the most important in another.

The Religious Life of Man is concerned with, on the one hand, the variety of religious expressions found in different traditions and, on the other, the similarities in the structures of religious life. The various forms are interpreted in terms of their cultural context and historical continuity, demonstrating both the diverse expressions and commonalities of religious traditions. Besides the single volumes on different religions, the series offers a core book on the study of religious meaning, which describes different study approaches and examines several modes and structures of religious awareness. In addition, each book presents a list of materials for further reading, including translations of religious texts and detailed examinations of specific topics.

During a decade of use the series has experienced a wide readership. A continuing effort has been made to update the scholarship, simplify the organization of material, and clarify concepts through the publication of revised editions. The authors have been gratified with the response to their efforts to introduce people to various forms of religious life. We hope readers will also find these volumes "Introductory" in the most significant sense: an introduction to a new perspective for understanding themselves and others.

Frederick J. Streng
Series Editor

Preface to the Third Edition

My main interests in this book are (1) to see Judaism as a whole, as a
system, and (2) to understand the principal epochs in the history of that
system, particularly the second and the third of the three epochs. I want
the student to know more than isolated facts about this holiday or that
custom. I want the student to know that within Judaism, holidays, beliefs,
practices, and ways of living and of shaping the life cycle all express a
single and whole conception of the world, of the human being, of the
character of humanity, and of the supernatural meaning of the Jewish people. For Judaism is not "this and that," but whole and encompassing—that
is, a mode of creating and of interpreting the world. It is a system of
holiness in which each and every element relates to all other elements, and
together they form a holy way of life and a holy world in time and beyond.
This particular mode of the sacred, moreover, is so shaped as to make
sense of and respond to the distinctive human situation of the Jewish people; hence, our attention focuses on the "ecology" of Judaism, a phrase I
shall define in a moment. I am certain that when students are able to enter
through their imaginations into the human situation of the Jews, they will
also grasp in some measure the human meaning of Judaism as a mode of
interpreting and shaping that human situation. Beyond that point, as students of religion, we cannot go. For that is the frontier between the realm
of interpretation and understanding, which belongs to us, and the kingdom of truth and faith, which belongs only to the Judaists, the believers
and practitioners of Judaism. The distinction between the Judaists and the
Jewish people (all those born of a Jewish mother or converted to Judaism)
becomes important at the end of Part I.

The changes in this third edition of *The Way of Torah* are important;
they reflect significant shifts in my own thinking about the character of
the history and structure of Judaism and the intellectual requirements of

the study of that subject. The new chapters—"The History of Judaism: The Three Periods," "The Mystic," and "Two Extraordinary Women"— and revisions and additions throughout the book show an opening toward a new range of questions and fresh approaches, about which I would like to add a word of explanation.

When I wrote this book in 1968, I was in a strongly negative frame of mind toward history. I had spent my whole adult life in that field and was just then making my break toward critical hermeneutics and the history of religions. As a result, I wanted to present a picture of Judaism essentially divorced from historical questions such as had occupied my *History of the Jews in Babylonia*. The move toward a different range of questions about literature and the structure of Judaism was completed in my *History of the Mishnaic Law of Purities*. Once I had perceived the central questions about the structure of Judaism and the capacity of that structure to respond to, and find a place within, the ecological system formed by the human situation of the Jewish people, I could once more entertain the prospect that history might have something to say. Still, I thought that history as presented by historians was intellectually bankrupt, and—the evidence being what it is in the field known as "Jewish history"—I hold the same opinion today.

It must be made clear, however, that structure without context—that is, the social and economic context defined by history—is insufficient either for description or for explanation. We may adequately describe a structure within the framework of religions and show how a system is constituted and how it functions. But without careful attention to the historical context in which a system functions, we cannot explain the way in which the system works. More importantly, we also cannot account for *changes* within the system itself. Consequently those structuralists (whom I admire and from whom I learn) who wish to provide systemic descriptions and analyses essentially outside the context of history and change seem to me to tell us something remarkably evanescent; they explain the condition of stasis in a world of change—that is, they explain a system for a single moment in its existence in its historical unfolding. True, the explanation is the thing, and out of structuralism come compelling explanations. But what is to be said of the explanation for the character of a system, when in yet a very little while the system undergoes modification and modulation? Surely the explanation offered to account for the character of the system must also change. This accounts for the ambivalent character of what follows. I try to describe and interpret the principal structure of Judaism; namely, the structure created on the foundations of Mishnah and Talmud and called rabbinic. But I also attempt to set that structure into the historical context of the life of the Jewish people from the first and second to the nineteenth and twentieth centuries and to relate structure to context. These are the considerations which account for the chapter on "ecology."

Obviously, by using the word *ecology*, borrowed from the natural sciences, I want to introduce an unusual metaphor into the study of religions. Ecology is a branch of science concerned with the interrelationship of organisms and their environments. By "ecology of religions" I mean the study of the interrelationship between a religious way of viewing the world and living life, and the historical and social situation of the people who view the world and live life in accord with the teachings of their religion. The Jewish people are a very small group, spread over many countries. One fact of their natural environment is that they form a distinct group in diverse societies. A second fact is that they constitute solely a faith-community in that they have few, if any, shared social or cultural traits. A third fact is that they look back upon an exceptionally long, and in some ways painful, history. A world view, to be suitable for the Jews, must make sense of their unimportance and explain their importance. It must deal with the issues of the long history of the group. Above all, it must make sense of the continuing life of the group, persuading people that their forming a distinct and distinctive community is important and worth carrying on. The interplay between the political, social, and historical life of the Jews and their conceptions of themselves in this world and under the aspect of God's will and Torah constitutes the focus for the inquiry—the "ecological" inquiry—that, I think, makes the study of Judaism accessible.

I may have made a mistake in introducing this metaphor—ecology of Judaism—into the intellectual framework of the book. But I think it is important to find language to focus upon the curious interplay between the history of Judaism and the history of the Jewish people and to do so without reducing the history of Judaism to a minor detail in the history of the Jewish people. Judaism cannot be studied, or even defined, outside the historical experience of the Jewish people. But it also cannot be studied solely within that experience—as if there is no such thing as Judaism, but merely the evanescent culture of the Jewish group. There *is* such a thing as Judaism, which may stand definition and analysis in the same way that any other religion may be defined and analyzed. Judaism is no less difficult to define and describe than any other religion. It holds no mysteries accessible only to people who originate in a Jewish family, and nothing about Judaism is inaccessible to the accepted methods and procedures of the academic study of religions. What is it, then, that makes Judaism especially interesting? In my judgment, it is that curious interplay between the social and historical environment of the Jews, on the one side, and the religious character of Judaism, on the other. The one defines the questions; the other answers them. In the interplay between question and answer is the work of ecology of religions—if, as I hope, I have not erred in converting to the present purpose a metaphor that may convey nothing but confusion. Time will tell.

What I am trying to do is to find my way between Jewish history which for a long time past has consisted merely in the discovery and recitation of facts (and which also expresses an irrelevant ideology of being Jewish), and those anthropologists and historians of religions who have taught me so much about the interpretation of facts, the description and analysis of systems, and the comparison of systems to systems, and of religions to religions. History presented by historians, even when they are literate (and few in Jewish history are), consists of accounts of one thing after another.

History of religions, applied to Judaism, yields vapid generalization and often is helpless in the face of contradictory facts. Anthropology of religions, not unlike history, provides us with interminable catalogs of trivia on the one side, and compelling and enduring explanations of a fleeting structure on the other. Between triviality and evanescent taxonomy divorced from all context (as between Mary Douglas and her critics) I prefer not to choose. Each side performs a magic of reductionism: the former, reduction of constants and structures to details and the latter, reduction of the flesh and blood of reality to neat matchboxes ("grid-group"). But if I must choose, let my lot be with the people who take seriously the ebb and flow of time and change; the others are reactionary. For all their talk of deep structure, their taxonomies are profoundly irrelevant to the encounter with the world of material reality and social being.

I must apologize to students for this reflection on what to me are very urgent issues, but what to you perhaps seem to emerge out of the opaque and unreal contentions of academic people. This book does make choices and does take stands on contended matters. Honesty surely requires me to say where I stand. Therefore I take my place wholly and fully under a strong light, even with imperfections of understanding clear to the naked eye. You can have interesting debates with your teachers and with me if you understand why I have done what I have done in this book. For there are choices. I made mine, and they make a difference.

I am totally unable to explain why, ten years ago, it did not seem to me so self-evident as it does now that serious attention should be paid to the role of women in Judaism. In this regard I have had the advantage of teaching many women students at Brown, who have instructed me in the intellectual range and concerns important to a perspective on women in the field of religions. In my teaching, long before now, I have tried to find appropriate units of study on the role and position of women in whatever theme or problem in Judaism was under analysis. The issue of women in Judaism now occupies the pride of place—the point at which we move from classical to modern times. The question of women's rights and responsibilities and women's own consciousness of their subordinated position has come to the fore and has become a principal expression of a new spirit. While I take pride in having encouraged many young women (and men) to take seriously careers of service in Judaism, I owe a special thanks to Naomi Janowitz and Margaret Wenig Rubenstein, who, as undergraduate students in my graduate seminar, taught me at least as much as I taught them. The graduate students with whom they studied went out of Brown with a deep respect for the field of women's studies and a hope to contribute in some small way to its literature when their own scholarship presents useful opportunities. This is because of the two delightful students just now mentioned. All of us are in their debt.

I have carefully corrected all sexist usages I could find in the earlier editions of this book. My friend and student, Alan Peck, did the same, and a third reader repeated the process. I hope that the basic language of the book has been brought into conformity with its purpose: to treat men and women as equals, and not to treat women as anomalies or as simply absent. I take pride in this effort, which has characterized my writing for some years now.

Besides this edition of *The Way of Torah*, new editions of textbooks I wrote on the eve of the 1970s have also gone to press. *There We Sat Down: Talmudic Judaism in the Making; American Judaism: Adventure in Modernity; An Anthological Essay;* and *From Politics to Piety: The Emergence of Pharisaic Judaism* have been reissued with new introductions by KTAV Publishing House, New York, in 1978. The other textbooks and textbook-anthologies of the early 1970s all remain in print and seem useful to sizable numbers of teachers and students. But *The Way of Torah* was the first of the sequence and closest to my heart. It emerged after eight years of reflection on teaching Judaism and (I do not mind saying) eight years of mistakes and failures. Indeed, now that eighteen years of teaching have come to completion, I realize that no course is ever without mistakes and failures committed with the best of intentions by an ever-fallible teacher. Yet we learn from our errors. I think this is a better book than it was in its first and second editions, and I know that if there is a fourth edition, it will be improved because of the criticism of those who will use the third, and because of the improved understanding yielded by my own experience as well.

The first edition of *The Way of Torah* emerged after four years of teaching at Dartmouth College. If it came into contact with some issues of importance to the study of religions in general, the reason was the persistent—not always gentle, but always constructive—questioning of my colleagues, Professors Hans H. Penner, Dartmouth College; Jonathan Z. Smith, now at the University of Chicago; Wayne A. Meeks, now at Yale University; Robin J. Scroggs, now at the Chicago Theological Seminary; David Kelsey, Yale University; and Fred Berthold, Dartmouth College. In many ways, Dartmouth's Department of Religion in the mid-1960s turned out for many of us to have been a remarkable personal and intellectual experience. The second and third editions of the book came out of ten years of teaching at Brown University. But the basic notion and design of the book are owing to my old friends—still, happily, enduring and dear friends—at Dartmouth.

While the editor of this series, Professor Fred Streng, Southern Methodist University, made formidable contributions both to the intellectual framework and to the detailed writing of the first two editions, his fresh and original perspectives on this edition have been of critical importance. He worked very hard on the manuscript and made numerous, fundamental proposals. I appreciated and adopted every one of them, which accounts for the reorganization of familiar materials and the presentation of new material. If this book is clearer and more accessible and some of its ideas make good sense, then Professor Streng deserves the larger part of the credit. But if that is not the case, then I do.

My dear friend and colleague, Professor Richard S. Sarason, took time off from his own scholarly projects to read this edition from cover to cover and make important corrections, observations, and additions. Many of the ideas added in this edition began in conversations with my companion and friend in all things scholarly, Professor Wendell S. Dietrich, to whom I owe an intellectual debt never to be repaid. I gain a great deal in conversations with colleagues at Brown and elsewhere, and owe much to many friends and associates. But these two—Professors Sarason and Dietrich—have been most important to the development of this book and of the course (Introduction to Judaism) out of which it flows and which it was meant to serve. All three of us, therefore, share in the dedication to our beloved colleague, Ernest S. Frerichs, Dean of the Graduate School of Brown University, in whom we take great pride, and to his wife.

Providence, Rhode Island   J.N.
1 September 1978
29 Ab 5738
The eve of Shmuel's bar
mitzvah *celebration*

Related Reading

Students will find extensive readings from primary sources complementing the several units of this book in its companion anthology, *The Life of Torah: Readings in the Jewish Religious Experience.* Appropriate selections illustrative of the main points of *The Way of Torah* are in *The Life of Torah* as follows:

The Way of Torah	*The Life of Torah*
History and Definition of Judaism, pp. 3-28	The Jewish Heritage, pp. 5-16
Mythic Structure of Classical Judaism, pp. 29-50	The Unity of God, Four Aspects of Torah, pp. 17-60
Way of Torah: A Way of Living, pp. 51-98	Rabbis: The Men of Torah, Torah as a Way of Life, pp. 61-154
Continuity and Change in Modern Times, pp. 99-132	Torah in America: Movements in American Judaism, Torah in the State of Israel, Zionism and Judaism, pp. 155-234

Acknowledgments

The author gratefully acknowledges permission to reprint copyrighted material:

From Judah Goldin, trans., *The Grace after Meals* (New York: Jewish Theological Seminary of America, 1955), pp. 9, 15ff.

From Philip Birnbaum, trans. and ed., *Daily Prayerbook* (New York: Hebrew Publishing Co., 1949), p. 424.

From Maurice Samuel, trans., *Haggadah of Passover* (New York: Hebrew Publishing Co., 1942), pp. 9, 13, 26, 27.

From Israel Abrahams, *Hebrew Ethical Wills*, II (Philadelphia: Jewish Publication Society, 1948), pp. 207–218.

From *Weekday Prayer Book*, ed. by Rabbinical Assembly of America Prayerbook Committee, Rabbi Gershon Hadas, Chairman, and Rabbi Jules Harlow, Secretary (New York: Rabbinical Assembly of America, 1962), pp. 42, 45–46, 50–54, 97–98.

From *A Rabbi's Manual*, ed. by Rabbi Jules Harlow (New York: Rabbinical Assembly of America, 1965), pp. 45, 96.

From A.S. Halkin, "The Judeo-Islamic Age," from *Great Ages and Ideas of the Jewish People*, ed. by Leo Schwarz (New York: Random House, Inc., 1956).

From Isaak Heinemann, *Judah Halevi, Kuzari* (London: East & West Library, 1957).

From Franz Kobler, *Letters of Jews Through the Ages*, II (London: East & West Library, 1952), pp. 565–567. Copyright © Horovitz Publishing Co. Ltd., 1952.

From *Prayer In Judaism*, by Bernard Martin, pp. 84–85, © 1968 by Basic Books, Inc., Publishers, New York.

From Sholom Alchanan Singer, trans., *Medieval Jewish Mysticism: The Book of the Pious* (Northbrook, Ill.: Whitehall Company, 1971), pp. 37–38.

xviii
Acknow-
ledgments

Reprinted from *Profiles of Eleven*, by Melech Epstein, p. 17, by permission of Wayne State University Press. Copyright © 1965 Wayne State University Press.

From "The Mystical Elements of Judaism," by Abraham J. Heschel in *The Jews: Their History, Culture, and Religion*, edited by Louis Finkelstein, vol. II, pp. 932–951. Copyright © 1949, 1955, 1960, 1971 by Louis Finkelstein. By permission of Harper & Row, Publishers, Inc.

Table of Dates

ca. 1200 B.C.	Exodus from Egypt under Moses; conquest of Canaan under Joshua
1200–1050	Period of the Judges
ca. 1050	Samuel
ca. 1013–973	David, king of Judah and then of Israel as well
973–933	Solomon
ca. 930	Kingdom divided
ca. 750	Amos
ca. 735	Hosea
ca. 725	Isaiah
722	Assyrians take Samaria; exile ten northern tribes
639–609	Josiah
620	Deuteronomic reforms
ca. 600	Jeremiah
586	Jerusalem Temple destroyed; Judeans exiled to Babylonia
ca. 590	Ezekiel
ca. 550	Second Isaiah
538	First return to Zion under Sheshbazzar
520	Zerubbabel, Haggai lay foundation for Temple
515	Temple completed
444	Ezra reads Torah
331	Alexander takes Palestine
168	Judaism prohibited by Antiochus IV; Maccabees revolt
165	Temple regained, purified by Maccabees
ca. 100	Community founded at Dead Sea, produces scrolls
63	Romans conquer Jerusalem
37–4	Herod rules as Roman ally
	Hillel
ca. 40	Gamaliel I heads Pharisees
70	Destruction of Jerusalem by Romans
	Yohanan ben Zakkai founds center for legal study and

	judicial and administrative rule at Yavneh
ca. 80–110	Gamaliel heads academy at Yavneh
	Final canonization of Hebrew Scriptures
	Promulgation of Order of Prayer by rabbis
115–117	Diaspora Jewries revolt against Trajan
120	Akiba leads rabbinical movement
132–135	Bar Kokhba leads messianic war against Rome
	Southern Palestine devastated
140	Rabbis reassemble in Galilee, restore Jewish government
ca. 200	Judah the Prince, head of Palestinian Jewish community, promulgates Mishnah
ca. 220	Babylonian academy founded at Sura by Rav
ca. 250	Pact between Jews and Persian king, Shapur I: Jews to keep state law; Persians to permit Jews to govern selves, live by own religion
297	Founding of school at Pumbedita, in Babylonia, by Judah b. Ezekiel
ca. 330	Pumbedita school headed by Abbaye, then Rava, lays foundation of Babylonian Talmud
ca. 400	R. Ashi begins to shape Babylonian Talmud
ca. 500	Babylonian Talmud completed in rough form
ca. 500–700	Saboraim complete the final editing of Babylonian Talmud
640	Moslem conquest of Middle East
ca. 750	*Problems* of Ahai Gaon; compilation of legal discourses
ca. 780	Death of Anan b. David, leader of Karaite revolt against rabbinic Judaism
882	Birth of Saadya, leading theologian, author of *Doctrines and Beliefs*
ca. 950	*Book of Creation*, mystical work, brief statement on how phenomena of world evolved from God
1040	Birth of Rashi, greatest medieval Bible and Talmud commentator
1096	First Crusade; Jews massacred in Rhineland by crusader armies
1138	Birth of Moses Maimonides
1141	Death of Judah Halevi
1179	Third Lateran Council issues anti–Semitic decrees
1180	Maimonides completes code of Jewish law
1187	Saladin recaptures Jerusalem from crusaders
1190	Riots at Lynn; massacre of Jews at York, England
1233	Inquisition at Aragon
1244	Ritual burning of Talmuds at Paris by church authorities
1247	Papal bull against ritual murder libel
1264	Charter of Boleslav the Pious
1283–1287	Riots against Jews in Rhineland
1290	Expulsion of Jews from England
1309	Expulsion of Jews from France
1328	Massacres in Navarre
1348–1349	Black death; Jews massacred; migration to Poland begins en masse
1385	Spanish Jews forbidden to live in Christian neighborhoods
1391	Massacres of Spanish Jewry

1492	Jews expelled from Spain
1496	Jews expelled from Portugal
1506	Secret Jews (*Maranos*) killed in Lisbon
1516	Ghetto introduced at Venice; Jews forced to live in separate neighborhood
1520	First printed edition of Babylonian Talmud
1521	Jewish migrations to Palestine
1546	Luther preaches against Jews
1553	Talmud burned in Italy
1567	Publication of *Shulhan Arukh*, code of Jewish law, by Joseph Karo
1624	Ghetto law instituted at Ferrara, Italy
1648	Massacres of Polish and Ukrainian Jews
1654	Jewish community founded in New Amsterdam (New York)
1655	Jews readmitted to England by Oliver Cromwell
1658	Newport, R.I., Jewish community founded
1665	Sabbetai Zevi proclaimed Messiah in Smyrna, Turkey
1670	Jews expelled from Vienna
1712	First public synagogue in Berlin
1760	Death of Baal Shem Tov, founder of Hasidism
1772	Rabbis of Vilna oppose Hasidism
1786	Death of Moses Mendelssohn, philosopher of Jewish Enlightenment
1789	U.S. Constitution guarantees freedom of religion
1791	Jews receive full citizenship in France
1796	Jews receive full citizenship in Batavia (Holland)
1807	Sanhedrin called by Napoleon
1812	Jews receive full citizenship in Prussia
1815	Polish Constitution omits Jewish rights
1825	Jews granted full citizenship in state of Maryland
1832	Jews receive full rights in Canada
1847	Birth of Solomon Schechter, leader of Conservative Judaism in the United States
1866	Emancipation of Jews of Switzerland
1868	Emancipation of Jews of Austria–Hungary
1870	Unification of Italy; ghettos abolished
1873	Founding of Union of American Hebrew Congregations (Reform)
1874	Death of Abraham Geiger, founder of German Reform
1881	Beginning of mass immigration of East European Jews to the United States, Britain, Canada, Australia, South Africa, Argentina
1882	Bilu Movement—beginning of Jewish immigration into Palestine
1885	Columbus Platform of Reform Rabbis renounces hope to return to Zion; affirms reason, progress
1886	Jewish Theological Seminary founded to train conservative rabbis
1888	Death of Samson R. Hirsch, leader of German Orthodoxy
1892	Anti–Semites elected to German Reichstag
1896	Herzl publishes *The Jewish State*

1897	Zionist movement founded at Basel, Switzerland
1909	Tel Aviv founded
1917	Balfour Declaration favors founding of Jewish national home in Palestine
1934	Nuremberg Laws in German; Jews lose rights
1937	Pittsburgh Platform of Reform Rabbis reaffirms Zionism, Jewish peoplehood
1938	Every synagogue in Germany burned down, 9 Nov.
1942	"Final Solution" adopted by German government, to exterminate all Jews in German-occupied Europe
1943	Warsaw ghetto revolt
1945	World War II ends; Jews in displaced persons camps
1948	Palestine partitioned; State of Israel created in Jewish part; Jews prohibited from sacred shrines in Jordanian Jerusalem
1967	Jerusalem reunited; ancient Temple wall recovered for Jewish veneration
1973	Yom Kippur War both calls into question the messianic spirit generated in 1967 and intensifies the messianic hope associated with the State of Israel and Jerusalem

PART ONE

The History and Definition of Judaism

CHAPTER 1

Prologue: In the Beginning

> In the beginning, two thousand years before the heaven and the earth, seven things were created: the Torah, written with black fire on white fire and lying in the lap of God; the Divine throne, erected in the heavens . . . ; Paradise on the right side of God; Hell on the left side; the Celestial Sanctuary directly in front of God, having a jewel on its altar graven with the name of the Messiah, and a Voice that cries aloud, *Return, Oh you children of men.*[1]

This creation account from classical talmudic Judaism may come as a surprise to readers more familiar with that creation legend of Scripture that states:

> *In the beginning God created the heavens and the earth. The earth was without form and void, and darkness was upon the face of the deep. The spirit of God was moving over the face of the waters. And God said, Let there be light, and there was light.*

> —Genesis 1:1–4

Genesis says nothing about what happened before creation. God alone is responsible for the works of creation, and what he made was heaven and earth. The talmudic creation legend, by contrast, begins with the creation of the Torah and concludes with the powerful "Voice that cries . . . ." Clearly, Judaism conceives of creation not solely within the biblical account, known to Christianity as well, but also within the rabbinic account cited here. What that means is simple: Judaism is not the religion of the "Old Testament"; rather, it is a development out of the ancient Hebrew Scriptures as much as Christianity is. But few people who are not Jewish, and not too many more who are Jewish, know that fact. Let us dwell on this observation: Judaism as it has flourished for many centuries has become, in modern times, an unknown religion even among its own community. If we say to a Jew today, "Tell me the Jewish story of creation," we may hear, "In the beginning God created . . . ." If, having the advantage of advanced education in the study of religions, we persist, "But what about the seven things created before creation?" an ordinary Jew will probably have no idea what we mean. The difficulty in studying Judaism is that in modern, Western society, the classic forms coexist, or compete, with strikingly different, but no less interesting, views, experiences, and definitions of Judaism.

To make the study of Judaism still more complicated, substantial numbers of Jews deny both that they are religious at all and that being Jewish has anything to do with religion. If Judaism is defined as the religion of the Jews, we might argue that its definition is to be sought in public opinion surveys of what Jews believe. And what Jews believe about most things is generally a function of their particular place in society and culture, on the one hand, and of their history as a segment of that society and culture, on the other. Studying Judaism would thus contribute little to the study of religions, interesting as Jews individually and collectively might be to anthropologists, sociologists, psychologists, and historians.

Furthermore, if religion is defined as, at the very least, a matter of faith in God, however liberal the definition of God, it is possible to conclude that Judaism is not to be studied as a living religion. If, similarly, by religious practices are meant forms familiar to American Protestants and Catholics, including prayers, churchgoing, and the like, we should almost certainly decide that whatever Jews do believe, many Jews, by ordinary American Christian standards, scarcely practice their religion.[2] Definitions of Judaism generally fail when measured against the realities of beliefs held by Jews who, if asked to describe what they really think about creation, refer neither to the legends of Genesis nor to those in the Talmud, but to physics and related sciences.

To understand the dynamics of Judaism, we need to distinguish between the Jewish people—all those born of a Jewish mother or converted to Judaism—and the Judaists—the believers and practitioners of the Torah. The Jewish people always were, and are today, a people of one religion, although their daily experiences have often been determined by a wider social and historical context. This context includes other peoples and cultures, changing political powers, and a variety of economic systems. At the same time Judaism—a broad collective term for the persisting theology, liturgy, moral code, and daily piety of Judaists—serves as a religion of one people. Judaism has persisted and flourished as the religion of the Jews for nearly the entire span of recorded history because it has created a world in which the Jewish people are able to make their lives. Judaism has responded to different cultural-historical contexts, and has reinterpreted the core of religious purpose according to the particular needs of the times. Thus, while Judaism has a great breadth of possible social expression, it nevertheless maintains a continuous structure that relates in a dynamic way to its larger social-historical habitat. By examining the interaction of Judaism with the life of the Jewish people in particular cultural contexts, we can become sensitive to the "ecology" of Judaism.

The Jews always were, and are today, a people of one religion, even though the framework of Judaism is so broad that it is not meant to be what it is—that is, a religion of one people. Still, the basic reason that Judaism has persisted and flourished as the religion of the Jewish people for nearly the entire span of recorded history and for the entire history of the Jews themselves is that Judaism, in all its forms and manifestations, succeeds in explaining to the Jews the world in which they live. Judaism further succeeds in creating for the Jews a world in which they are able to make their lives. So Judaism relates in a dynamic way to its "ecological" context.

In trying to enter into the human imaginative and emotional world created by Judaism, in trying to reckon how this group of people is able to make sense of the world through this particular religious expression, we have first of all to ask about the traits of the social environment that Judaism must explain and make meaningful. The "ecology"—the interaction of Jews with the whole, encompassing social and historical framework in which Judaism takes shape as a complete system—is defined, to begin with, by the social and historical condition of the Jewish people.

What are the traits of the social environment that Judaism must explain? The first is that the Jews are a small group; in the United States, for example, they comprise less than 3 percent of the population. The second is that from the decades before the destruction of Jerusalem in 586 B.C., the Jews have lived both in "their own land" and outside it. Indeed, the presence of Jews among other groups and peoples and in lands other than those in which they formed a majority is the best attested and most continuing trait both of the history of the Jewish people and the history of Judaism. It is rather unusual, in fact, for sizable numbers of Jews to live in the Holy Land, which Jews call the Land of Israel (*Erets Yisrael*) and which today encompasses the State of Israel. The majority of the Jewish people has not lived in the Holy Land since the second century A.D. and does not do so today.

The Jews, then, are not only a small group; they also have been and are today a group that relates to a great many other groups over the face of the earth. Moreover, the Jews take on the traits of these other groups: their languages, their patterns of life, their social and economic and political characters. So the questions of how the Jews are distinctive; of how they explain and justify—to themselves and to others—the fact that, in some ways, they are different are perennial and central questions. Small in numbers, diverse in character, living in many different cultural and national settings, the Jews form an international people. What links them to one another has to be explained. What does not link them to one another is clear: There is no common culture or language, nor are there common social, cultural, and economic traditions characteristic of all Jews everywhere.

A basic question which must be dealt with by any mode of Judaism is the effects of that long and therefore uneven experience of society which is known, as we shall see, as Jewish history. Any group that persists for a long time in human history also suffers and has much to remember—not all of it happy, by any means. So, too, with the Jews: Their history consists both of long periods of peace and serenity and long periods of war, persecution, oppression, and tragedy. History is made by both kinds of events, but historians and theologians prefer to talk about what is dramatic and compelling. The story of how seven or eight generations of Jews lived reasonably peaceful lives—were born, grew up, married, had children, raised their children, and then died—attracts little attention. What attracts interest is the tale of what happened to the eleventh generation: How it was forced to move, after three hundred years in peace, to some other place, or how some of its members suffered injury or death at the hands of enemies. So a central conception in the imaginative and emotional life of the Jews is the message of their history. That is, the meaning must be adduced from those past experiences which are perceived as eventful, critical, and fraught with significance. When we isolate those events which are deemed history and therefore held to require interpretation and to be made intelligible, we find time and again that the issue is translated into the meaning of that long history, perceived as an endless tale of suffering.

Judaism in any form is going to have to make sense of the uneven and sometimes difficult life of a small group of people always threatened with extinction through cultural assimilation, yet remarkably persistent through the generations. Judaism must help group the larger of the Jewish people—those who live outside the Holy Land—to secure some sense of its continuity and meaningful difference from others, without either understating or overstating the importance of the difference. It must explain through the message of the faith—Judaism—why the Jews are what they are and not something else. It must narrate and explain in a context rich in personal significance the history of the Jewish people. Judaism must shape and account for the particular social and psychological experience of living the Judaic life—that is, of pursuing human existence in accord with the distinctive teachings and life pattern of Judaism. These teachings, as we shall see, for the longest stretch of the history of Judaism have been and are the way of Torah.

If we are to experience what it means to be a Jew, we must apprehend Judaism as it has been experienced for twenty centuries and that is, in part, through the study of the written word, of the holy books. At the same time, we should bear in mind that the Judaic religious tradition is shaped by the historical life of the Jewish people. What happens to that people sets the themes and problems of Judaic theology. Events, such as, in biblical times, the bondage in Egypt, the monarchy of David, and the destruction of the Temple, become problems for religious reflection.

CHAPTER 2

The History of Judaism: The Three Periods

From a contemporary perspective, the history of Judaism can be divided into three periods: the beginnings, inclusive of the biblical period; the classical period, from the first century to the nineteenth century; and modern and contemporary times, the nineteenth and twentieth centuries. The middle or classical period forms the center of our interest because that was the point at which Judaism in its paramount form came to full expression and predominated in the life of the Jewish people. The modern and contemporary period has been marked by significant variations in the character and pattern of Judaism from the fairly uniform and cogent traits paramount in the classical age. And before the first century, there was a very long period of time out of which the classical expression of Judaism took shape and in which other forms and kinds of Judaism were explored as well. In this chapter we shall deal with these three periods in the history of Judaism.

THE BIBLICAL PERIOD

The history of Judaism begins with the Hebrew Bible. But the history of the Hebrew Bible does not begin with the events depicted in it. It starts long afterward. As Morton Smith points out: "The Hebrew Bible . . . is primarily evidence of the interests of the Pharisees, who not only selected and interpreted the books but also carefully determined and corrected their texts. Behind the Pharisees, the previous critical period of selection was probably the Maccabean revolt . . . . Thus the Hebrew Bible is the product not merely of partisan collection and revision but of a long series of partisan collections and revisions. . . . It represents, therefore, the literature of a large number and long succession of parties."[1] But seen as a whole, from the perspective of the history of Judaism, the Hebrew Bible is a single, unitary document telling the story of the faith and destiny of the people of Israel—the Jewish people.

Israel's history begins, in the biblical narrative, with the creation of the world and ends with the redemption of mankind and the conclusion of history. The Jews traced their origin to Abraham, who migrated from Mesopotamia and became a sojourner in the land of Canaan (the present-day land of Israel). That migration was given religious significance: Abraham left the gods of this world—idols and no-gods—to serve the Lord, Creator of heaven and earth. His descendants, Isaac and Jacob, were bearers of the promise God had made to Abraham that, through him, the families of man would bless themselves and that Abraham would be the father of a great people. Jacob, called Israel, went down to Egypt in the time of famine, when his son Joseph served Pharoah, and there his children multiplied. A pharaoh arose who did not know Joseph; he oppressed the children of Israel until they cried out to the God of their fathers. God sent Moses to redeem Israel from the bondage of Egypt—to bring them through the wilderness to the Promised Land.

So goes the biblical legend. It has been adopted by many peoples. Jews see it not as a merely spiritual paradigm but as a personal, concrete history, the family history of Israel after the flesh. The history of Israel probably ceases to be legend with Moses, but the shift from legends to relatively secure historical facts makes little theological difference. Great events called forth, and continue to call forth, a singular two-part response among Jews: first, to provide a written record of those events; second, to reflect on their meaning.

In retrospect, we see that the great event of the Exodus from Egypt produced the Mosaic revelation; the monarchy of King David, several centuries afterward, so shaped the Israelite imagination as to produce histories, psalms, and, above all, the messianic hope attached to the Davidic line. The destruction of the northern part of the kingdom, the ten tribes of Israel, in 722 B.C. provoked magnificent prophecy. The end of the southern kingdom, Judah—that is, the destruction of its city and the Temple of Jerusalem in 586 B.C., and the exile of Judeans (Jews or *Yehudim*) to Babylonia—resulted in the formation of much of the Hebrew Bible as we know it.

The conquest of Jerusalem by the Romans in A.D. 70 led to the foundation of classical, rabbinic Judaism under the leadership of Yohanan ben Zakkai and other great rabbis. The Moslem conquest of the Middle East in A.D. 640 afterward renewed the philosophical and mystical inquiry. The advent of modern times—marked by the political emancipation of Western European Jewry, the destruction of European Jewry, and the creation of the State of Israel—this, too, has had important religious consequences.

The fate of the Jewish people and the faith of Judaism were forever bound up with one another. One became a Jew—that is, part of the Jewish people—not through ethnic or territorial assimilation, but through profession of faith in one God and adoption of the laws of the Torah. Professing that faith and practicing those laws make a person into a Jew.

The beginning of Israel-the-people marked the appearance, not only of a new group, but also of an entirely new religious ideal—monotheism. To understand what was new in the biblical legacy, one must know what was old. Biblical writers invariably misrepresented paganism, calling it the worship of wood and stone, of dumb idols—that is, fetishism. What was actually central to paganism was the deification of worldly phenomena (not the simple carving of idols), the view that all manifestations of nature are aspects of a "mysterious supernatural vitality."[2] Israel began with the affirmation that God is transcendent over creation. God created the world and is wholly different from it. He has no myth, no birth. He is not subject to nature, to anything above himself, to any primordial reality. He is sovereign, and there is no realm beyond him.

Moses transformed the liberation of slaves into the birth of a nation[3] and made the birth of a nation into the creation of a new faith. He did so by pronouncing the redemption to be the work of the supreme God who revealed his will through the liberation from Egyptian slavery. The Lord further made a covenant at Sinai, a contract, that Israel should be his people and he should be their God, that Israel should do his will and he should protect and defend them. That will was both universal and specific. Some of the commandments concerned only Israel; others, including the respect for the sanctity of life, marriage, property, and justice, pertained to everyone. Ethics applied to the entire nation. A new moral category, the people, was created, which bore ethical and legal responsibilities beyond those that earlier pertained to individuals.

The creation of the monarchy, ca. 1000 B.C., a political event, called forth prophecy of religious significance. The king was not to be deified; he, too, was not God but subject to the law of God. When political and military disasters produced social disintegration, prophets came forward as apostles of God, emphasizing the primacy of morality. What was new was the conviction that the cult had no intrinsic value. God demanded justice, mercy, and loving-kindness. History was decided, not by force, but by the moral condition of the people. Idolatry, a religious matter, and social corruption, a moral one—these were the predominating facts in the shaping of the people's political destiny. The prophets looked forward to the end of days, when God would make himself known to the nations as he was now known to Israel. Thus history was seen as a succession of events that were not meaningless, but rather pointed toward a goal, the fulfillment of the divine, moral law. Through prophecy, Israelite religion created the notion of a single, all-encompassing universal history of mankind.

The destruction of Jerusalem in 586 B.C. produced a crisis of faith,[4] because ordinary folk supposed that the god of the conquerors had conquered the God of Israel. Israelite prophets saw matters otherwise. Israel had been punished for her sins, and it was God who had carried out the punishment. God was not conquered but vindicated. The pagans were merely his instruments. God could, moreover, be served anywhere, not only in the holy and promised land of Israel. Israel in Babylonian exile continued the cult of the Lord through worship, psalms, and festivals; the synagogue, a place where God was worshipped without sacrifice, took shape. The Sabbath became Israel's sanctuary, the seventh day of rest and sanctification for God. When, for political reasons, the Persians chose to restore Jewry to Palestine and many returned (ca. 500 B.C.), the Jews were not surprised, for they had been led by prophecy to expect that with the expiation of sin through suffering and atonement, God would once more show mercy and bring them homeward. The prophets' message was authenticated by historical events.

In the early years of the Second Temple (ca. 450 B.C.), Ezra, the priest-scribe, came from Babylonia to Palestine and brought with him the Torah-book, the collection of ancient scrolls of law, prophecy, and narrative. Jews resolved to make the Torah the basis of national life. The Torah was publicly read on New Year's Day in 444 B.C., and those assembled pledged to keep it. Along with the canonical Scriptures, oral traditions, explanations, instructions on how to keep the law, and exegeses of Scripture were needed to apply the law to changing conditions of everyday life. A period of creative interpretation of the written Torah began, one that has yet to come to conclusion in the history of Judaism. From that time forward, the history of Judaism became the history of the interpretation of Torah and its message for each successive age.

The next great event in the history of the Jews was the destruction of the Second Temple in A.D. 70. A political and military event, its religious consequences were drawn by Yohanan ben Zakkai and other great rabbis of the age. These rabbis, heirs of the tradition of oral interpretation and instruction in Torah and the continuators of the prophets of old, taught that the God of Israel could still be served by the Jewish people, who had not been abandoned by God but once more chastised. The rabbis in the following talmudic story taught that by obedience to Torah, Israel would again be restored to its land:

> When a disciple of Yohanan ben Zakkai wept at seeing the Temple mount in ruins, Yohanan asked him, "Why do you weep, my son?"
> "This place where the sins of Israel were atoned, is in ruins, and should I not weep?" the disciple replied.
> "Let it not be grievous to your eyes, my son," Yohanan replied, "For we have another means of atonement, as effective as Temple sacrifice. It is deeds of lovingkindness, as it is said [Hosea 6:6], *For I desire mercy and not sacrifice.*"

Once again a historical event produced a major religious revolution in the life of Judaism. That revolution is embodied in the pages of the Palestinian and Babylonian Talmuds, compendia of Judaic law, lore, and theology produced by the rabbis of Palestine and Babylonia on the basis of the ancient oral tradition and finally edited in the fifth and sixth centuries A.D.[5] Once and for all, the rabbis defined "being Jewish" in terms of laws universally applicable, laws that might be kept by Jews living in every civilization. Wherever Jews might go, they could serve God through prayer, study of Torah, practice of the commandments, and acts of lovingkindness. All Jews were able to study. No clerical class was required—only learned men. So rabbis took the priests' place as teachers of the people. The Jews thus formed a commonwealth within an empire,[6] a religious nation within other nations, living in conformity with the laws of alien governments, but in addition carrying out their own Torah. It was a commonwealth founded on religious belief, a holy community whose membership was defined by obedience to laws believed given at Sinai and interpreted and applied by rabbinical sages to each circumstance of daily life.

We see, therefore, that the biblical period, down to before the first century A.D., was a period of approximately fourteen centuries, in which religious experiences and beliefs of various kinds, among diverse groups, took shape among the Jewish people, the people of ancient (and modern) Israel. One principal development in that long period was the Hebrew Scriptures, called by Christians the Old Testament and by Jews *Tanakh* (for the letters beginning the Hebrew words for the three parts of the document: *Torah* or Pentateuch, *Nebi'im* or Prophets, and *Ketubim* or Writings, hence *T–N–K*). As we must realize, the Hebrew Scriptures are a mosaic of different kinds of books—about different sorts of religious experiences and teachings—all addressed to a single group of people, ancient Israel, and all brought together and united solely by their common audience.

The formative generations of rabbinic Judaism—the next period before us—drew upon more than the ancient Hebrew Scriptures. The formative generations flowed out of particular groups in the world of Judaism which read these Scriptures in a particular way and which had a distinctive approach to the religious life of the community of Israel. There were three main components of the religious life of the Jews in the last two centuries B.C. and the first century A.D. to which we must pay attention. These components were: the priests, with their commitment to the Temple of Jerusalem and its sacred offerings and to governance of the people of Israel in accord with the orderly world created by and flowing out of the Temple; the scribes, with their commitment to the ancient Scriptures and their capacity to interpret and apply these Scriptures to the diverse conditions of the life of the people; and the messianic Zealots, who believed that God would rule the Jews when foreign rulers had been driven out of the Holy Land. Obviously, these three components were talking about different things to different people.

Of these three groups, one predominated in the shaping of events in the first century A.D., and the other two fused thereafter. The messianic Zealots were the most powerful force in the history of the Jews until the destruction of the Temple of Jerusalem in A.D. 70. We know that simply because we know the single most important event of the time was the war fought against Rome from A.D. 66 to 73, climaxed by the fall of Jerusalem in A.D. 70. And the messianic Zealots must have remained paramount for another three generations, since the next major event in the history of the Jews was yet a second, and still more disastrous, holy and messianic war against Rome fought under the leadership of Ben Kosiba (also called *Bar Kokhba*, the Star's Son) from A.D. 132 to 135.

The other two groups—the priests and the scribes—with their interest in continuity, order, and regularity lost out both times. The priests of the

Temple saw the destruction of their sanctuary in A.D. 70 and realized after A.D. 135 that it would not be rebuilt for a long time. The scribes who taught Scriptures and administered their law witnessed the upheavals of society and the destruction of the social order that war inevitably brings in its aftermath. While both groups doubtless shared in the messianic hopes, they most certainly could not have sympathized with the policies and disastrous programs of the messianic Zealots. We shall now see how rabbinic (or classical) Judaism emerged out of the two groups under discussion (the scribes and the priests) in the period before A.D. 70.

THE CLASSICAL PERIOD: RABBINIC JUDAISM

The urgent question is: What is this classical period of nineteen centuries, and how shall we characterize that paramount form of Judaism which was normal and normative in its time? For it is from the middle that we may look both backward, into the formative, biblical age, and forward, toward the disintegration and reconstruction of modern and contemporary times. The classical period ran from the end of the first century A.D. into the nineteenth century. This is an amazingly long time for something so volatile as a religion to have remained essentially stable and to have endured without profound shifts in symbolic structure, ritual life, or modes of social organization for the religious community. The Judaism which predominated during that long period and which has continued to flourish in the nineteenth and twentieth centuries bears a number of names: *rabbinic* because of the nature of its principal authorities, who are rabbis; *talmudic* because of the name of its chief authoritative document after the Hebrew Scriptures, which is the Talmud; *classical* because of its basic quality of endurance and prominence; or, simply, *Judaism* because no other important alternative was explored by Jews.

What proved the stability and essential cogency of rabbinic Judaism during the long period of its predominance was the capacity of rabbinic Judaism—its modes of thought, its definitions of faith, worship, and the right way to live life—to take into itself and to turn into a support and a buttress for its own system a wide variety of separate and distinct modes of belief and thought. Of importance were, first, the philosophical movement, and, second, the mystical one. Both put forward modes of thought quite distinct from those of rabbinic Judaism.

Philosophers of Judaism raised a range of questions and dealt with those questions in ways essentially separate from the established and accepted rabbinic ways of thinking about religious issues. But all of the philosophers of Judaism not only lived in accord with the rabbinic way of life; all of them were entirely literate in the Talmud and related literature, and many of the greatest philosophers also were great Talmudists. The same is to be said of the mystics. Their ideas about the inner character of God, their quest for a fully realized experience of union with the presence of God in the world, their particular doctrines, with no basis in the talmudic literature produced by the early rabbis, and their intense spirituality, were all thoroughly "rabbinized"—that is, brought into conformity with the lessons and way of life taught by the Talmud. In the end, rabbinic Judaism received extraordinary reinforcement from the spiritual resources generated by the mystic quest. Both philosophy and mysticism found their way into the center of rabbinic Judaism. Both of them were shaped by minds that, to begin with, were infused with the content and spirit of rabbinic Judaism.

The first document of rabbinic Judaism, the Mishnah, was a compilation of laws: some for the present age before the coming of the Messiah and some for the age to come, in which the Temple would be rebuilt. The document came into existence in about A.D. 200, but its contents strongly suggest that its roots go back for something more than a century before that time. So, looking backward from the basic holy book distinctive to rabbinic Judaism, we may expect to find the principal components in significant antecedent groups of that period. And, in fact, we can discover two distinctive and definitive traits of the rabbinic form of Judaism: the method of the priests and the contents of the writings of the scribes. Rabbinic Judaism is a system of regularity, interacting elements, and order, in which the holy life is lived in accord with a plan and a pattern revealed in heaven. The method of the holy life is expressed in Temple ritual and priestly activities. But the contents of the holy life come from a different group—the scribes of the period before A.D. 70—who held that knowledge of the Torah and its proper interpretation were the most important thing.

The method of rabbinic Judaism is to live the holy life in a regular and orderly pattern. This is the method of the Temple and its priests, with their formal and patterned ritual. One half of the Mishnah, the first document of rabbinic Judaism, is devoted to the concerns of the Temple priesthood: laws of the cult, of purity in the cult, and of the agricultural taxes to be paid to the priesthood and the cult. So Mishnah is a document that devotes a great deal of time to the priests' interests.

The contents of rabbinic Judaism speak of Torah—that is, of divine revelation contained in the Five Books of Moses and, by extension, in the *Tanakh*. Now, on the face of it, this conception of what is important derives from the scribes, who before A.D. 70 formed a profession. Their professional ideal was that of learning: of acquiring knowledge of Torah and learning how to apply that knowledge to numerous concrete situations. The rabbis of the third and possibly even the second century, however, had a special doctrine of Torah, distinct from that of the scribes (as represented by the apocryphal book, *Ben Sira*, for example). The rabbinical doctrine held that when God revealed the Torah to Moses at Mount Sinai, God gave the Torah in two parts. One part was in writing, the written Torah, which we know as *Tanakh*. The other part was not written down, but was meant to be handed on through memorization and repetition of the precise language that had been memorized from one generation to the next. This other half of the Torah is called, therefore, the Oral Torah, or the Torah which is memorized. Together the two halves of the Torah constitute, in the language of rabbinic Judaism, "the whole Torah of Moses, our rabbi," for it goes without saying that Moses too was a rabbi, as were all of the great biblical heroes.

The contents of rabbinic Judaism, therefore, consist of Torah as the rabbis teach it. Learning in Torah promises the experience of transcendence and opens the way to God through the learning of Torah—that is, through the *holy act of study*. Learning in Torah, as rabbis teach it, is the holy life for Judaism. Futhermore, the Mishnah itself, a second-century document, and the great commentaries generated by the Mishnah (the Babylonian Talmud and the Palestinian Talmud—that is, the commentaries created in the schools of the two countries in which Jews were subject to rabbinic authority) also are called Torah. Indeed, to the revelation received by Moses from God at Mount Sinai is attributed the beginning of Mishnah itself. The whole of the holy literature of rabbinic Judaism would, in time to come, be called Torah, and then would include both the written Scriptures and the rabbinic writings which were, in toto, claimed to be Oral Torah—that is, the other half of the revelation at Sinai transmitted orally to Moses and from him, in an unbroken chain, down to the rabbis themselves.

In a single word, the contents of rabbinic Judaism we have just examined, the kind of holy leader of such a religion, the principal religious activity, and the nature of the central religious institution all call to mind the ideals of the scribal profession. For it was the scribe who, before the second century, stood for learning in Torah. It was the scribe who saw the learned person (but, in rabbinic Judaism, only the learned *man*) as the authority. It was the scribe who regarded learning as the important thing to do. It was the scribe who regarded the school as the principal institution for society—the school that functioned also as the court and the center for the administration of society.

Rabbinic Judaism began in Mishnah, a (1) scribal document about the concerns of (2) the priests. But what it does *not* choose to talk about (3) is as important as what it wants to say. A religion, or a distinctive form of a religion, is defined both by its center and its perimeter; by its beliefs, and by the things it finds incredible and implausible. What Mishnah does not mention, and what later rabbinic Judaism treats with a considerable measure of reticence and with a clear policy of subordination, is what the messianic Zealots thought most important: the Messiah, the coming of the messianic age, the fighting of the messianic war, and similar concerns. The message of rabbinic Judaism is that the coming of the Messiah depends upon adherence to the Torah. When all the Jewish people will keep a single Sabbath in the proper way—that is, the way the rabbis teach—then the Messiah will come. This and similar sayings treat the coming of the Messiah as secondary to, and dependent upon, the keeping of the Torah. True, the prayerbook of Judaism, the *Siddur* (Order of Prayer), is so rich in messianic references and allusions as to be a near-messianic handbook. But throughout the history of Judaism, from the second century to the nineteenth, the pattern was the same: Messiahs came and Messiahs went; rarely, if ever, winning the credence of the rabbinic authorities of the time and place, but at the same time capturing the credence of the masses. That

Messiahs

is to say, the Jewish people would put forward in every age one candidate after another for the messianic role. And, in every age, the message of leading exponents of Judaism would be: Not this one, not here, not now. But there always was a reason: The time has not yet come. Given the sorts of expectations associated with the coming of the Messiah from the writings of the prophets of ancient Israel onward, we need hardly be surprised at the consistent position of Judaism: The Messiah will come, but this is not the Messiah, because the promise made in behalf of the Messiah has not yet been kept.

There is, then, this balance to be struck: a way of life infused with (1) the ancient ideal of the scribal profession, shaped along the lines—the methods—of the orderly and correct rites of (2) the Temple priesthood and infused with the hope for an age of perfection and of holiness put forward by (3) messianic doctrine from the biblical prophets onward. One final element acts as a kind of catalyst of the system, and that is (4) the claim that, within the way of life of Torah, one might have a foretaste of the world to come, of the messianic age. This allegation is definitive of the way of Torah—that is, rabbinic Judaism. It promises eternity in the here and now, the world to come in the creation of time. It may take the form of the view that the Sabbath is a moment of eternity in time. It may take expression in the notion that through study of Torah, particularly of the Talmud and its commentaries, one attains revelation, a fully realized experience of the knowledge of heaven. It may be stated in the idea that God in heaven lives in accord with Torah. When the Jew visits the sick and buries the dead and helps the weak and the suffering, then the Jew acts "like God" and becomes godly. It may also take the form of mystical concentration on the proper fulfillment of God's commandments and proper intention in prayer, by which the cosmic forces of redemption are activated. Through these forces little acts of messianic redemption may be constantly made to take place.

If all of this salvation is here and now, what need is there, in the end, for a radical change in the nature of history and of being, to be brought on by the coming of the Messiah? What place is there for a Messiah in the life of people who strive to do the things God wants them to do, to be the things that make them like God—that is—*in our likeness, after our image,* as Genesis 1:26 states the matter? In the end, the holy life is to be lived here and now, and in the living of that life, people attain sanctification and imitate God. Life in accord with Torah is more than an amalgam of scribal and priestly ideals and a subversion of the disruptive hope of messianic Zealots. Life in accord with Torah comes out as a distinctive and particular mode of holiness.

The way of Torah was for a long time, and remains today, the paramount definition of Judaism, a definition chosen in the face of, and against, alternatives. People might have been many things. This is what they chose to be. Through the ages there were many candidates for the title "Judaism." But it was the way of Torah that the Jewish people took and that vast numbers today continue to take. This is the way in which they make their path through time and toward eternity.

From the destruction of the Second Temple to the beginning of the nineteenth century—nearly nineteen hundred years—Jews lived among two great civilizations, Islam and Christendom, but under their own law and within their own community. They did not seek to be integrated with "the nations," but to endure as a singular people among them. We can hardly reduce to a few generalizations the complex facts of their history and culture. The religious events of those long centuries likewise cannot be summarized in a brief catalogue: mysticism, philosophy, study of the law through talmudic commentary, logical codification, the issuing of concrete decisions. To the outside world, Jewish history was the tale of persecution and massacre, degradation and restriction to despised occupations, then riot and expulsion, and the discovery of new homes elsewhere. To the medieval Jew, such dates as 1290, when Jews were expelled from England; 1309, when the same took place in France; 1391, when the great and flourishing communities of Spain were overtaken by destruction; 1492, when the Jews were expelled from Christian Spain; 1648, when Polish Jews were massacred in vast numbers—such dates marked times for penitence and reaffirmation of Torah.

THE MODERN PERIOD

It is only in modern times that other than religious consequences have been drawn from cataclysmic historical events. Because Judaism had developed prophecy and rabbinic leadership, it was able to overcome the disasters of 586 B.C. and A.D. 70. The challenge of modern times comes not only from the outside but also from within: the nurture of new religious leadership for Jews facing a world of new values and ideals.

Religion provides a particularly subtle problem for students of the process of modernization. While in such other areas as politics and economics, that which is "modern" may meaningfully be set apart and against that which is "traditional," in religion the complexities of the process of social change become most evident, the certainties less sure. Even the very definition of the problem to be studied poses difficulty.

We refer to "the impact of cultural modernization upon traditional religion," as though religion is a *given*, "a compact entity inherited from the past in a particular form," and as though modernization is also a *given*, a process with a fixed direction.[7] According to the "impact theory," it is *modern* culture that acts upon *traditional* religion, just as economic and political patterns are "modernized."

As Wilfred Cantwell Smith points out, the "impact theory" is altogether too "externalist," for it minimizes the "*interiorization* of modernity in the religious life of all communities," a process that takes place from within as much as from without. It underestimates the dynamism of the so-called tradition, ignoring its own evolution, as in the development of Hasidism and Enlightenment we are about to study. We speak of "the impact" of one thing upon another only at the risk of vast oversimplification. The dynamic is *within* as well as *upon* the tradition.

Smith further asks whether we can speak of "traditional religion *and* modern culture" and finds difficulty in so doing. He points out that the supposed dichotomy between "religion" and "culture" emerges uniquely in the West, which "not only conceptualizes, but institutionalizes, the two separately." "Traditional religion and modern culture" is not only a Western concept, but a Western *phenomenon*, Smith says. *If* Judaism is a Western religion, then the dichotomy fails even here. Smith raises the issue: Is it meaningful to speak of "religion" at all in non–Western contexts? "Hinduism is a modern Western concept, which formulates in Western cultural terms that which can more accurately . . . be characterized as Hindu culture," Smith says, and the same may be said of Judaism. He concludes: "In non–Western societies there is no such thing as religion, there is only culture." Many of the specifically Jewish problems we shall consider derive from that fact.

Smith thus emphasizes that the very concept of a "religious phenomenon" existing apart from culture is one of the very *significations* of "modernization." Hence the isolation of something called "traditional religion" is similarly a byproduct of modernization. The very recognition of the category of *tradition* represents the first step toward the disintegration of that tradition. As a Muslim theologian said: "There is no hope in returning to a traditional faith after it has once been abandoned, since the essential condition in the holder of a traditional faith is that he should not know he is a traditionalist." Smith seems to offer a paraphrase: "The emergence of Hinduism and Islam as 'traditional religions' is itself a symptom of modern culture." So, too, he states, "Curiously, this modern-cultural phenomenon of something called 'traditional religions' turns out to be not only not traditional, but also not religious." By "religious," Smith refers to two qualities—first, timelessness, and, second, a sense of daily presence: "If religion is anything at all, it is something that links the present moment to eternity." So long as religion is a "living reality," immediately present in the lives of the communicants, so long as the law is practiced, not merely obeyed, so long as society represents the corporate stage for living out the divinely ordained duty—then so long is "the religious tradition" fully *traditional*.

The issue is, therefore, more adequately stated by Smith as follows: "*To discern and to delineate what is happening to man's religiousness in the flux and turmoil of the modern world.*" A corollary, peculiarly modern issue, which will be of special concern here, is: What is happening to the "religiousness" of people who, in Smith's words, "either do not express their religiousness formally at all, or, if they do, express it in new, untraditional ways?" The question is a broad one. Religious phenomena in the past expressed an inner orientation in the lives of people. If so, what is happening today to the human person and to the qualities of life that those traditions used to represent and to foster? It is this investigation that is here subsumed under the narrow and yet exemplary rubric of "Judaism": What has happened to Jewish human beings?

Two points come clear: first, Jews persisted in an extraordinary belief rooted not in reality but in their own fantasies, that some day things would be better, that somehow problems would find solutions, and that people were not fated to repeat their old mistakes forever and ever. They retained the faith that times would change for the better and that faith called forth from them extraordinary changes in their normal patterns of behavior. In 1665–66—the time of the (false) Messiah, Sabbetai Zevi—that faith led them to sell all their possessions and await the great day. In the years after 1897—the time of the beginning of modern Zionism, the political movement that created the State of Israel—that faith demanded that they leave their homelands for a Mediterranean country previously known only in prayer, dream, and Scripture. So the very substance of the "tradition" continued unchanged. The psychic realities embodied in it seem, in retrospect, to have endured amid all kinds of changes.

On the other hand, Jews so fundamentally changed that they could no longer talk about reality in the arcane metaphysics of the tradition, but had rather to adapt for their own use the equally metaphysical language of democratic socialism and nineteenth-century romantic nationalism. Sabbetai Zevi and Theodor Herzl could not have been more different; and yet, had their followers met, they might have seen in the sparkle of one another's eyes, in the radical willingness to act, in the hopeful, frenzied optimism, something not wholly unfamiliar.

From such a perspective, one may readily perceive the unreality of the "impact theory" and of formulating the issue in terms of "modernization *and* religion." What we want to know is not how matters *progressed* to their present state, but rather: What changed? And what remained the same? What is constant in the human experience, and what has been altered in the passage of time, in the movement of people from one place to another, and in the alteration of inherited patterns of economic, social, and political behavior? And of greatest interest in the Jewish paradigm: How has the inherited tradition shaped, as much as it has been shaped by, the processes of change we call, for convenience, modernization? These questions will occupy us for a long time in Part IV.

Yet another question must be raised at the outset of our discussion, when we consider the three principal periods in the history of Judaism, and this question is of the most fundamental character: What made the modern period *modern*? The break with those long centuries in which Judaism was defined by the rabbis of the Talmud was marked by the fact that classical Judaism became implausible in the face of the contemporary context. Many Jews, emerging from the perspectives of rabbinic world views, found that the promise of modernity was closed off by those world views. The longtime reticence about Messiah and the messianic age did not credibly explain that wonderful age people thought had dawned—an age of liberalism in acceptance of difference in general and an age in which Jews in particular might find themselves citizens like all others, subject to a common law and enjoying common rights. One important component in the shift of Judaism in the modern period, therefore, is the demise of long-established skepticism in the face of claims of Messiahs and new dawns and new ages. Through much of the nineteenth century and even down to World War II, that skepticism proved to be incredible and implausible.

The second reason that classical Judaism was found to be unlikely contradicts the first. From the last third of the nineteenth century onward, many Jews began to understand that the promises of Enlightenment and of emancipation would never be kept; indeed, were false to begin with. There was no place in Western civilization for the Jews, who had to build their own state as a refuge from the storms that were coming upon them. These Jews rejected that fundamental teleological optimism, rationalism, yielding patience, and quietism with which classical Judaism had viewed the world. They did not believe that the world was so orderly and reliable as Judaism had supposed. They regarded Judaism as a misleading and politically unwise view of the Jewish people and their worldly context. What was needed was not prayer, study of Torah, and a life of compassion and good deeds. What the hour demanded was renewed action, a reentry into politics, and the repoliticization of the Jewish people. Zionism was the movement that redefined the Jewish people into a nation and revived the ancient political status of the Jews. So far as Zionism saw the world as essentially irrational and unreliable, unable to proceed in the orderly, calm, reasonable fashion in which Judaism assumed the world would always do its business, Zionism marked an end to Judaism as it had been known. The fact that, in time to come, Zionism would, as we shall see, take up the old messianic language and symbolism of Judaism and make over these ancient vessels into utensils bearing new meaning is not to be ignored. But at its beginning, Zionism marked a break from Judaism, not because of Zionism's messianic fervor, but because of its rejection of the quiet confidence, rationalism, and optimism of rabbinic Judaism.

Thus, these two things—the promise of emancipation and the advent of racist and political anti–Semitism—fell so far outside the world view of rabbinic Judaism that they could not be satisfactorily interpreted and explained within the established system. The result, as we shall observe later on, is the breakdown of the Judaic system for many, many Jews. The system of Judaism was not overturned; for these people, it simply had become implausible. It had lost the trait of self-evidence.

To state matters very simply: rabbinic Judaism was and is a system of balance between cosmic, teleological optimism and short-term skepticism—a system of moderation and restraint, of rationalism and moderated feeling. Just as it came into being in response to the collapse of unrestrained Messianism, feelings unleashed and hopes unbounded by doubt, so it came to an end, where and when it did come to an end, in a renewed clash with those very emotions and aspirations which, in the beginning, it had overcome: passionate hope and unrestrained, total despair. A system of optimistic skepticism and skeptical optimism, a world grasped with open arms and loved with a breaking heart, could never survive those reaches toward the extremes, those violations of the rules and frontiers of moderate and balanced being, that characterize modern times.

When the balance was upset, it hardly mattered whether it was shifted toward one extreme—optimism become Messianism—or toward the other—skepticism turned into utter despair and nihilism. The extremes would meet, in due course, in the messianization of Zionism in the last third of the twentieth century. But at that point, it would appear, even the avatars and exponents of rabbinic Judaism would take up the messianic fervor of the moment. That unanticipated phenomenon—the Messianism of rabbinic Judaism in the persons of its most "authentic" exponents—would mark a moment in the history of Judaism so completely contemporary and so utterly unanticipated as to permit no comment whatsoever.

Yet as students of religions, we do have to take note of the unpredictable character of religions. If, as is argued, Juadism today constitutes, both in its Israeli Orthodox and (in a measure) its American Orthodox forms, a kind of remessianization of a Judaism formerly distinctly skeptical of messianic claims, then there can be no more certainties; only surprises. The one thing not to be predicted even as recently as 1967 was that Orthodoxy would invoke messianic language and symbolism in behalf of the State of Israel. Nor could anyone have imagined that a claim to return to the promises to the patriarchs through settlement in the territories of Judea and Samaria would impress the sober and cautious intellects of that enduring world view. Yet in the 1970s that is precisely what took place. In the face of the advent of what any reasonable student of Judaism would have declared impossible, what is there to be said? Only that religions have a way of surprising students of religions.

return to wonder

CHAPTER 3

Defining Judaism:
The Jew and the Judaist

The third and final part of the work of introducing the study of Judaism is to define the thing we study, Judaism. The work of definition is not easy. Indeed, what we do when we study religions is to define religions—that is, describe the things we deem religious, put them together into some sort of workable system, and interpret the way that system works and makes sense to people within its boundaries. Definitions may serve more than a single purpose. Some may tell us the principal theological convictions of a religion. Others may deal solely with the cultural traits of a religious community. Still others may serve the needs of the social study of religions.

Since the approach of this book falls within the range of history of religions, it is natural for us to ask Judaism to define itself—that is, to deal with the successive statements of self-understanding and self-perspective that, in the history of Judaism, have constituted its self-definition.

Let us begin with the hero of classical Judaism, Hillel, a Pharisaic sage who lived at the beginning of the common era. He once was asked by a Gentile to define all of Judaism while standing on one foot. Instead of regarding the man's question as impertinent, he replied:

> What is hateful to yourself do not do to your fellow-man. That is the whole Torah. All the rest is commentary. Now go and study
>
> —Talmud, b. Shabbat, 31(a)

Hillel was neither the first nor the last to attempt a pithy definition of Judaism.[1] He chose four elements for his definition. First, he selected, from among many available Scriptures, Leviticus 19:18: *You shall love your neighbor as yourself: I am the Lord.* This commandment, Hillel held, summarized everything. Second, he referred to the central, dominating motif of the Judaic consciousness: Torah. He did not speak of Judaism but of Torah when referring to the tradition. Third, he regarded everything else in the tradition as "commentary"—that is to say, as illustration of this single, primary principle. So he did think a definition was possible. Finally, he told the man to go, not to the synagogue for prayer or to the Temple for sacrifice; not to the contemporary Dead Sea monastery for meditation and for a holy life or to the zealot bands for a holy war to bring the messianic day; but to the schoolhouse for study of Torah.

Fifty years later, Hillel's great disciple, Yohanan ben Zakkai, taught: "If you have done much in study of Torah, do not take credit for yourself, for to this end were you created."[2] The purpose of man is to study revelation, truth—that is, Torah.

Still a further definition of Judaism derives from later rabbis of the Talmud. Rabbi Simlai expounded:

> Six hundred and thirteen commandments were given to Moses, three hundred and sixty-five negative ones, corresponding to the number of the days of the solar year, and two hundred forty-eight positive commandments, corresponding to the parts of man's body. . . .
>
> David came and reduced them to eleven: *A Psalm of David* [Psalm 15]. *Lord, who shall sojourn in thy tabernacle, and who shall dwell in thy holy mountain?* (i) *He who walks uprightly and* (ii) *works righteousness and* (iii) *speaks truth in his heart and* (iv) *has no slander on his tongue and* (v) *does no evil to his fellow and* (vi) *does not take up a reproach against his neighbor,* (vii) *in whose eyes a vile person is despised but* (viii) *honors those who fear the Lord.* (ix) *He swears to his own hurt and changes not.* (x) *He does not lend on interest.* (xi) *He does not take a bribe against the innocent.* . . .
>
> Isaiah came and reduced them to six [Isaiah 33:25–26]: (i) *He who walks righteously and* (ii) *speaks uprightly,* (iii) *he who despises the gain of oppressions,* (iv) *shakes his hand from holding bribes,* (v) *stops his ear from hearing of blood* (vi) *and shuts his eyes from looking upon evil, he shall dwell on high.*
>
> Micah came and reduced them to three [Micah 6:8]: *It has been told you, man, what is good, and what the Lord demands from you,* (i) *only to do justly, and* (ii) *to love mercy, and* (iii) *to walk humbly before God.* . . .
>
> Isaiah again came and reduced them to two [Isaiah 56:1]: *Thus says the Lord,* (i) *Keep justice and* (ii) *do righteousness.*
>
> Amos came and reduced them to a single one, as it is said, *For thus says the Lord to the house of Israel. Seek Me and live.*
>
> Habakkuk further came and based them on one, as it is said [Habakkuk 2:4], *But the righteous shall live by his faith.*
>
> —Talmud, b. Makkot, 24(a)

This long passage illustrates in both form and substance the very essential attributes of definitions of Judaism produced within the classical tradition. First, we notice, as expected, an emphasis on the Hebrew Bible as the source of authoritative teaching. But the Scriptures are not cited in a slavish, unimaginative way. Rather, they are creatively used to serve as the raw material for the rabbi's own insights. By now it is obvious that while Judaism is based upon the Hebrew Scriptures, it is not only what is contained in those Scriptures, but rather a religious tradition built upon their foundation. Second, the reference to "commandments" (in Hebrew, *mitzvot*) concerning both what people are supposed to do and what they are to refrain from doing tells us that Judaism is going to have much to say about the conduct of life—about every aspect of human existence. Third, we once again observe emphasis placed on ethical and moral deeds and attributes. If Torah means revelation, then according to the rabbis, what was in fact revealed was mostly ethical teachings. Yet the direction of ethics is the search for God, and the good life consists of that search—*The righteous man shall live by his faith*—for in Hebrew, the word for faith is *emunah*, meaning trust, loyalty, commitment. Thus, what keeps a person alive, what renders life real and meaningful, is trust in and loyalty to God. In modern times Judaism has been described as a religion of ethical monotheism, meaning a religion in which belief in one God is expressed through ethical behavior. Here, as in many other passages, we find an illustration of that principle.

So far, we have chosen to define Judaism in terms selected by the rabbis, who created classical Judaism. Yet in doing so we have discovered the obvious fact that the rabbis themselves did not issue definitions of Judaism, but spoke in terms of Torah, commandments, moral requirements, loving-kindness, and good-heartedness. They addressed themselves, not to a self-conscious ethnic group seeking meaning for its peculiarity, but rather to the condition of ordinary humanity. To the Jew living within the classical tradition, a definition of Judaism is meaningless, for Judaism is too narrow, limited, one-dimensional, abstract, and altogether too philosophical. To be a classical Jew is to live a way of life—a life so whole, integrated, and complete, that no aspect may be singled out and called ritual, ethics, theology, culture, or religion.

As Wilfred Cantwell Smith points out: "Fundamentally, it is the outsider who names a religious system."[3] It is understandable, therefore, that the Hebrew language contains no word for Judaism. When referring to their religious tradition, Jews have made use of a variety of words, images, symbols, and concepts; but until modern times, when self-consciousness imposed the necessity to explain themselves—to summarize, spell out, explicate their "religion"—Jews did not need to tell outsiders or themselves about the 3, or 10, or 613 principles defining something they called Judaism. Their religious way of life was not an "ism."

As we turn, finally, for a definition of Judaism derived from modern times, we had best begin with the simplest one: Who is a Jew according to Jewish law? According to Jewish law as codified in the Talmud and defined by rabbis from late antiquity to the present day, a Jew is a person who was born of a Jewish mother or who has been converted to Judaism. This definition is circular, however, for we immediately need to ask: What constitutes the Jewishness of that Jewish mother? All we know, so far, is that the status of being a Jew is conferred from birth through the female parent or attained through faith and ritual. To escape the circularity, we might, for example, ask: What is the term of reference, the purpose, for a definition? Who is a Jew for purposes of automatic entitlement to an Israeli passport? What is a Jew for purposes of synagogue membership?

Raphael Loewe, a British Judaica scholar who attempts to define Judaism, points out that one may offer as a valid answer to who is Jew: "Any person . . . who has been victimized by antisemitic forces on grounds of his being of Jewish origin, whether those grounds may be substantiated or not."[4] This is a functional definition.

In considering the question of who is a Jew, we enter into one of the central enterprises of contemporary Jewish life: the debate on this very issue. The historical, legal definition is adequate only for historical and legal questions. Yet, when we reflect on the history of the term *Jew*, we realize the ambiguities even of such a definition. In biblical times, the people of "Israel" were divided into the ten tribes of northern Israel and the two of Judea, the latter consisting of Judah and Benjamin. When in 722 B.C. the northern nation was destroyed, leaving only the Judeans (*Yehudim*) in the south, the term "Jew" (*Yehudi*) became coextensive with "Israel," meaning the children of Abraham, Isaac, and Jacob, heirs of those who had received the Torah at Mount Sinai and thus participants in the sacred history of the covenant between God and humanity.

Yet others claimed to inherit that sacred history, its promises, and its covenant. These included, for example, the Samaritans who continued to live in the northern territories of Palestine and claimed to possess the Torah; the various sects who claimed to be true heirs of the Mosaic revelation; the Christians, who said they were the "true Israel"; the medieval Karaites, who regarded followers of rabbinic Judaism as in error but said the Karaites alone possessed the Torah; the Sabbateans, and—last but not least—the modern Israeli, who holds that to be a Jew is to be part of the Jewish nation, which is the State of Israel today.

The answers to the questions: "Who is a Jew?" "Who is Israel?" depend not merely on historical or sociological realities, but upon matters of conviction. And that is why discussing who is a Jew brings the student into the theological framework of modern Judaic existence: The answers to the questions contain within them a whole set of affirmations and denials.

Loewe begins with the following conditions:

1. The assertion of the party concerned, in good faith, that he or she is a Jew by parentage or formal conversion;

2. Neither practice of, nor unavowed adherence to, any theistic religion other than Judaism;

3. The evincing of some positive indication, according to circumstances, of solidarity with the Jewish people.[5]

Loewe holds that the status attained by appropriate replies to these questions is to be called "Jewishness." Pretty much anyone may be called "a Jewish person" who is of Jewish parentage or has converted to Judaism, who in addition adheres to no other religion and gives indication of affirming identity with other Jews.

The undeniable fact is that there are Jews who deny the tenets of Judaic religion, however these may be formulated. A Jew who repudiates Judaism most often remains actively a part of the Jewish community. A Methodist who gives up his or her religion does not often remain an active member of the Methodist church. The two are hardly analogous.

To distinguish between Jews who are religious and those who are not, Loewe proposes an additional term. *Judaicity,* yielding *Judaic* for an adjective. By Judaicity, Loewe means "all actions and behavior that are 'in character' with the ethical values enunciated by the classical Jewish sources." Our usage is somewhat broader, for by Judaic we mean that which derives from, or is characterized by, Judaism. In light of our earlier remarks, we should quickly revise Judaism to read *Judaic tradition.*

Who is a Judaist—that is, one who professes to believe and participate in the Judaic tradition? Loewe's definition is satisfactory:

1. Acknowledgment of the uncompromisingly absolute, monotheistic sanction for Jewish ethical behavior, including acknowledgment of its binding validity for oneself;

2. A sense of the meaningfulness of Jewish history;

3. An appreciation . . . of the fact that Judaism enunciates its doctrines for the most part symbolically and by implication, using Jewish social self-regulation (that is, *halakhah,* "procedure, law") as its principal medium.[6]

Loewe defines Judaism not merely as a religion, because it applies no dogmatic tests and enforces no ritual observances. He also does not see it as a civilization, for Jews have no common language and folk culture; it is also not a political movement, for Zionism has affected a minority of the Jews. By Judaism, Loewe means:

. . . a complex of faith and social ethics, of universal significance and possibly universal relevance [resting] upon the sanction of . . . absolute monotheism; expressing itself mainly through a pattern of religious symbolism, the cultural features of which are predominantly concrete, and the transmission of which is predominantly by descent; and having as its object the general sublimation of the material concerns of humanity, by pervading them with such spiritual considerations as will not compromise the monotheistic basis of the whole.[7]

We began by asking for some simple definitions and ended with a theological statement. We have rapidly moved into the realm of contemporary Jewish discourse, which is *both* religious and secular. We have thus experienced at the end one of the chief meanings of being a Jew: To be a Jew means to argue about what being a Jew means, though not everyone who joins the argument is a Jew.

This long prologue cannot be concluded without some clear and simple definitions. First, let us distinguish between *Jew* and *Judaist*. The former is one who belongs to the ethnic group of the *Jews*, a group existing in various parts of the world and defining what is Jewish *about* Jews in various sorts of ways relative to particular societies and cultures. The latter is one who, in addition, affirms the Judaic tradition in important ways.

We consequently distinguish between *Jewishness* and *Judaism*. Jewishness refers to the conglomeration of those traits which, in various settings, are regarded as peculiarly and characteristically Jewish; but those traits may have little, if anything, to do with the Judaic tradition. Judaism consists of the religious tradition enshrined in the holy books and expressed by the holy words, deeds, way of living, and principles of faith subsumed under the word *Torah*.

PART TWO

---

*The Mythic Structure
of Classical Judaism*

CHAPTER 4

The Evidence

In a history of nearly forty centuries, the Jews have produced rich and complex religious phenomena. Indeed, Judaic religious and historical data, like those of other religions, may seem at the outset to defy adequate description. The varieties of historical settings, rituals, intellectual and religious expressions, exegetical and theological literature can scarcely be satisfactorily apprehended in the modest framework of a lifetime of study. In working toward a definition of any religion, we must confront the same formidable complexities.

Our operative criteria of selection ought to be: What phenomena are most widely present and meaningful? What, further, is important as a representation of the reality both viewed and shaped by Judaism? The answers surely cannot be found only in philosophical, legal, mystical, or theological literature produced by and for a religious elite. We cannot suppose sophisticated conceptions of extraordinary people were fully grasped by common folk. Theological writings, while important, testify to the conceptions of reality held by only a tiny minority. The legal ideals and values of Judaism were first shaped by the rabbis, a class of religious virtuosi, and then imposed upon the life of ordinary people. Excluding learned theological and legal writings, the religious materials best conforming to our criteria are liturgical. The myths conveyed by prayer and associated rituals are universal, everywhere present and meaningful in the history of Judaism. Of greatest importance, they provide the clearest picture of how Jews in archaic times envisioned the meaning of life and of themselves.

Before proceeding, we had best clarify the meaning of "mythic structure." By myth, historians of religion do *not* mean something that is not true. They mean, in Streng's words: "That the essential structure of reality manifests itself in particular moments that are remembered and repeated from generation to generation."[1] These moments are preserved in myths. This meaning is wholly congruent to the Judaic data we shall now consider. If, in general, myth has the power to transform life because "it reveals the truth of life," as Streng says,[2] then what is the nature of Judaic myth?

If a myth is present, it must be everywhere present, somehow hidden in every ceremony and rite, every liturgy, every sacred gesture and taboo. We must be able to locate it in commonplace, not merely extraordinary, events of piety. Liturgy provides the clearest and, at the same time, the most reliable evidence of the structure of Judaic myth.

The overall mythic structure of Judaism has three principal components: a story of creation, one of revelation, and one of redemption. God created the world, revealed the Torah, and will redeem the people of Israel—to whom God revealed the Torah—at the end of time through the sending of the Messiah. Sometimes the same elements will be given the shape of a story about God, Israel (the Jewish people), and the covenant effected through the keeping of the Torah—that is, through doing God's will for Israel. (This set of mythic statements is called by the New Testament scholar E. P. Sanders "covenantal nomism," meaning the keeping of the religious requirements of the Torah as an expression of loyalty to the covenant between God and Israel.[3]) In many of the religious statements we shall see, the main themes again and again are God's creation of the world, revelation of the Torah, and redemption of Israel. Naturally, it is possible to express these same themes in diverse ways, so that creation takes the form of the Garden of Eden story, redemption is symbolized by the going forth from Egypt, and revelation is reflected throughout in the use of Torah-symbols.

We shall consider several sorts of liturgies, for the Judaic Prayerbook—the *Siddur*—is what all forms and aspects of the Judaic tradition have in common and constitutes the corpus of Judaic dogma, rite, and myth. First comes the *Shema*, containing the fundamental principles of faith. Then we shall turn to the marriage liturgy to see how the vital myth reshapes a private experience into a moment of public and communal meaning. Third, we shall consider two disparate liturgies of self-consciousness, the family together at the Passover *seder* and the community on the threshold of going forth from worship. Each prayer tells us about how the Jew sees and defines himself in, and apart from, the world. We shall see, in the Grace after Meals, how the land and Jerusalem enter the Judaic imagination. We shall read a folk song, a message of prophecy, a stanza of a modern nationalist anthem, and a messianic prayer in the daily service, all addressed to the question: *How long O Lord?*

As we proceed in our study, we draw on materials from the Hebrew Scriptures—for instance, Psalms—as much as from documents generally credited to talmudic rabbis, just as the rabbis themselves drew on the Scriptures for a definition of Judaism. What we see in the profoundly biblical orientation of Judaism is that the talmudic rabbis did not start something essentially new, but reshaped something that had been in existence for a very long time. That means that the ecological framework to be interpreted by Judaism—that is, the context framed and shaped in the life of the Jewish people—remained fairly stable, so that old ideas con-

tinued to be found plausible and self-evident. In this respect, the claim of
the rabbinic version of Judaism to continue the Torah of Moses "our
rabbi" is by no means incredible, except as plain history. And (it goes
without saying) the fact that a great many sources we shall adduce in evidence of the inner life of Judaism are not distinctive to rabbinic perspectives of Judaism changes nothing. These are materials talmudic rabbis
found congenial to their conceptions. And they found them so because
they could and did read them as statements of ideas particular to the
talmudic rabbis themselves.

Why should this expression of Judaism—that is, the world view expressed through the symbols of creation, revelation, and redemption—have
made sense and proved plausible for the Jews over a long period of time?
The reason is that the critical issues of the Jews' historical life—Why do we
matter? Why should we go forward? How long will this situation last?—
are dealt with in a profound and transcendent way. Keep in mind that the
Jews have had to suffer for their faith and accept the condition of a despised minority, a pariah people, everywhere they have lived. Even in
America today many people look down on the Jews and think ill of them.
The Jews, for their part, have always had the choice of accepting the dominant religion of their place of residence—Christianity in the West, Islam in
the Middle East—and so of leaving their condition as a pariah people. And
some did. But most did not, just as the Jews of the modern period chose
and continue to choose to be Jews, no matter what. Why should they do
this? Why do they do this? And what does it mean?

In the classical myth, the meaning is found in the correspondence of
heaven and earth. The world was created for the sake of the Torah; the
Torah was revealed for the sake of Israel; and Israel, keeping the covenant
through the Torah, will be redeemed in the end of time. To the world, the
Jews may seem to be pariahs, but Judaism knows they are God's children—
princes and princesses. The life of Torah is a sweet and serene life. The
rhythms of creation and Sabbath, revelation and Torah-study, and redemption and the festivals (Passover, Tabernacles, Pentecost) join the lives
of individual men and women to the patterns of the transcendent and the
holy. From the perspective of Judaism lived by the Jewish people, why
should the Jew not choose to be Judaic, since God has chosen him and her
to be just that? From the perspective of the Jewish people, the suffering
has been the proof and vindication of the faith of Torah. The very
regularity of creation—the waves on the ocean, the majesty and perman-
ence of the mountains and the valleys—stands as witness to the truth of
the faith of Torah. These are the lines of thought to be explored: the
relationship between the Jews' historical and social realities and their self-
understanding as shaped and expressed through their religion, Judaism.

We begin with the *Shema*, the proclamation of God's unity recited
morning and evening in Judaic worship. This highly theological
statement—that God is one and singular—is set into a context of prayers
that convey much insight into the classical Judaic view of reality.

CHAPTER 5

Hear, O Israel

Evening and morning, the pious Jew proclaims the unity and uniqueness of God. The proclamation is preceded and followed by blessings. The whole constitutes the credo of the Judaic tradition. It is "what the Jews believe." Components recur everywhere. Let us first examine the prayer called *Shema* (Hear).

The recital of the *Shema* is introduced by a celebration of God as Creator of the world. In the morning, one says:

> Praised are You, O Lord our God, King of the universe.
> You fix the cycles of light and darkness;
> You ordain the order of all creation
> You cause light to shine over the earth;
> Your radiant mercy is upon its inhabitants.
> In Your goodness the work of creation
> Is continually renewed day by day. . . .
> O cause a new light to shine on Zion;
> May we all soon be worthy to behold its radiance.
> Praised are You, O Lord, Creator of the heavenly bodies.[1]

The corresponding prayer in the evening refers to the setting of the sun:

> Praised are You. . . .
> Your command brings on the dusk of evening.
> Your wisdom opens the gates of heaven to a new day.
> With understanding You order the cycles of time;
> Your will determines the succession of seasons;
> You order the stars in their heavenly courses.
> You create day, and You create night,
> Rolling away light before darkness. . . .
> Praised are You, O Lord, for the evening dusk.[2]

Morning and evening, the Jew responds to the natural order of the world with thanks and praise of God who created the world and who actively guides the daily events of nature. Whatever happens in nature gives testimony to the sovereignty of the Creator. And that testimony is not in unnatural disasters, but in the most ordinary events: sunrise and sunset. These, especially, evoke the religious response to set the stage for what follows.

For the Jew, God is not merely Creator, but purposeful Creator. The works of creation serve to justify and to testify to Torah, the revelation of Sinai. Torah is the mark not merely of divine sovereignty, but of divine grace and love, source of life here and now and in eternity. So goes the second blessing:

> Deep is Your love for us, O Lord our God;
> Bounteous is Your compassion and tenderness.
> You taught our fathers the laws of life,
> And they trusted in You, Father and king,
> For their sake be gracious to us, and teach us,
> That we may learn Your laws and trust in You.
> Father, merciful Father, have compassion upon us:
> Endow us with discernment and understanding.
> Grant us the will to study Your Torah,
> To heed its words and to teach its precepts. . . .
> Enlighten our eyes in Your Torah,
> Open our hearts to Your commandments. . . .
> Unite our thoughts with singleness of purpose
> To hold You in reverence and in love. . . .
> You have drawn us close to You;
> We praise You and thank You in truth.
> With love do we thankfully proclaim Your unity.
> And praise You who chose Your people Israel in love.[3]

Here is the way in which revelation takes concrete and specific form in the Judaic tradition: God, the Creator, revealed his will for creation through the Torah, given to Israel his people. That Torah contains the "laws of life."

The Jew, moved to worship by the daily miracle of sunrise and sunset, responds with the prayer that he or she, like nature, may enjoy divine compassion. But what does that compassion consist of? The ability to understand and the will to study Torah! This is the mark of the relationship between God and the human being—the Jewish person in particular: that a person's eyes are open to Torah and that a person's heart is open to the commandments. These are the means of divine service and of reverence and love for God. Israel sees itself as "chosen"—close to God—because of Torah, and it finds in its devotion to Torah the marks of its chosenness. The covenant made at Sinai—a contract on Israel's side to do and hear the Torah; on God's side, to be the God of Israel—is evoked by natural events and then confirmed by the deeds and devotion of men.

In the *Shema*, Torah—revelation—leads Jews to enunciate the chief teaching of revelation:

> Hear O Israel, the Lord Our God, the Lord is One.

This proclamation is followed by three Scriptural passages. The first is Deuteronomy 6:5–9:

> *You shall love the Lord your God with all your heart, with all your soul, with all your might.*

And further, one must diligently teach one's children these words and talk of them everywhere and always, and place them on one's forehead, doorposts, and gates. The second Scripture is Deuteronomy 11:13–21, which emphasizes that if Jews keep the commandments, they will enjoy worldly blessings; but that if they do not, they will be punished and disappear from the good land God gives them. The third is Numbers 15:37–41, the commandment to wear fringes on the corners of one's garments. The fringes are today attached to the prayer shawl worn at morning sevices and they remind the Jew of *all* the commandments of the Lord.

The proclamation is completed and yet remains open, for having created humanity and revealed his will, God is not unaware of events since Sinai. Humanity is frail, and in the contest between the word of God and the will of humanity, Torah is not always the victor. We inevitably fall short of what is asked of us and Jews know that their own history consists of divine punishment for human failure time and again. The theme of redemption, therefore, is introduced.

Redemption—in addition to creation and revelation, the third element in the tripartite world view—resolves the tension between what we are told to do and what we are able actually to accomplish. In the end it is the theme of God, not as Creator or Revealer, but God as Redeemer that concludes the twice-daily drama:

> You are our King and our father's King,
> Our redeemer and our father's redeemer.
> You are our creator. . . .
> You have ever been our redeemer and deliverer
> There can be no God but You. . . .
> You, O Lord our God, rescued us from Egypt;
> You redeemed us from the house of bondage. . . .
> You split apart the waters of the Red Sea,
> The faithful you rescued, the wicked drowned. . . .
> Then Your beloved sang hymns of thanksgiving. . . .
> They acclaimed the King, God on high,
> Great and awesome source of all blessings,
> The everliving God, exalted in his majesty.
> He humbles the proud and raises the lowly;
> He helps the needy and answers His people's call. . . .
> Then Moses and all the children of Israel
> Sang with great joy this song to the Lord:
> Who is like You O Lord among the mighty?

Who is like You, so glorious in holiness?
So wondrous your deeds, so worthy of praise!
The redeemed sang a new song to You;
They sang in chorus at the shore of the sea,
Acclaiming Your sovereignty with thanksgiving:
The Lord shall reign for ever and ever.
Rock of Israel, arise to Israel's defense!
Fulfill Your promise to deliver Judah and Israel.
Our redeemer is the Holy One of Israel,
The Lord of hosts is His name.
Praised are You, O Lord, redeemer of Israel.[4]

Redemption is both in the past and in the future. That God not only creates but also redeems is attested by the redemption from Egyptian bondage. The congregation repeats the exultant song of Moses and the people at the Red Sea, not as scholars making a learned allusion, but as participants in the salvation of old and of time to come. Then the people turn to the future and ask that Israel once more be redeemed.

But redemption is not only past and future. When the needy are helped, when the proud are humbled and the lowly are raised—in such commonplace, daily events redemption is already present. Just as creation is not only in the beginning, but happens every day, morning and night, so redemption is not only at the Red Sea, but every day, in humble events. Just as revelation was not at Sinai alone, but takes place whenever people study Torah, whenever God opens their hearts to the commandments, so redemption and creation are daily events.

The great cosmic events of creation in the beginning, redemption at the Red Sea, and revelation at Sinai—these are everywhere, every day near at hand. The Jew views secular reality under the mythic aspect of eternal, ever-recurrent events. What happens to the Jew and to the world, whether good or evil, falls into the pattern revealed of old and made manifest each day. Historical events produce a framework in which future events will find a place and by which they will be understood. Nothing that happens cannot be subsumed by the paradigm.

The myths of creation, of the Exodus from Egypt, and of the revelation of Torah at Sinai are repeated, not merely to tell the story of what once was and is no more, but rather to recreate out of the raw materials of everyday life the "true being"—life as it was, always is, and will be forever. Streng says, "Myth and ritual recreate in profane time what is eternally true in sacred reality. To live in the myth is to live out the creative power that is the basis of any existence whatever."[5] We here see an illustration of these statements. At prayer the Jew repeatedly refers to the crucial elements of his or her mythic being, thus uncovering the sacred both in nature and in history. We therefore cannot say that Judaic myth does not emphasize a repetition of a cosmic pattern in cyclical or mythical time, for what happens in the proclamation of the *Shema* is just that: the particular events of creation—sunset, sunrise—evoke in response the celebration of the power and the love of God, of his justice and mercy, and of revelation and redemption.

CHAPTER 6

Coming Together

For the Jew the most intimate occasion—the marriage ceremony—is also intrinsically public. Here a new family begins. Individual lover and beloved celebrate the uniqueness, the privacy of their love. One should, therefore, expect the nuptial prayer to speak of him and her, natural man and natural woman. Yet the blessings that are said over the cup of wine of sanctification are as follows:

> Praised are You, O Lord our God, King of the universe, Creator of the fruit of the vine.
>
> Praised are You, O Lord our God, King of the universe, who created all things for Your glory.
>
> Praised are You, O Lord our God, King of the universe, Creator of man.
>
> Praised are You, O Lord our God, King of the universe, who created man and woman in his image, fashioning woman from man as his mate, that together they might perpetuate life. Praised are You, O Lord, Creator of man.
>
> May Zion rejoice as her children are restored to her in joy. Praised are You, O Lord, who causes Zion to rejoice at her children's return.
>
> Grant perfect joy to these loving companions, as You did to the first man and woman in the Garden of Eden. Praised are You, O Lord, who grants the joy of bride and groom.
>
> Praised are You, O Lord, our God, King of the universe, who created joy and gladness, bride and groom, mirth, song, delight and rejoicing, love and harmony, peace and companionship. O Lord our God, may there ever be heard in the cities of Judah and in the streets of Jerusalem voices of joy and gladness, voices of bride and groom, the jubilant voices of those joined in marriage under the bridal canopy, the voices of young people feasting and singing. Praised are You, O Lord, who causes the groom to rejoice with his bride.[1]

These seven blessings say nothing of private people and of their anonymously falling in love. Nor do they speak of the community of Israel, as one might expect on a public occasion. In them are no hidden sermons to be loyal to the community and faithful in raising up new generations in it. Lover and beloved rather are transformed from natural to mythical figures. The blessings speak of archetypical Israel, represented here and now by the bride and groom.

Israel's history begins with creation—first, the creation of the vine, symbol of the natural world. Creation is for God's glory. All things speak to nature, to the physical as much as the spiritual, for all things were made by God. In Hebrew, the blessings end, "who formed the *Adam*." All things glorify God; above all creation is Adam. The theme of ancient paradise is introduced by the simple choice of the word *Adam*, so heavy with meaning. The myth of man's creation is rehearsed: man and woman are in God's image, together complete and whole, creators of life, "like God." Woman was fashioned from man together with him to perpetuate life. And again, "blessed is the creator of Adam." We have moved, therefore, from the natural world to the archetypical realm of paradise. Before us we see not merely a man and a woman, but Adam and Eve.

But this Adam and this Eve also are Israel, children of Zion the mother, as expressed in the fifth blessing. Zion lies in ruins, her children scattered:

> If I forget you, O Jerusalem, may my right hand forget its skill . . . if I do not place Jerusalem above my greatest joy.

> —Psalm 137

Adam and Eve cannot celebrate together without thought to the condition of the mother, Jerusalem. The children will one day come home. The mood is hopeful yet sad, as it was meant to be, for archaic Isreal mourns as it rejoices and rejoices as it mourns. Quickly then, back to the happy occasion, for we do not let mourning lead to melancholy: "Grant perfect joy to the loving companions," for they are creators of a new line in mankind—the new Adam, the new Eve—and their home: May it be the garden of Eden. And if joy is there, then "praised are you for the joy of bride and groom."

The concluding blessing returns to the theme of Jerusalem. This time it evokes the tragic hour of Jerusalem's first destruction. When everyone had given up hope, supposing with the end of Jerusalem had come the end of time, only Jeremiah counseled renewed hope. With the enemy at the gate, he sang of coming gladness:

> Thus says the Lord:

> In this place of which you say, "It is a waste, without man or beast," in the cities of Judah and the streets of Jerusalem that are desolate, without man or inhabitant or beast,

> There shall be heard again the voice of mirth and the voice of gladness, the voice

of the bridegroom and the voice of the bride, the voice of those who sing as they
bring thank-offerings to the house of the Lord. . . .

For I shall restore the fortunes of the land as at first, says the Lord.

—Jeremiah 33:10–11

The closing blessing is not merely a literary artifice or a learned allusion to the ancient prophet. It is rather the exultant, jubilant climax of this acted-out myth: Just as here and now there stand before us Adam and Eve, so here and now in this wedding, the olden sorrow having been rehearsed, we listen to the voice of gladness that is coming. The joy of this new creation prefigures the joy of the Messiah's coming, hope for which is very present in this hour. And when he comes, the joy then will echo the joy of bride and groom before us. Zion the bride, Israel the groom, united now as they will be reunited by the compassionate God—these stand under the marriage canopy.

In classical Judaism, who are Jewish man and woman? They are ordinary people who live within a mythic structure and who thereby hold a view of history centered upon Israel from the creation of the world to its final redemption. Political defeats of this world are by myth transformed into eternal sorrow. The natural events of human life—here, the marriage of ordinary folk—are by myth heightened into a reenactment of Israel's life as a people. In marriage, individuals stand in the place of mythic figures, yet remain, after all, boys and girls. What gives their love its true meaning is the myth of creation, revelation, and redemption, here and now embodied in that love. But in the end, the sacred and secular are in most profane, physical love united.[2]

The wedding of symbol and reality—the fusion and confusion of the two—these mark the classical Judaic experience shaped by myths of creation, of Adam and Eve, of the Garden of Eden, and by the historical memory of the this-worldly destruction of an old, unexceptional temple. Ordinary events, such as a political and military defeat or success, are changed into theological categories such as divine punishment and heavenly compassion. If religion is a means of ultimate transformation, rendering the commonplace into the paradigmatic, changing the here and now into a moment of eternity and of eternal return, then the marriage liturgy serves to exemplify what is *religious* in Judaic existence.

CHAPTER 7

Going Forth

At the festival of Passover, in the spring, Jewish families gather around their tables for a holy meal. There they retell the story of the Exodus from Egypt in times long past. With unleavened bread and sanctified wine, they celebrate the liberation of slaves from Pharaoh's bondage. How do they see themselves?

> *We* were the slaves of Pharaoh in Egypt; and the Lord our God brought us forth from there with a mighty hand and an outstretched arm. And if the Holy One, blessed be He, had not brought our fathers forth from Egypt, then surely we, and our children, and our children's children, would be enslaved to Pharaoh in Egypt. And so, even if all of us were full of wisdom and understanding, well along in years and deeply versed in the tradition, we should still be bidden to repeat once more the story of the exodus from Egypt; and he who delights to dwell on the liberation is a man to be praised.[1]

Through the natural eye, one sees ordinary folk, not much different from their neighbors in dress, language, or aspirations. The words they speak do not describe reality and are not meant to. When Jewish people say of themselves, "We were the slaves of Pharaoh in Egypt," they know they never felt the lash; but through the eye of faith that is just what they have done. It is *their* liberation, not merely that of long-dead forebears, they now celebrate.

To be a Jew means to be a slave who has been liberated by God. To be Israel means to give eternal thanks for God's deliverance. And that deliverance is not at a single moment in historical time. It comes in every generation and is always celebrated. Here again, events of natural, ordinary life are transformed through myth into paradigmatic, eternal, and ever-recurrent sacred moments. Jews think of themselves as having gone forth from Egypt, and Scripture so instructs them. God did not redeem the dead generation of the Exodus alone, but the living too—especially the living. Thus the family states:

> Again and again, in double and redoubled measure, are we beholden to God the All-Present: that He freed us from the Egyptians and wrought His judgment on them; that He sentenced all their idols and slaughtered all their first-born; that He gave their treasure to us and split the Red Sea for us; that He led us through it dry-shod and drowned the tyrants in it; that He helped us through the desert and fed us with the manna; that He gave the Sabbath to us and brought us to Mount Sinai; that He gave the Torah to us and brought us to our homeland—there to build the Temple for us, for atonement of our sins.[2]

> This is the promise which has stood by our forefathers and stands by us. For neither once, nor twice, nor three times was our destruction planned; in every generation they rise against us, and in every generation God delivers us from their hands into freedom, out of anguish into joy, out of mourning into festivity, out of darkness into light, out of bondage into redemption.[3]

> For ever after, in every generation, *every man must think of himself as having gone forth from Egypt* [italics added]. For we read in the Torah: "In that day thou shalt teach thy son, saying: All this is because of what God did for me when I went forth from Egypt." It was not only our forefathers that the Holy One, blessed be He, redeemed; us too, the living, He redeemed together with them, as we learn from the verse in the Torah: "And He brought us out from thence, so that He might bring us home, and give us the land which he pledged to our forefathers."[4]

Israel was born in historical time. Historians, biblical scholars, and archaeologists have much to say about that event. But to the classical Jew their findings, while interesting, have little bearing on the meaning of reality. The redemptive promise that stood by the forefathers and "stands by us" is not a mundane historical event, but a mythic interpretation of historical, natural events. Oppression, homelessness, extermination—like salvation, homecoming, renaissance—are this-worldly and profane, supplying headlines for newspapers. The myth that a Jew must think of himself or herself as having gone forth from Egypt (or as we shall see, from Auschwitz) and as being redeemed by God renders ordinary experience into a moment of celebration. If "us, too, the living, He [has] redeemed," then the observer no longer witnesses only historical men in historical time, but an eternal return to sacred time.

The "going forth" at Passover is one sort of exodus. Another comes morning and night when Jews complete their service of worship. Every synagogue service concludes with a prayer prior to going forth, called *Alenu*, from its first word in Hebrew. Like the Exodus, the moment of the congregation's departure becomes a celebration of Israel's God, a self-conscious, articulated rehearsal of Israel's peoplehood. But now it is the end, rather than the beginning, of time that is important. When Jews go forth, they look forward:

Let us praise Him, Lord over all the world;
Let us acclaim Him, Author of all creation.
He made our lot unlike that of other peoples;
He assigned to us a unique destiny.
We bend the knee, worship, and acknowledge
The King of kings, the Holy One, praised is He.
He unrolled the heavens and established the earth;
His throne of glory is in the heavens above;
His majestic Presence is in the loftiest heights.
He and no other is God and faithful King,
Even as we are told in His Torah:
Remember now and always, that the Lord is God;
Remember, no other is Lord of heaven and earth.
We, therefore, hope in You, O Lord our God,
That we shall soon see the triumph of Your might,
That idolatry shall be removed from the earth,
And false gods shall be utterly destroyed.
Then will the world be a true kingdom of God,
When all mankind will invoke Your name,
And all the earth's wicked will return to You.
Then all the inhabitants of the world will surely know
That to You every knee must bend,
Every tongue must pledge loyalty.
Before You, O Lord, let them bow in worship,
Let them give honor to Your glory.
May they all accept the rule of Your kingdom.
May you reign over them soon through all time.
Sovereignty is Yours in glory, now and forever.
So it is written in Your Torah:
The Lord shall reign for ever and ever.[5]

In secular terms Jews know that in some ways they form a separate, distinct group. In mythical reality they thank God they enjoy a unique destiny. They do not conclude with thanks for their particular "being," but sing a hymn of hope merely that he who made their lot unlike that of all others will soon rule as sovereign over all. The secular difference, the unique destiny, is for the time being only. When the destiny is fulfilled, there will be no further difference. The natural eye beholds a social group with some particular cultural characteristics defining that group. The myth of peoplehood transforms *difference* into *destiny*.

The existence of the natural group means little, except as testimony to the sovereignty of the God who shaped the group and rules its life. The unique, the particular, the private now are no longer profane matters of culture, but become testimonies of divine sovereignty, pertinent to all people, all groups. The particularism of the group is for the moment alone; the will of God is for eternity. When that will be done, then all people will recognize that the unique destiny of Israel was intended for everyone. The ordinary facts of sociology no longer predominate. The myth of Israel has changed the secular and commonplace into a paradigm of true being.

CHAPTER 8

The Only Kid and the Messiah

And what of Israel's long and pathetic history? Is it merely a sucession of meaningless disasters—worldly happenings without end or purpose? The answer comes in a folk song sung at the Passover *seder*, the ceremonial meal commemorating the Exodus from Egypt:

> An only kid, an only kid
> My father bought for two pennies,
> An only kid, an only kid.
> But along came the cat and ate up the kid,
> My father bought for two pennies,
> An only kid, an only kid.

And so goes the dreary story. Here is the final verse:

> Then the Holy One, blessed be He, came along
> And slew the angel of death
> Who slew the slaughterer
> Who slew the ox
> Who drank the water
> That put out the fire
> That burned the stick
> That beat the dog
> That bit the cat
> That ate the kid
> My father bought for two pennies,
> An only kid, an only kid.[1]

Here is the whole of Israel's history embodied in the little lamb the father bought for next to nothing, his only kid. The fate of Israel, the lamb slaughtered not once but many times over, is suffering that has an end and a purpose in the end of days. Death will die, and all who shared in the lamb's suffering will witness the divine denouement of history. The history of sin, suffering, atonement, reconciliation is a cycle not destined forever and ever to repeat itself.

Yet in the worst hour, when all hope is lost, the memories of ancient days, of redemption in olden times, serve to remind Israel of God's enduring concern and divine pathos. For not once but many times in the thousands of years of Israel's history, it appeared that the final chapter at last was to be inscribed—and inscribed in blood—on the pages of history. Ezekiel's vision of the dry bones—elevated and exalted in contrast to the humble song of the only kid—ever seemed addressed, not to the days of old, but to the very present hour:

> *The hand of the Lord was upon me, and he brought me out by the Spirit of the Lord, and set me down in the midst of the valley; it was full of bones . . . and lo, they were very dry. And he said to me, "Son of man, can these bones live?" And I answered, "O Lord, God, you know."*

> *And again he said to me, "Prophesy to these bones, and say to them, O dry bones, hear the word of the Lord. Thus says the Lord God to these bones, Behold I will cause breath to enter you, and you shall live. And I will lay sinews upon you and will bring flesh upon you and cover you with skin and put breath in you and you shall live, and you shall know that I am the Lord."*

Ezekiel did as he was told:

> *So I prophesied as he commanded me, and the breath came into them and they lived and stood upon their feet, an exceedingly great host.*

> *Then he said to me, "Son of man, these bones are the whole house of Israel. Behold, they say, 'Our bones are dried up, and our hope is lost, we are clean cut off.' Therefore prophesy and say to them, Thus says the Lord God, Behold, I will open your graves . . . O my people, and I will bring you home into the land of Israel. And you shall know that I am the Lord, and when I open your graves . . . and I will put my Spirit within you, and you shall live . . . then you shall know that I, the Lord, have spoken, and I have done it, says the Lord."*

> —**Ezekiel 37**

As elsewhere, so here we read words that come to one generation after another as if addressed particularly to its own time and place. What is remarkable about the mythic life of the Judaic tradition is the capacity of historical events to produce recurrent, consistent responses—indeed, to evoke a single response from varied and unrelated people in all sorts of places. Ezekiel spoke twenty-five centuries ago. His words, "our hope is lost," provide the theme of the Israeli national anthem, *Hattigvah*, "The Hope":

> . . . Our hope is *not* yet lost
> The hope of two thousand years
> To be a free people in our land
> In the land of Zion and Jerusalem.

But of such continuities we shall say more later on.

What unites the discrete, unrelated events in the life of the "only kid" and provokes a singular response among varied men is the pervasive conviction that an end *is* coming. Nothing is meaningless, for the random happenings of the centuries are in truth leading to the Messiah. The messianic hope lies at the end of the mythic life of Israel and illuminates every moment in it.

As we shall see, in modern times the Messiah became the "messianic hope," and Jews talked of a "messianic age" rather than of a single wonderful man. Actually, hope for the ideal king of the messianic age, the *mashiah* (anointed one; in Greek, *Christos*), first occurs in biblical times. The first detailed picture of the future ideal king comes in Isaiah 9:1-6, 11:1-10, and 32:1-5. Jeremiah and Ezekiel likewise look forward to the perfect dominion of God's anointed. The Messiah will be of the house of David. The spirit of God will rest on him. He will not conquer nations, but inaugurate a time of peace. He will bring peace, order, and prosperity. Nature will be perfected, so the lamb will not fear the wolf; society will be made whole, so tyranny and violence will end. Ezekiel emphasizes that in the time of the Messiah, the kingdom of Israel will be restored and reunited. Second Isaiah (ca. 550 B.C.) sees Israel, the people, in the messianic role. Israel is the servant of God who will achieve the regeneration of mankind through suffering and service. In pre–Christian times the messianic hope took the form of a personal Messiah, a scion of David who would end the rule of pagans over the people of God and inaugurate an age of peace and justice.

After the Second Temple was destroyed in A.D. 70, the rabbis who led Jewry looked forward to an earthly Messiah. The form their expectation took is best seen in the prayers they included for daily recitation in Jewish worship:

> Sound the great shofar to herald man's freedom;
> Raise high the banner to gather all exiles;
> Restore our judges as in days of old;
> Restore our counsellors as in former times;
> Remove from us sorrow and anguish.
> Reign over us alone with loving kindness;
> With justice and mercy sustain our cause.
> Praised are You, O Lord, King who loves justice.[2]

The restoration of the exiles to Zion and the gathering of the dispersed are followed naturally by the prayer for good government, government under God's law. Then comes the concrete reference to the Messiah himself:

> Have mercy, O Lord, and return to Jerusalem, Your city;
> May Your presence dwell there as You promised.
> Rebuild it now, in our days and for all time;
> Re-establish there the majesty of David, Your servant.
> Praised are You, O Lord, who rebuilds Jerusalem.
> Bring to flower the shoot of Your servant David.

Hasten the advent of the Messianic redemption;
Each and every day we hope for Your deliverance.
Praised are You, O Lord, who assures our deliverance.[3]

As we have repeatedly seen, the messianic hope thus is inextricably bound with the restoration of the people, the city, the Temple cult, and the house of David.

The history of Israel, the Jewish people, is the history of the only kid; at the end, the Holy One, blessed be He, comes to slaughter the angel of death, vindicate the long sufferings of many centuries, and bring to a happy and joyful end the times of trouble. Among the elements of the mythic structure of classical Judaism, the messianic hope—made concrete in the figure of the Messiah, son of David and king of Israel—stands forth everywhere and dominates throughout.

CHAPTER 9

The Land and Jerusalem

Israel's history did not end with the entry into the land of Canaan, but rather began. That history, in a worldly sense, consisted of the secular affairs of a seldom important kingdom, able to hold its own only when its neighbors permitted or could not prevent it. In a mythic context, however, Jews looked back upon the history of the people as a continuing revelation of divine justice and mercy. Israel, the people, kept the Torah; therefore, they enjoyed peace and prospered. Then Israel sinned, so God called forth instruments of his wrath: the Philistines, Assyrians, Babylonians, Persians, Greeks, Romans—there was no end to the list as time went on. But when Israel was properly chastised, God restored their prosperity and brought them back to the land.

Perhaps the single most powerful worldly experience in the history of Judaism was the destruction of the First Temple in 586 B.C., followed by the restoration of Jews to their land by the Persians approximately a half-century later. The worldly motives of the Persians are of no interest here, for they never played a role in the interpretation of historical events put forward by Judaic tradition. What the Jews understood was simply this: God had punished them, but when they repented and atoned, he had forgiven and redeemed them. And they further believed that the prophets who had foretold just this pattern of events were now vindicated, so that much else that they said was likely to be true. From the fifth century B.C. to the present, Jews have seen their history within the paradigm of sin, punishment, atonement, reconciliation, and then restoration.

The land entered the Judaic imagination as a powerful—indeed overwhelming—symbol. It was holy, the stage for sacred history. We have already noted numerous references to the land, Jerusalem, Zion, and the like. These references all represent concrete exemplifications of myth. Redemption is not an abstract concept, but rather it is what happened when Moses led the people through the Sea of Reeds, or what happened with the

return to Zion when the Second Temple was built (ca. 500 B.C.), or what
will happen when God again shines light on Zion and brings the scattered
people back to their homes. In classical Judaism, the sanctity of the land,
the yearning for Zion, the hope for the restoration of Jerusalem and the
Temple cult are all symbols by which the redemption of the past is projected on to the future. The equivalent of the salvation at the sea will be the
restoration of Israel to the land and the reconstruction of the Temple and
of Jerusalem: The one stands at the beginning of Israel's history; the
other, its counterpart, at the end.

How do the several salvific symbols fit together in the larger mythic
structure of creation, revelation, and redemption? In the Grace after
Meals, recited whenever pious Jews eat bread, we see their interplay. To
understand the setting, we must recall that in classical Judaism the table at
which meals were eaten was regarded as the equivalent of the sacred altar
in the Temple. Judaism taught that each Jew before eating had to attain the
same state of ritual purity as the priest in the sacred act of making a
sacrifice. So in the classic tradition the Grace after Meals is recited in a
sacerdotal circumstance.

On Sabbaths and festivals—times of eternity in time—Jews first sing
Psalm 126: *When the Lord brought back those that returned to Zion, we were
like dreamers. Our mouth was filled with laughter, our tongue with singing.
Restore our fortunes, O Lord, as the streams in the dry land. They that sow in
tears shall reap in joy* . . . Then they recite the grace:

> Blessed art Thou, Lord our God, King of the Universe, who nourishes all the
> world by His goodness, in grace, in mercy, and in compassion: He gives
> bread to all flesh, for His mercy is everlasting. And because of His great
> goodness we have never lacked, and so may we never lack, sustenance—for
> the sake of His great Name. For He nourishes and feeds everyone, is good to
> all, and provides food for each one of the creatures He created.

> Blessed art Thou, O Lord, who feeds everyone.

> We thank Thee, Lord our God, for having given our fathers as a heritage a
> pleasant, a good and spacious land; for having taken us out of the land of
> Egypt, for having redeemed us from the house of bondage; for Thy cove-
> nant, which Thou hast set as a seal in our flesh, for Thy Torah which Thou
> hast taught us, for Thy statutes which Thou hast made known to us, for the
> life of grace and mercy Thou hast graciously bestowed upon us, and for the
> nourishment with which Thou dost nourish us and feed us always, every
> day, in every season, and every hour.

> For all these things, Lord our God, we thank and praise Thee; may Thy
> praises continually be in the mouth of every living thing, as it is written,
> And thou shalt eat and be satisfied, and bless the Lord thy God for the good
> land which He hath given thee.

> Blessed art thou, O Lord, for the land and its food.

> O Lord our God, have pity on Thy people Israel, on Thy city Jerusalem, on

Zion the place of Thy glory, on the royal house of David Thy Messiah, and on the great and holy house which is called by Thy Name. Our God, our Father, feed us and speed us, nourish us and make us flourish; unstintingly, O Lord our God, speedily free us from all distress.

And let us not, O Lord our God, find ourselves in need of gifts from flesh and blood, or of a loan from anyone save from Thy full, generous, abundant, wide-open hand; so we may never be humiliated, or put to shame.

O rebuild Jerusalem, the holy city, speedily in our day. Blessed art Thou, Lord, who in mercy will rebuild Jerusalem. Amen.

Blessed art Thou, Lord our God, King of the Universe, Thou God, who art our Father, our powerful king, our creator and redeemer, who made us, our holy one, the holy one of Jacob, our shepherd, shepherd of Israel, the good king, who visits His goodness upon all; for every single day He has brought good, He does bring good, He will bring good upon us; He has rewarded us, does reward, and will always reward us, with grace, mercy and compassion, amplitude, deliverance and prosperity, blessing and salvation, comfort, and a living, sustenance, pity and peace, and all good—let us not want any manner of good whatever.[1]

The context of grace is enjoyment of creation, through which God nourishes the world in his goodness. That we have had this meal—however humble—is not to be taken for granted, but rather as a gift. Whenever one eats, he or she must reflect on the beneficence of the Creator. The arena for creation is the land, which to the ordinary eye is commonplace, small, dry, rocky; but which to the eye of faith is pleasant, good, spacious. The land lay at the end of redemption from Egyptian bondage. Holding it, enjoying it—as we saw in the *Shema*—is a sign that the covenant is intact and in force and that Israel is loyal to its part of the contract and God to his. The land, the Exodus, the covenant—these all depend upon the Torah, statutes, and a life of grace and mercy, here embodied in and evoked by the nourishment of the meal. Thanksgiving wells up, and the paragraph ends with praises for the land and its food.

Then the chief theme recurs—that is, redemption and hope for return, and then future prosperity in the land: "May God pity the people, the city, Zion, the royal house of the Messiah, the holy Temple." The nourishment of this meal is but a foretaste of the nourishment of the messianic time, just as the joy of the wedding is a foretaste of the messianic rejoicing.

Still, it is not the messianic time, so Israel finally asks not to depend upon the gifts of mortal men but only upon those of the generous, wide-open hand of God. And then "rebuild Jerusalem." The concluding paragraph summarizes the whole, giving thanks for creation, redemption, divine goodness, every blessing.

In some liturgies creation takes the primary place, as here and in the wedding ceremony. In others, the chief theme is revelation. Redemptive and concrete salvific symbols occur everywhere.

PART THREE

The Way of Torah:
A Way of Living

CHAPTER 10

The Spirit of the Law

The mythic structure built upon the themes of creation, revelation, and redemption finds expression, not only in synagogue liturgy, but especially in concrete, everyday actions or action-symbols—that is, deeds that embody and express the fundamental mythic life of the classical Judaic tradition.

Deeds

These action-symbols are set forth in *halakhah*. This word is normally translated as "law," for the *halakhah* is full of normative, prescriptive rules about what one must do and refrain from doing in every situation of life and at every moment of the day. But *halakhah* derives from the root *halakh*, which means "go," and a better translation would be "way." The *halakhah* is "the way": *The way* man lives his life; *the way* man shapes his daily routine into a pattern of sanctity; *the way* man follows the revelation of the Torah and attains redemption.

For the Judaic tradition, this *way* is absolutely central. Belief without the expression of belief in the workaday world is of limited consequence. The purpose of revelation is to create a kingdom of priests and a holy people. The foundation of that kingdom, or sovereignty, is the rule of God over the lives of humanity. For the Judaic tradition, God rules much as people do, by guiding others on the path of life, not by removing them from the land of living. Creation lies behind; redemption, in the future; Torah is for here and now. To the classical Jew, Torah means revealed law or commandment, accepted by Israel and obeyed from Sinai to the end of days.

The spirit of the Jewish way (*halakhah*) is conveyed in many modes, for law is not divorced from values, but rather concretizes human beliefs and ideals. The purpose of the commandments is to show the road to sanctity, the way to God. In a more mundane sense, the following provides a valuable insight:

Rava [a fourth-century rabbi] said, "When a man is brought in for judgment in the world to come, he is asked, 'Did you deal in good faith? Did you set aside time for study of Torah? Did you engage in procreation? Did you look forward to salvation? Did you engage in the dialectics of wisdom? Did you look deeply into matters?' "

—Talmud, b. Shabbat, 31(a)

Rava's interpretation of the Scripture *and there shall be faith in thy times, strength, salvation, wisdom and knowledge* (Isaiah 33:6) provides one glimpse into the life of the classical Jew who followed the way of Torah. The first consideration was ethical: Did the man conduct himself faithfully? The second was study of Torah, not at random but every day, systematically, as a discipline of life. Third came the raising of a family, for celibacy and abstinence from sexual life were regarded as sinful; the full use of man's creative powers for the procreation of life was a commandment. Nothing God made was evil. Wholesome conjugal life was a blessing. But, fourth, merely living day-by-day according to an upright ethic was not sufficient. It is true that people must live by a holy discipline, but the discipline itself was only a means. The end was salvation. Hence the pious people were asked to look forward to salvation, aiming their deeds and directing their hearts toward a higher goal. Wisdom and insight—these completed the list, for without them, the way of Torah was a life of mere routine, rather than a constant search for deeper understanding.

If in this context we have not referred also to women, it is not because they were wholly excluded from the system, but because in this setting the principal activities—study of Torah, for example—were done by men only. The *halakhah*, in fact, clearly recognized that there were religious duties incumbent on both men and women, but there were some required only of men. Women were excluded, in particular, from the requirement to perform those religious acts which had to be done at a particular time. The reason was that their responsibilities to their families overrode their responsibilities to heaven. If at the same time a woman had to perform a particular commandment and also take care of her daughter or her son, she could not do the former with a whole heart. Therefore from the very beginning the law excluded her. On the other hand, we shall later survey a religious world from which, in point of fact, women were excluded when there was no reason for their exclusion intrinsic to the law and the system. That is a separate problem to which we shall return.

CHAPTER 11

Hear Our Prayer, Grant Us Peace

Life under the law means praying—morning, noon, night, and at meals—both routinely and when something unusual happens. To be a Jew in the classical tradition, one lives his or her life constantly aware of the presence of God and always ready to praise and bless God. The way of Torah is the way of perpetual devotion to God. What is the substance of that devotion? For what do pious Jews ask when they pray?

The answers to these questions tell us about more than the shape and substance of Judaic piety. They tell us, too, what manner of person would take shape, for the constant repetition of the sacred words and moral and ethical maxims in the setting of everyday life is bound to affect the personality and character of the individual and the quality of communal life as well. Prayer expresses the most solemn aspirations of the praying community; it is what gives that community a sense of oneness and of shared hopes; it embodies the values of the community. But if it is the community in its single most idiomatic hour, it also presents the community at its least particular and self-aware, for in praying, people stand before God without the mediation of culture and ethnic consciousness. But, as we shall see, that does not mean in Judaic prayer we do not find an acute awareness of history and collective destiny. These are very present.

In the morning, noon, and evening prayers are found the Eighteen Benedictions. Some of these, in particular those at the beginning and the end, recur in Sabbath and festival prayers. They are said silently. Each individual prays by and for himself or herself, but together with other silent, praying individuals. The Eighteen Benedictions are then repeated aloud by the prayer leader, for prayer is both private and public, individual and collective. To contemplate the meaning of these prayers, one should imagine a room full of people, all standing by themselves yet in close proximity, some swaying this way and that, all addressing themselves directly and intimately to God in a whisper or in a low tone. They do not move their feet, for they are now standing before the King of kings, and it is not mete to shift and shuffle. If spoken to, they will not answer. Their attention is fixed upon the words of supplication, praise, and gratitude. When they begin, they bend their knees—so too toward the end—and at the conclusion they step back and withdraw from the presence. These, on ordinary days, are the words they say:

WISDOM—REPENTANCE
You graciously endow man with intelligence;
You teach him knowledge and understanding.
Grant us knowledge, discernment, and wisdom.
Praised are You, O Lord, for the gift of knowledge.

Our Father, bring us back to Your Torah;
Our King, draw us near to Your service;
Lead us back to you truly repentant.
Praised are You, O Lord who welcomes repentance.

FORGIVENESS—REDEMPTION
Our Father, forgive us, for we have sinned;
Our King, pardon us, for we have transgressed;
You forgive sin and pardon transgression.
Praised are You, gracious and forgiving Lord.

Behold our affliction and deliver us.
Redeem us soon for the sake of Your name,
For You are the mighty Redeemer.
Praised are You, O Lord, Redeemer of Israel.

HEAL US—BLESS OUR YEARS
Heal us, O Lord, and we shall be healed;
Help us and save us, for You are our glory.
Grant perfect healing for all our afflictions,
O faithful and merciful God of healing.
Praised are You, O Lord, Healer of His people.

O Lord our God! Make this a blessed year;
May its varied produce bring us happiness.

Bring blessing upon the whole earth.

Bless the year with Your abounding goodness.
Praised are You, O Lord, who blesses our years.

GATHER OUR EXILES—REIGN OVER US
Sound the great shofar to herald [our] freedom;
Raise high the banner to gather all exiles;
Gather the dispersed from the corners of the earth.
Praised are You, O Lord, who gathers our exiles.

Restore our judges as in days of old;

Restore our counsellors as in former times;
Remove from us sorrow and anguish.
Reign over us alone with loving kindness;
With justice and mercy sustain our cause.
Praised are You, O Lord, King who loves justice.

HUMBLE THE ARROGANT—SUSTAIN THE RIGHTEOUS
Frustrate the hopes of those who malign us;
Let all evil very soon disappear;
Let all Your enemies be speedily destroyed.
May You quickly uproot and crush the arrogant;
May You subdue and humble them in our time.
Praised are You, O Lord, who humbles the arrogant.

Let Your tender mercies, O Lord God, be stirred
For the righteous, the pious, the leaders of Israel,
Toward devoted scholars and faithful proselytes.
Be merciful to us of the house of Israel;
Reward all who trust in You;
Cast our lot with those who are faithful to You.
May we never come to despair, for our trust is in You.
Praised are You, O Lord, who sustains the righteous.

FAVOR YOUR CITY AND YOUR PEOPLE
Have mercy, O Lord, and return to Jerusalem, Your city;
May Your Presence dwell there as You promised.
Rebuild it now, in our days and for all time;
Re-establish there the majesty of David, Your servant.
Praised are You, O Lord, who rebuilds Jerusalem.

Bring to flower the shoot of Your servant David.
Hasten the advent of the Messianic redemption;
Each and every day we hope for Your deliverance.
Praised are You, O Lord, who assures our deliverance.

O Lord, our God, hear our cry!
Have compassion upon us and pity us;
Accept our prayer with loving favor.
You, O God, listen to entreaty and prayer.
O King, do not turn us away unanswered,
For You mercifully heed Your people's supplication.
Praised are You, O Lord, who is attentive to prayer.

O Lord, our God, favor Your people Israel;
Accept with love Israel's offering of prayer;
May our worship be ever acceptable to You.
May our eyes witness Your return in mercy to Zion.
Praised are You, O Lord, whose Presence returns to Zion.

OUR THANKFULNESS
We thank You, O Lord our God and God of our fathers,
Defender of our lives, Shield of our safety;

Through all generations we thank You and praise You.
Our lives are in Your hands, our souls in Your charge.

We thank You for the miracles which daily attend us,
For Your wonders and favor morning, noon, and night.
You are beneficent with boundless mercy and love.
From of old we have always placed our hope in You.
For all these blessings, O our King,
We shall ever praise and exalt You.

Every living creature thanks You, and praises You in truth.
O God, You are our deliverance and our help. Selah!
Praised are You, O Lord, for Your goodness and Your glory.

PEACE AND WELL-BEING
Grant peace and well-being to the whole house of Israel;
Give us of Your grace, Your love, and Your mercy.

Bless us all, O our Father, with the light of Your Presence.
It is Your light that revealed to us Your life-giving Torah,
And taught us love and tenderness, justice, mercy, and peace.

May it please You to bless Your people in every season,
To bless them at all times with Your gift of peace.
Praised are You, O Lord, who blesses Israel with peace.[1]

The first two petitions pertain to intelligence. The Jew thanks God for mind: knowledge, wisdom, discernment. But knowledge is for a purpose, and the purpose is knowledge of Torah. Such discernment leads to the service of God and produces a spirit of repentance. We cannot pray without setting ourselves right with God, and that means repenting for what has separated us from God. Torah is the way to repentance and to return. So knowledge leads to Torah, Torah to repentance, and repentance to God. The logical next stop is the prayer for forgiveness. That is the sign of return. God forgives sin; God is gracious and forgiving. Once we discern what we have done wrong through the guidance of Torah, we therefore seek to be forgiven. It is sin that leads to affliction. Affliction stands at the beginning of the way to God; once we have taken that way, we ask for our suffering to end; we beg redemption. This is then specified. We ask for healing, salvation, a blessed year. Healing without prosperity means we may suffer in good health or starve in a robust body. So along with the prayer for healing goes the supplication for worldly comfort.

The individual's task is done. But what of the community? Health and comfort are not enough. The world is unredeemed. Jews are enslaved, in exile, and alien. At the end of days a great *shofar*, or ram's horn, will sound to herald the Messiah's coming. This is now besought. The Jewish people at prayer ask first for the proclamation of freedom, then for the ingathering of the exiles to the Promised Land. Establishing the messianic kingdom, God needs also to restore a wise and benevolent government, good judges, good counsellors, and loving justice.

Meanwhile Israel, the Jewish people, finds itself maligned. Arrogant men hating Israel hate God as well. They should be humbled. And the pious and righteous—the scholars, the faithful proselytes, the whole House of Israel that trusts in God—should be rewarded and sustained. Above all, remember Jerusalem. Rebuild the city and dwell there. Set up Jerusalem's messianic king, David, and make him to prosper. These are the themes of the daily prayer: personal atonement, good health, and good fortunes; collective redemption, freedom, the end of alienation, good government, and true justice; the final and complete salvation of the land and of Jerusalem by the Messiah. At the end comes a prayer that prayer may be heard and found acceptable; then an expression of thanksgiving, not for what may come, but for the miracles and mercies already enjoyed morning, noon, and night. And at the end is the prayer for peace—a peace that consists of wholeness for the sacred community.

People who say such prayers do not wholly devote themselves to this world. True, they ask for peace, health, and prosperity. But these are transient. At the same moment they ask, in so many different ways, for eternity. They arise in the morning and speak of Jerusalem. At noon they make mention of the Messiah. In the evening they end the day with talk of the *shofar* to herald freedom and the ingathering of the exiles. Living here in the profane, alien world, they constantly talk of going there—to the Holy Land and its perfect society. They address themselves to the end of days and the Messiah's time. The praying community above all seeks the fulfillment and end of its—and humanity's—travail.

CHAPTER 12

Sabbaths for Rest,
Festivals for Rejoicing

The classical Jew keeps the Sabbath both as a memorial of creation and as a remembrance of the redemption from Egypt. The primary liturgy of the Sabbath is the reading of the Scripture lesson from the Torah in the synagogue service. So the three chief themes—creation, revelation, and redemption—are combined in the weekly observance of the seventh day—that is, from sunset Friday to sunset Saturday.

The Sabbath is protected by negative rules: One must not work; one must not pursue mundane concerns. But the Sabbath is also adorned with less concrete but affirmative laws: One must rejoice; one must rest.

How do pious Jews keep the Sabbath? All week long they look forward to it, and the anticipation enhances the ordinary days. By Friday afternoon they have bathed, put on their Sabbath garments, and set aside the affairs of the week. At home, the wife will have cleaned, cooked, and arranged her finest table. The Sabbath comes at sunset and leaves when three stars appear Saturday night. After a brief service the family comes together to enjoy its best meal of the week—a meal at which particular Sabbath foods are served. In the morning comes the Sabbath service—including a public reading from the Torah, the Five Books of Moses, and prophetic writings—and an additional service in memory of the Temple sacrifices on Sabbaths of old. Then home for lunch and very commonly a Sabbath nap, the sweetest part of the day. As the day wanes, the synagogue calls for a late afternoon service, followed by Torah-study and a third meal. Then comes a ceremony, *havdalah* (separation)—effected with spices, wine, and candlelight—between the holy time of the Sabbath and the ordinary time of weekday.

This simple, regular observance has elicited endless praise. To the Sabbath-observing Jew, the Sabbath is the chief sign of God's grace:

> For thou hast chosen us and sanctified us above all nations, in love and favor has given us thy holy Sabbath as an inheritance.[1]

So states the Sanctification of the Sabbath wine. Likewise in the Sabbath
morning liturgy:

> You did not give it [the Sabbath] to the nations of the earth, nor did you
> make it the heritage of idolators, nor in its rest will unrighteous men find a
> place.

> But to Israel your people you have given it in love, to the seed of Jacob
> whom you have chosen, to that people who sanctify the Sabbath day. All of
> them find fulfillment and joy from your bounty.

> For the seventh day did you choose and sanctify as the most pleasant of
> days, and you called it a memorial to the works of creation.

Here again we find a profusion of themes, this time centered upon the
Sabbath. The Sabbath is a sign of the covenant. It is a gift of grace, which
neither idolators nor evil people may enjoy. It is the testimony of the
chosenness of Israel. And it is the most pleasant of days. Keeping the Sabbath *is* living in God's kingdom:

> Those who keep the Sabbath and call it a delight will rejoice in your
> kingdom.

So states the additional Sabbath prayer. Keeping the Sabbath now is a
foretaste of the redemption: "This day is for Israel light and rejoicing."
The rest of the Sabbath is, as the afternoon prayer affirms, "a rest granted
in generous love, a true and faithful rest. . . . Let your children realize
that their rest is from you, and by their rest may they sanctify your
name."
   That people need respite from the routine of work is no discovery of the
Judaic tradition. That the way in which they accomplish such a routine
change of pace may be made the very heart and soul of their spiritual existence is the single absolutely unique element in Judaic tradition. The
word *Sabbath* simply renders the Hebrew *Shabbat*; it does not translate it,
for there is no translation. In no other tradition or culture can an
equivalent word be found. Certainly those who compare the Sabbath of
Judaism to the somber, supposedly joyless Sunday of the Calvinists know
nothing of what the Sabbath has meant and continues to mean to Jews.
   In his account of the Sabbath, Abraham J. Heschel builds his theology
around the meaning of the Sabbath day. He reflects:

> Judaism is a religion of time aiming at the sanctification of time. . . .
> Judaism teaches us to be attached to holiness in time, to be attached to sacred
> events, to learn how to consecrate sanctuaries that emerge from the magnifi-
> cent stream of a year. The Sabbaths are our great cathedrals, and our Holy of
> Holies is a shrine that neither the Romans nor the Germans were able to
> burn. . . . Jewish ritual may be characterized as the art of significant forms
> in time as architecture of time.[2]

Heschel finds in the Sabbath "the day on which we are called upon to
share in what is eternal in time, to turn from the world of creation to the
creation of the world."[3]

From this brief description of what the Jew actually does on the seventh day, we can hardly derive understanding of how the Sabbath can have meant so much as to elicit words such as those of the Jewish Prayerbook and of Rabbi Heschel. Those words, like the laws of the Sabbath—not to mourn, not to confess sins, not to repent, not to do anything that might lead to unhappiness—describe something only the participant can truly comprehend and feel. Only a family whose life focuses upon the Sabbath week by week, year by year, from birth to death, can know the sanctity of which the theologian speaks, the sacred rest to which the prayers refer. The heart and soul of the Judaic tradition, the Sabbath cannot be described—only experienced. For the student of religions, it stands as that element of Judaism that is absolutely unique and therefore a mystery.

The festivals mark the passage of time: not of the week but of the seasons. Passover is the Jewish spring festival, and the symbols of the Passover *seder*—hard-boiled eggs and vegetable greens—are not unfamiliar in other spring rites. But here the spring rite has been transformed into a historical commemoration. The natural course of the year, while important, is subordinated to the historical events remembered and relived on the festival. Called the feast of unleavened bread and the season of our freedom, the Passover festival preserves very ancient rites in a new framework.

It is, for example, absolutely prohibited to make use of leaven, fermented dough, and the like. The agricultural calendar of ancient Canaan was marked by the grain harvest, beginning in the spring with the cutting of barley and ending with the reaping of the wheat approximately seven weeks later.[4] The farmers would get rid of all their sour dough, which they used as yeast, and old bread as well as any leaven from last year's crop. The origins of the practice are not clear, but that the Passover taboo against leaven was connected with the agricultural calendar is beyond doubt. Just as the agricultural festivals were historicized, likewise much of the detailed observance connected with them was supplied with historical "reasons" or explanations. In the case of the taboo against leaven, widely observed today even among otherwise unobservant Jews, the "reason" was that the Israelites had to leave Egypt in haste and therefore had to take with them unleavened bread, for they had no time to permit the bread to rise properly and be baked. Therefore we eat the *matzah*, unleavened bread.

The Feast of Weeks, *Shavuot* or Pentecost, comes seven weeks after Passover. In the ancient Palestinian agricultural calendar, it marked the end of the grain harvest and was called the feast of harvest. In Temple times, two loaves of bread were baked from the wheat of the new crop and offered as a sacrifice, the firstfruits of wheat harvest. So *Shavuot* came to be called the day of the firstfruits. Pharisaic Judaism added a historical "explanation" to the natural ones derived from the land and its life. The rabbis held that the Torah was revealed on Mount Sinai on that day and celebrated it as "the time of the giving of our Torah."[5] Nowadays, confirmation and graduation ceremonies of religious schools take place on *Shavuot*.

Sukkot, the feast of tabernacles, is the autumnal festival. It marks the end of agricultural toil. The fall crops by then were gathered in from the fields, orchards, and vineyards. The rainy season was about to begin. It was time both to give thanks for what had been granted and to pray for abundant rains in the coming months. Called festival of the ingathering, it was the celebration of nature par excellence. The principal observance is still the construction of a frail hut, or booth, for temporary use during the festival. In it Jews eat their meals out-of-doors. The huts are covered over with branches, leaves, fruit, and flowers, but light shows through, and at night, the stars. We do not know the origin of the practice. Some have held that during the harvest it was common to build an ordinary shack in the fields for shelter from the heat of the day. In any event, the ancient practice naturally was given a historical context: When the Jews wandered in the wilderness they lived, not in permanent homes, but in frail booths. At a time of bounty it is good to be reminded of man's travail and dependence upon heavenly succor.

The three historical-agricultural festivals pertain, in varying ways and combinations, to the themes we have already considered. Passover is the festival of redemption and points toward the Torah-revelation of the Feast of Weeks; the harvest festival in the autumn celebrates not only creation, but especially redemption.

The New Year, *Rosh Hashanah,* and the Day of Atonement, *Yom Kippur,* together mark the Days of Awe, of solemn penitence, at the start of the autumn festival season; they are followed by *Sukkot.* These are solemn times. In the myth of classical Judaism, at the New Year humanity is inscribed for life or death in the heavenly books for the coming year, and on the Day of Atonement the books are sealed. The synagogues on that day are filled with penitents. The New Year is called the birthday of the world: "This day the world was born." It is likewise a day of remembrance on which the deeds of all creatures are reviewed. On it God asserts his sovereignty, as in the New Year Prayer:

> Our God and God of our Fathers, Rule over the whole world in Your honor . . . and appear in Your glorious might to all those who dwell in the civilization of Your world, so that everything made will know that You made it, and every creature discern that You have created him, so that all in whose nostrils is breath may say, "The Lord, the God of Israel is king, and His kingdom extends over all."[6]

The themes of the liturgy are divine sovereignty, divine memory, and divine disclosure. These correspond to creation, revelation, and redemption. Sovereignty is established by creation of the world. Judgment depends upon law: "From the beginning You made this, Your purpose known . . . ." And therefore, since people have been told what God requires of them, they are judged:

> On this day sentence is passed upon countries, which to the sword and which to peace, which to famine and which to plenty, and each creature is judged today for life or death. Who is not judged on this day? For the

remembrance of every creature comes before You, each man's deeds and destiny, words and way . . . .

The theme of revelation is further combined with redemption; the ram's horn, or *shofar*, which is sounded in the synagogue during daily worship for a month before the *Rosh Hashanah* festival, serves to unite the two:

> You did reveal yourself in a cloud of glory. . . . Out of heaven you made them [Israel] hear Your voice. . . . Amid thunder and lightning You revealed yourself to them, and while the shofar sounded You shined forth upon them. . . . Our God and God of our fathers, sound the great Shofar for our freedom. Lift up the ensign to gather our exiles. . . . Lead us happily to Zion Your city, Jerusalem the place of Your sanctuary.

The complex themes of the New Year, the most "theological" of Jewish holy occasions, thus weave together the central mythic categories we have already discovered elsewhere.

The most personal, solemn, and moving of the Days of Awe is the Day of Atonement, *Yom Kippur*, the Sabbath of Sabbaths. It is marked by fasting and continuous prayer. On it, the Jew makes confession:

> Our God and God of our fathers, may our prayer come before You. Do not hide yourself from our supplication, for we are not so arrogant or stiff-necked as to say before You . . . . We are righteous and have not sinned. But we have sinned.
>
> We are guilt laden, we have been faithless, we have robbed . . . .
>
> We have committed iniquity, caused unrighteousness, have been presumptuous . . . .
>
> We have counseled evil, scoffed, revolted, blasphemed . . . .[7]

The Hebrew confession is built upon an alphabetical acrostic, as if by making certain every letter is represented, God, who knows human secrets, will combine them into appropriate words. The very alphabet bears witness against us before God. Then:

> What shall we say before You who dwell on high? What shall we tell You who live in heaven? Do You not know all things, both the hidden and the revealed? You know the secrets of eternity, the most hidden mysteries of life. You search the innermost recesses, testing men's feelings and heart. Nothing is concealed from You or hidden from Your eyes. May it therefore be Your will to forgive us for our sins, to pardon us for our iniquities, to grant remission for our transgressions.

A further list of sins follows, built on alphabetical lines. Prayers to be spoken by the congregation are all in the plural: "For the sin which we have sinned against You with the utterance of the lips . . . . For the sin which we have sinned before You openly and secretly . . . ." The community takes upon itself responsibility for what is done in it. All Israel is part of one community, one body, and all are responsible for the acts of each. The sins confessed are mostly against society, against one's fellowmen; few pertain to ritual laws. At the end comes a final word:

> O my God, before I was formed, I was nothing. Now that I have been formed, it is as though I had not been formed, for I am dust in my life, more so after death. Behold I am before You like a vessel filled with shame and confusion. May it be Your will . . . that I may no more sin, and forgive the sins I have already committed in Your abundant compassion.

So the Jew in the classical Judaic tradition sees himself or herself before God: possessing no merits, yet hopeful for God's love and compassion. To be a classical Jew is to be intoxicated by faith in God, to live every moment in God's presence, and to shape every hour by the paradigm of Torah. The day with its worship in the morning and evening, the week with its climax at the Sabbath, the season marked by nature's commemoration of Israel's sacred history all shape life into rhythms of sanctification, and thus make all of life an act of worship. How does an individual enter into and leave that life? That is the question we answer in the next chapter.

CHAPTER 13

Birth,
Maturity,
Death

The covenant between God and Israel is not a mere theological abstraction, nor is it effected only through laws of community and family life. It is quite literally engraved on the flesh of every male Jewish child through the rite of circumcision, *brit milah* (the covenant of circumcision).

Circumcision must take place on the eighth day after birth, normally in the presence of a quorum of ten adult males. Elijah is believed to be present. A chair is set for him, based upon the legend that Elijah complained to God that Israel neglected the covenant (I Kings 19:10–14).[1] God therefore ordered him to come to every circumcision so as to witness the loyalty of the Jews to the covenant. The *mohel*, or circumciser, is expert at the operation. The traditional blessing is said: "Praised are You . . . who sanctified us with Your commandments and commanded us to bring the son into the covenant of Abraham our father." The wine is blessed: "Praised are You, Lord our God, who sanctified the beloved from the womb and set a statute into his very flesh, and his parts sealed with the sign of the holy covenant. On this account, Living God, our portion and rock, save the beloved of our flesh from destruction, for the sake of his covenant placed in our flesh. Blessed are You . . . who makes the covenant."

The advent of puberty is marked by the *bar mitzvah* rite, at which a young man becomes obligated to keep the commandments; *bar* means son, or subject to, and *mitzvah* means commandment. The young man is called to pronounce the benediction over a portion of the Torah lection in the synagogue and is given the honor of reading the prophetic passage as well. In olden times it was not so important an occasion as it has become in modern America.

Only when a Jew achieves intelligence and self-consciousness, normally at puberty, is he expected to accept the full privilege of *mitzvah* (commandment) and to regard himself as *commanded* by God. Judaism per-

ceives the commandments as expressions of one's acceptance of the yoke
of the kingdom of heaven and submission to God's will. That acceptance
cannot be coerced, but requires thoughtful and complete affirmation. The
bar mitzvah thus represents the moment that the young Jew first assumes
full responsibility before God to keep the commandments. In America a
girl at the same age is able to become a *bat mitzvah*.

At the onset of death, the dying Jew says a confession.

> My God and God of my fathers, accept my prayer. . . .
> Forgive me for all the sins which I have committed in my lifetime. . . .
> Accept my pain and suffering as atonement and forgive my wrong-doing for
>   against you alone have I sinned. . . .
> I acknowledge that my life and recovery depend on You.
> May it be Your will to heal me.
> Yet if You have decreed that I shall die of this affliction,
> May my death atone for all sins and transgressions which I have committed
>   before You.
> Shelter me in the shadow of Your wings.
> Grant me a share in the world to come.
> Father of orphans and Guardian of widows, protect my beloved
>   family. . . .
> Into Your hand I commit my soul. You redeem me, O Lord God of truth.
> Hear O Israel, the Lord is our God, the Lord alone.
> The Lord He is God.
> The Lord He is God.[2]

The corpse is carefully washed and always protected. The body is
covered in a white shroud, then laid in a coffin and buried. Normally
burial takes place on the day of death or on the following day. Once the
body has been placed in the grave, three pieces of broken pottery are laid
on eyes and mouth as signs of their vanity. A handful of dirt from the
Land of Israel is laid under the head.[3] The family recites the *kaddish*, an eschatological prayer of sanctification of God's name that looks forward to
the messianic age and the resurrection of the dead. The prayer expresses
the hope that the Messiah will soon come, "speedily, in our days," and
that "he who brings harmony to the heavens will make peace on earth."
The mourners remain at home for a period of seven days and continue to
recite the memorial *kaddish* for eleven months.

CHAPTER 14

The Center of Life: Study of Torah

The central myth of classical Judaism is the belief that the ancient Scriptures constituted divine revelation, but only a part of it. At Sinai God had handed down a dual revelation: the written part known to one and all, but also the oral part preserved by the great scriptural heroes, passed on by prophets to various ancestors in the obscure past, and finally and most openly handed down to the rabbis who created the Palestinian and Babylonian Talmuds. The "whole Torah" thus consisted of both written and oral parts. The rabbis taught that that "whole Torah" was studied by David, augmented by Ezekiel, legislated by Ezra, and embodied in the schools and by the sages of every period in Israelite history from Moses to the present. It is a singular, linear conception of a revelation preserved only by the few, pertaining to the many, and in time capable of bringing salvation to all.

The Torah myth further regards Moses as "our rabbi," the first and prototypical figure of the ideal Jew. It holds that whoever embodies the teachings of Moses "our rabbi" thereby conforms to the will of God—and not to God's will alone but also to his *way*. In heaven God and the angels study Torah just as rabbis do on earth. God dons phylacteries like a Jew. He prays in the rabbinic mode. He carries out the acts of compassion called for by Judaic ethics. He guides the affairs of the world according to the rules of Torah, just as does the rabbi in his court. One exegesis of the creation legend taught that God had looked into the Torah and therefrom had created the world.

The myth of Torah is multidimensional. It includes the striking detail that whatever the most recent rabbi is destined to discover through proper exegesis of the tradition is as much a part of the way revealed to Moses as is a sentence of Scripture itself. It therefore is possible to participate even in the giving of the law by appropriate, logical inquiry into the law. God himself, studying and living by Torah, is believed to subject himself to these same rules of logical inquiry. If an earthly court overrules the testimony, delivered through miracles, of the heavenly one, God would rejoice, crying out, "My sons have conquered me! My sons have conquered me!"

In a word, before us is a mythical-religious system in which earth and heaven correspond to one another, with Torah as the nexus and model of both. The heavenly paradigm is embodied upon earth. Moses "our rabbi" is the pattern for the ordinary sage of the streets of Jerusalem, Pumbedita, Mainz, London, Lvov, Bombay, Dallas, or New York. And God himself participates in the system, for it is his image that, in the end, forms that cosmic paradigm. The faithful Jew constitutes the projection of the divine on earth. Honor is due to the learned rabbi more than to the scroll of the Torah, for through his learning and logic he may alter the very content of Mosaic revelation. He *is* Torah, not merely because he lives by it, but because at his best he forms as compelling an embodiment of the heavenly model as does a Torah scroll itself.

The final element in the rabbinic Torah myth concerns salvation. It takes many forms. One salvific teaching holds that had Israel not sinned—that is, disobeyed the Torah—the Scriptures would have closed with the story of the conquest of Palestine. From that eschatological time, the sacred community would have lived in eternal peace under the divine law. Keeping the Torah was therefore the veritable guarantee of salvation. The opposite is said in many forms as well. Israel had sinned; therefore, God had called the Assyrians, Babylonians, and Romans to destroy the Temple of Jerusalem; but in his mercy he would be equally faithful to restore the fortunes of the people when they, through their suffering and repentance, had expiated the result and the cause of their sin.

So in both negative and positive forms, the Torah myth tells of a necessary connection between the salvation of the people and of the world and the state of Torah among them. For example, if all Israel would properly keep a single Sabbath, the Messiah would come. Of special interest here is the rabbinic saying that the rule of the pagans depends upon the sin of Israel. If Israel would constitute a full and complete replication of "Torah"—that is, of heaven—then pagan rule would come to an end. It would end because all Israel then, like some few rabbis even now, would attain to the creative, theurgical powers inherent in Torah. Just as God had created the world through Torah, so saintly rabbis could now create a sacred community. When Israel makes itself worthy through its embodiment of Torah—that is, through its perfect replication of the heavenly way of living—then the end will come.

Learning thus finds a central place in a classical Judaic tradition because of the belief that God had revealed his will to mankind through the medium of a written revelation given to Moses at Mount Sinai, accompanied by oral traditions taught in the rabbinical schools and preserved in the Talmuds and related literature. The text without the oral traditions might have led elsewhere than into the academy, for the biblicism of other groups yielded something quite different from Jewish religious intellectualism. But belief in the text was coupled with the belief that oral traditions were also revealed. In the books composed in the rabbinical academies, as much as in the Hebrew Bible itself, was contained God's will for man.

The act of study, memorization, and commentary upon the sacred books is holy. The study of sacred texts therefore assumes a *central* position in Judaism. Other traditions had their religious virtuosi whose virtuosity consisted in knowledge of a literary tradition; but few held, as does Judaism, that everyone must become such a virtuoso.

Traditional processes of learning are discrete and exegetical. Creativity is expressed not through abstract dissertation, but rather through commentary upon the sacred writings, or, more likely in later times, commentary upon earlier commentaries. One might also prepare a code of the law, but such a code represented little more than an assemblage of authoritative opinions of earlier times, with a decision being offered upon those few questions the centuries had left unanswered.

The chief glory of the commentator is his *hiddush* (novelty). The *hiddush* constitutes a scholastic disquisition upon a supposed contradiction between two earlier authorities chosen from any period, with no concern for how they might in fact relate historically, and upon a supposed harmonization of their "contradiction." Or a new distinction might be read into an ancient law, upon which basis ever more questions might be raised and solved. The focus of interest quite naturally lies upon law rather than theology, history, philosophy, or other sacred sciences. But within the law it rests upon legal theory, and interest in the practical consequences of the law is decidedly subordinated.

The devotion of the Jews to study of the Torah, as here defined, is held by them to be their chief glory. This sentiment is repeated in song and prayer and shapes the values of the common society. The important Jew is the learned man. The child many times is blessed, starting at birth. "May he grow in Torah, commandments, good deeds."

The central *ritual* of the Judaic tradition, therefore, is study. Study as a natural action entails learning of traditions and executing them—in this context, in school or in court. Study becomes a *ritual action* when it is endowed with values *extrinsic* to its ordinary character—that is, when set into a mythic context. When a disciple memorizes his master's traditions and actions, he participates in that myth. His study is thereby endowed with the sanctity that ordinarily pertains to prayer or other cultic matters. Study loses its referent in intellectual attainment. The *act* of study itself becomes holy, so that its original purpose, which was mastery of particular information, ceases to matter much. What matters is piety—piety expressed through the rites of studying. Repeating the words of the oral revelation, even without comprehending them, produces reward, just as imitating the master matters, even without really being able to explain the reasons for his actions.

The separation of the value, or sanctity, of the act of study from the natural, cognitive result of learning therefore transforms study from a natural to a ritual action. That separation is accomplished in part by myth and in part by the powerful impact of the academic environment itself.

A striking illustration of the distinction between mere learning and learning as part of ritual life derives from the comment of Mar Zutra, a fifth-

century A.D. Babylonian rabbi, on Isaiah 14:5: *The Lord has broken the*
staff of the wicked, the scepter of rulers. He said, "These are disciples of the
sages who teach public laws to boorish judges" (Talmud, b. Shabbat,
139*a*). The fact that the uncultivated judge would know the law did not
matter, for he still was what he had been—a boor, not a disciple of the
sages. Mere knowledge of the laws does not transform an ordinary person,
however powerful, into a sage. Learning carried with it more than
naturalistic valence, as further seen in the saying of Amemar, a contemporary of Mar Zutra: "A sage is superior to a prophet, as Scripture [Psalm
90:12] says, *And a prophet has a heart of wisdom*" (Talmud, b. Bava Batra,
12*a*). What characterized the prophet was, Amemar said, sagacity. Since
the prophet was supposed to reveal the divine will, it was not inconse-
quential that his revelation depended *not* upon gifts of the spirit but upon
learning.

The talmudic rabbis' emphasis on learning as a ritual act ought not to
obscure their high expectations of actual accomplishment in learning.
While they stressed the act of study without reference to its achievement,
at the same time they possessed very old traditions on how best to pursue
their task. These traditions included much practical advice on how to acquire and preserve learning. Another Babylonian sage, R. Mesharsheya,
advised his sons:

> When you wish to come before your teacher to learn, first review your
> Mishnah and then go to your teacher. When you are sitting before your
> teacher look at the mouth of your teacher, as it is written, *But thine eyes shall
> see thy teacher* [Isaiah 30:20]; and when you study any teaching, do so by
> the side of water, for as the water is drawn out, so your learning may be
> prolonged. Be on the dustheaps of Mata Mehasia [a great center of learn-
> ing] rather than in the palaces of Pumbedita [where Torah was lacking].

> —Talmud, b. Keritot, 6(a)

Part of that advice was perfectly reasonable. Reviewing before classes,
concentrating on the teacher, staying near the great schools would make
sense anywhere. On the other hand, the advice to study by a body of water
"so that your learning may be prolonged" has little to do with the practical
problems of memorizing and reasoning. It, rather, reflects the rabbis' view
of a correspondence between their own study and those aspects of nature
which the rabbis looked upon as symbolic of their activities—and they
many times compared Torah to living waters.

No role whatever was assigned to women. They did not study in the
schools, and the life of Torah effectively was closed to them. On the other
hand, mothers would encourage their sons to study Torah. Rabina, a late
fourth-century master, explained how the merit of study of the Torah applied to womenfolk: Women acquire merit when they arrange for their
sons' education in Scripture and Mishnah and when they wait for their
husbands to return from the schools. Since that return was often
postponed by months or even years, it was no small sacrifice. But the
schools were entirely male institutions, and no equivalent religious life was
available for women.

CHAPTER 15

The Rabbi and the School

The rabbi functioned in the Jewish community as judge and administrator. But he lived in a society in some ways quite separate from that of Jewry as a whole. The rabbinical academy was, first, a law school. Some of its graduates served as judges and administrators of the law. The rabbinical school was by no means a center for merely legal study. It was, like the Christian monastery, the locus for a peculiar kind of religious living. Only one of its functions concerned those parts of the Torah to be applied in everyday life through the judiciary. In ancient, medieval, and modern times these activities and institutions remained remarkably stable.

The school, or *yeshiva* (literally, session), was a council of Judaism, a holy community. In it men learned to live a holy life, to become saints. When they left, sages continued to live by the discipline of the school. They invested great efforts in teaching that discipline by example and precept to ordinary folk. Through the school, classical Judaism transformed the Jewish people into its vision of the true replica of Mosaic revelation.

The schools, like other holy communities, imposed their own particular rituals intended, in the first instance, for the disciples and masters. Later, it was hoped, all Jews would conform to those rituals and so join the circle of master and disciples.

As with study, the schools' discipline transformed other ordinary, natural actions, gestures, and functions into rituals—the rituals of "being a rabbi." Everyone ate. Rabbis did so in a "rabbinic" manner. That is to say, what others regarded as matters of mere etiquette—formalities and conventions intended to render eating aesthetically agreeable—rabbis regarded as matters of "Torah," something to be *learned*. It was "Torah" to do things one way, and it was equally "ignorance" to do them another (though not heresy, for theology was no issue).

The master of Torah, whether disciple or teacher, would demonstrate

his mastery not merely through what he said in the discussion of legal
traditions or what he did in court. He would do so by how he sat at the table, by what ritual formulas he recited before eating one or another kind of fruit or vegetable, by how he washed his hands. Everyone had to relieve himself. The sage would do so according to "Torah." The personality traits of men might vary. Those expected of, and inculcated into, a sage were of a single fabric.

We must keep in mind the fundamental difference between the way of Torah and ways to salvation explored by other holy men and sacred communities. The rabbi at no point would admit that his particular rites were imposed upon him alone, apart from all Israel. He ardently "spread Torah" among the Jews at large. He believed he had to, because Torah was revealed to all Israel at Sinai and required of all Israel afterward. If he was right that Moses was "our rabbi" and even God kept the commandments as he did, then he had to ask of everyone what he demanded of himself: conformity to the halakhah, the way of Torah. His task was facilitated by the widespread belief that Moses had indeed revealed the Torah and that some sort of interpretation quite naturally was required to apply it to everyday affairs. The written part of Torah generally shaped the life of ordinary pious folk. What the rabbi had to accomplish was to persuade the outsider that the written part of the Torah was partial and incomplete, requiring further elaboration through the oral traditions he alone possessed and embodied.

The central human relationship in the schools was between the disciple and the master. Long ago it was taught that the master took the place of the father. The father brought the son into this world; the master would lead him into the world to come. Whatever honor was due the father was all the more so owing to the master. But the master did not merely replace the father. He also required the veneration and reverence owing to the Torah. The extreme forms of respect which evolved over the centuries constitute the most striking rituals attached to "being a rabbi." If study was an act of piety, then the master was partly its object. That is not to suggest that the master, though a saint, was regarded as in any sense divine. But the forms of respect reserved for the divinity or for the Torah were not too different, in appropriate circumstances from those owing to the master.

The forms of respect for the master constituted part of the ritual of being a rabbi. The service of the disciples of the sages separated the true sage from the merely learned man. It had earlier been taught that if one had studied Scripture and Mishnah but did not attend upon disciples of the sages, he was regarded as a boor, an 'am ha'ares. To these epithets, a fourth-century rabbi added: "Behold, such a one is a Magus," and the talmudic discussion then cited a popular saying: "The Magus mumbles and does not know what he is saying, just as the Tanna [the professional memorizer and reciter of Mishnah] who has not attended on the sages recites and does not know what he is saying" (b. Sotah, 22a). The sage claimed to see no difference between a learned Jew and a learned Zoroastrian except that the disciple served the sages. That service—

meaning not merely personal attendance but imitation and study of the *master* as much as of the Torah—constituted a vital part of the Torah. The master exemplified the whole Torah, including the oral part of it. Scripture and Mishnah, written and Oral Torah, meant little without observation and imitation of the sage. The whole Torah was not in books nor in words to be memorized. Torah was to be found in whole and complete form in the master. That is why the forms of respect for the master were both so vital and so unique to the mythic life of the schools.

Ordinary folk could reasonably be expected to carry out most of the rites we have called characteristic of the rabbinical estate. True, common people were supposed to honor all rabbis, but that honor was quite different from the perpetual humility displayed by a disciple before his particular master. The real difference was not the depth of submission, but the constant attendance and attention. On the rare occasions when a great rabbi appeared in public, the ordinary people could be just as humble as his private entourage. But the one thing they could not do was keep it up, wait on him constantly, and so learn all his ways. They just did not have the time. Of all human relationships open to rabbis, therefore, the one between master and disciple was most thoroughly ritualized, most utterly divorced from natural forms of human intercourse. If the master is a living Torah, source of revelation of the oral tradition given at Sinai and embodied now in the master himself, then the disciple had best humbly imitate each and every gesture of that living Torah and so prepare himself as the nexus of the transmission of this same oral tradition to the coming generation.

Submission to the master produced several sorts of tensions: First the master's knowledge, so much greater than the disciple's, must have intimidated the latter; and as this phenomenon reproduced itself one generation after the other, it led to exaggerating the attainments of the ancients and denigrating one's own. Rava said, "We are like a finger in wax as regards reasoning." R. Ashi said, "We are like a finger in the well as regards forgetting";—that is to say, "just as a finger cannot penetrate wax, so we cannot penetrate reasoning; just as a finger cannot bring up water from a well, so easily do we forget what we have learned" (b. 'Eruvin, 53a). Both similes come at the end of a long line of sayings on the glories of the ancients and the limitations of the moderns. It was an attitude inculcated by the schools, inherent in the belief that perfection had been revealed at Sinai, only to be slowly but inevitably forgotten—to suffer attrition through the ages.

CHAPTER 16

The Philosopher

Alongside study of Torah—meaning spending one's life in learning the Babylonian Talmud and later codes, commentaries, and rabbinical court decisions—a different sort of intellectual-religious life flourished in classical Judaism. It was the study of the tradition through the instruments of reason and the discipline of philosophy.

For the whole history of the classical tradition, "study of Torah" predominated. The philosophical enterprise attracted small numbers of elitists and mainly served their specialized spiritual and intellectual needs. That does not mean the philosophical way was unimportant. Those who followed it included the thoughtful and the perplexed—those who took the statements of the tradition most seriously and, through questioning and reflection, intended to examine and then effect them. The philosophers, moreover, were not persons who limited their activities to study and teaching; they frequently both occupied high posts within the Jewish community and served in the high society of politics, culture, and science outside the community as well. Though not numerous, the philosophers exercised considerable influence, particularly over the mind of an age that believed reason and learning, not wealth and worldly power, were what really mattered.

The philosophical way proved attractive only at specific times and under unique circumstances, while the way of Torah was always and everywhere characteristic in premodern times. Philosophy proved uniquely important to Jews living in close contact with other cultures and traditions, like those of Hellenistic Alexandria in the first century A.D., of ninth-century Muslim Baghdad, of Spain in the eleventh and twelfth centuries, of Christian Germany in the nineteenth century, and of twentieth-century America. In such settings, Jews coexisted in an open society with Gentiles—pagans, Muslims, Christians, Zoroastrians. They did not live isolated from, or in ignorance of, the dominant spiritual currents of the day. On the contrary, each particular group felt called upon to explain its chief ideas and doctrines in terms accessible to all others. Reason was conceived as the medium for such discourse.

All groups in the day-to-day encounter of differing cultures and traditions, therefore, attained a high degree of self-consciousness; so that something called Judaism or Christianity or Islam could be defined by contrast to—against the background of—other sorts of "isms" and "ities." The total, all-encompassing world view of Torah, on the other hand, quite unself-consciously spoke of "person," in the assumption that people were pretty much alike because they were Jews. "The good way" for a human being could be defined in a homogeneous setting. The doctrines of Judaism had to be defined because of the heterogeneous situation.

But the heterogeneity was only one of detail. Philosophy flourished in a world of deep religious conviction—a conviction common to the several disparate communities. The issues of philosophy were set, not by lack of belief, but by deep faith. Few, if any, denied providence, a personal God, and a holy book revealed by God through his chosen messenger.[1] Everyone believed in reward and punishment, in a last judgment, and in a settling of accounts.

The Jewish philosopher had to cope with problems imposed not only by the classical faith, but also by the anomalous situation of the Jews themselves. What was the meaning of the strange, unfortunate history of the Jews? How was philosophy to account reasonably for the homelessness of God's people, who were well aware that they lived as a minority among powerful, prosperous majorities—Christian or Muslim? If Torah were true, why did different revelations claiming to be based upon it—but to complete it—flourish, while the people of Torah suffered? Why, indeed, ought one to remain a Jew, when every day one was confronted by the success of the daughter religions? Conversion was always a possibility—an inviting one even under the best of circumstances—for a member of a despised minority.[2]

These problems pressed upon the philosopher in particular—a marginal figure both in Jewry and in the urban civilization of the day. For him, the easy answers—we are still being punished for our sins, or, we suffer now but our reward will be all the greater later on—were transparent, self-serving, and unsatisfactory because they were too easy. He was, further, concerned with the eternal questions facing all religious people: Is God just? What is the nature of humanity? What is the meaning of revelation? Where were answers to be found?

The search was complicated by the formidable appeal of Greek philosophy to medieval Christian and Islamic civilization. Its rationalism, its openness, its search for pure knowledge challenged all revelations. Philosophy called into question all assertions of truth verifiable not through reason, but only through appeals to a source of truth not universally recognized. Reason thus stood, it seemed, against revelation. Mysterious divine plans came into conflict with allegations of the limitless capacity of human reason. Free inquiry might lead anywhere and so would not reliably lead to the synagogue, church, or mosque. And not merely

traditional knowledge, but the specific propositions of faith and the assertions of a holy book had to be measured against the results of reason. Faith
or reason—this seemed to be the choice.

For the Jews, moreover, the very substance of faith—in a personal,
highly anthropomorphic God who exhibited traits of character not always
in conformity with humanity's highest ideals and who in rabbinic hands
looked much like the rabbi himself—posed a formidable obstacle. Classical
conundrums of philosophy were further enriched by the obvious con-
tradictions between belief in free will and belief in divine providence. Is
God all-knowing? Then how can people be held responsible for what they
do? Is God perfect? Then how can he change his mind or set aside his laws
to forgive people?

No theologian in such a cosmopolitan, rational age could begin with an
assertion of a double truth or a private, relative one. The notion that something could be true for one party and not for another, or that faith and
reason were equally valid and yet contradictory were ideas that had little
appeal. And the holy book had to retain the upper hand: "Scripture as the
word of God contained, of course, absolute truth, while philosophy as a
human activity could find its truth only in reasoning."[3] The two
philosophers we shall now consider represent the best efforts of medieval
Judaic civilization to confront these perplexities.

The first is Moses Maimonides (1141–1205), who was at the same time
a distinguished student of the Talmud and of Jewish law in the classical
mode, a community authority, a great physician, and a leading thinker of
his day. His achievement was to synthesize a neo–Platonic Aristotelianism
with biblical revelation. His *Guide to the Perplexed*, published in 1190, was
intended to reconcile the believer to the philosopher and the philosopher
to faith. For him philosophy was not alien to religion but identical with it,
for truth was, in the end, the sole issue. Faith is a form of knowledge;
philosophy is the road to faith.

His proof for the existence of God was Aristotelian. He argued from
creation to Creator, but accepted the eternity of the world:

> Since, in addition to bodies which are both moving and moved, there are
> other bodies which are moved and yet are not causes of movement, there
> must also exist a being which moves without being moved. The second proof
> is based not on the movement of bodies but on their transition from potency
> to act: the transition presupposes the existence of an actualizing principle
> which is external to the being thus changed. The impossibility of an infinite
> regression of causes, just as it led in the first proof to prime mover, now
> serves to establish the existence of a first actualizing principle, free of all
> potentiality and hence also immaterial in nature. . . . Maimonides can
> prove the origin of the world as a whole, from God, only by deduction from
> the contingent existence of things.[4]

God becomes, therefore an "absolutely simple essence from which all
positive definition is excluded."[5] One can say nothing about the attributes
of God. He is purged of all sensuous elements. One can say only that God
is God—nothing more—for God can only be *known* as the highest cause of
being.

What then of revelation? Did God not say anything about himself? And if he did, what need for reasonings such as these? For Maimonides, prophecy, like philosophy, depends uopn the Active Intellect. But in the case of the prophets, "the Active Intellect impresses itself especially upon their imaginative faculty, which is why they express their teachings in a poetic or literary form, rather than in the ratiocinative form of the philosophers."[6] Prophecy is a gift bestowed by God upon man. The Torah and commandments are clearly important, but are not ultimately beyond question or reasonable inquiry. They, however, survive the inquiry unimpaired. The Torah fosters a sound mind and body:

> All its precepts and teachings conspire to guide a man to the greatest benefits, moral and intellectual. Everything in the Torah, whether it be a law or a narrative or genealogy, is significant . . . intended to inculcate a moral or intellectual truth, to wean men away from wrong beliefs, harmful excesses, or dangerous indulgences. In its entirety, the Law is the supreme means whereby man realizes himself most fully.[7]

The greatest good, however, is not to study Torah in the sense described earlier, but rather to know God—that is, to worship and love him. Piety and knowledge of Torah serve merely to prepare people for this highest achievement. Study of Torah loses its character as an end in itself and is rendered into a means to a philosophical goal. This constituted the most striking transformation of the old values. Philosophical knowledge of physical and metaphysical truths "culminates in a purified conception of the nature of God. It is this kind of understanding that engenders the longing for God and the love of him."[8]

Maimonides provided a definition of Judaism—a list of articles of faith he thought obligatory on every faithful Jew. These are as follows: (1) existence of God; (2) his unity; (3) his incorporeality; (4) his eternity; (5) the obligation to worship him alone; (6) prophecy; (7) Moses as the greatest of the prophets; (8) the divine origin of Torah; (9) the eternal validity of Torah; (10) God's knowledge of man's deeds; (11) his punishment of evil and rewarding of goodness; (12) his promise to send a Messiah; and (13) his promise to resurrect the dead. These philosophical principles were hotly debated and much criticized, but ironically, achieved a place in the life of Judaic piety. Although subjected to debate and criticism, in the end they were sung as a prayer in a hymn at the conclusion of synagogue prayer.

1. The living God we praise, exalt, adore
   He was, he is, he will be evermore.
2. No unity like unto his can be
   Eternal, inconceivable is he.
3. No form or shape has the incorporeal one
   Most holy he, past all comparison.
4. He was ere aught was made in heaven or earth
   But his existence has no date or birth.
5. Lord of the Universe is he proclaimed
   Teaching his power to all his hand has framed.

6. He gave his gift of prophecy to those
   In whom he gloried, whom he loved and chose.
7. No prophet ever yet has filled the place
   Of Moses, who beheld God face to face.
8. Through him (the faithful in his house) the Lord
   The law of truth to Israel did accord.
9. This Law of God will not alter, will not change
   For any other through time's utmost range.
10. He knows and heeds the secret thoughts of man:
    He saw the end of all ere aught began.
11. With love and grace doth he the righteous bless,
    He metes out evil unto wickedness.
12. He at the last will his anointed send
    Those to redeem who hope and wait the end.
13. God will the dead to life again restore.
    Praised be his glorious name for evermore.[9]

The esoteric words of the philosopher were thus transformed into a message of faith, at once sufficiently complex to sustain critical inquiry according to the canons of the day and simple enough to bear the weight of the faith of ordinary folk and to be sung. The "God without attributes" is still guide, refuge, stronghold. It is a strange and paradoxical fate for the philosopher's teachings. Who would have supposed at the outset that the way of the philosopher would lead to the piety of the people?

Many, indeed, came to no such supposition. They found the philosophers presumptuous, inadequate, and incapable of investigating the truths of faith. But the critics of "philosophy" were themselves philosophers. The greatest was Judah Halevi (1080–1141), who produced *not* a work of sustained philosophical argument and analysis, but a set of dialogues between a king in search of true religion and the advocates of the several religious and philosophical positions of the day, including Judaism. Judah Halevi, poet and mystic, objected to the indifference of philosophy to the comparative merits of the competing traditions. In philosophy's approach, "the ultimate objective is the knowledge of God. Religion is recommended because it inculcates the proper moral qualities in men, but no attention is paid to the question of *which* system of religious morality one ought to follow."[10] For the majority religions in the West—Islam and Christianity—such an indifference may have been tolerable, but *not* for a minority destined any day to have to die for the profession of faith.

Martyrdom will not be evoked by the unmoved mover, the God anyone may reach either through revelation or through reason. Only for the God of Israel will a Jew give up his or her life. By its nature, philosophy is insufficient for the religious quest: "It starts with assumptions and ends with mere theories."[11] It can hardly compete with—let alone challenge—the *history* of the Jewish people—a history recording extraordinary events starting with revelation. What has philosophy to do with Sinai, with the land, with prophecy? On the contrary, the Jew, expounding religion to the king of the Khazars, begins not like the philosopher with a disquisition on divine attributes, nor like the Christian who starts with the works of creation and expounds the Trinity, nor like the Moslem who acknowledges the unity and eternity of God, but as follows:

> I believe in the God of Abraham, Isaac, and Israel, who led the Israelites out of Egypt with signs and miracles; who fed them in the desert and gave them the Land, after having made them traverse the sea and the Jordan in a miraculous way; who sent Moses with His Torah and subsequently thousands of prophets, who confirmed His law by promises to those who observed and threats to the disobedient. We believe in what is contained in the Torah—a very large domain.[12]

The king then asks: Why did the Jew not say he believes in the creator of the world and in similar attributes common to all creeds? The Jew responds that the evidence for Israel's faith is *Israel*, the people, its history and endurance, and not the kinds of reasonable truths offered by other traditions. The *proof* of revelation is the testimony of those who were *there* and wrote down what they heard, saw, and did.

If so, the king wonders, what accounts for the despised condition of Israel today? The Jew compares Israel to the dry bones of Ezekiel:

> . . . these bones, which have retained a trace of vital power and have once been the seat of a heart, head, spirit, soul, and intellect, are better than bones formed of marble and plaster, endowed with heads, eyes, ears, and all limbs, in which there never dwelt the spirit of life.[13]

God's people is Israel; he rules them and keeps them in their present status:

> Israel amid the nations is like the heart amid the organs: it is the most sick and the most healthy of them all. . . . The relationship of the Divine power to us is the same as that of the soul to the heart. For this reason it is said, *You only have I known among all the families of the earth, therefore I will punish you for all your iniquities* [Amos 3:2]. . . . Now we are oppressed, while the whole world enjoys rest and prosperity. But the trials which meet us serve to purify our piety, to cleanse us, and to remove all taint from us.[14]

The pitiful condition of Israel is, therefore, turned into the primary testimony and vindication of Israel's faith. That Israel suffers is the best assurance of divine concern. The suffering constitutes the certainty of coming redemption. In the end, the Jew parts from the king in order to undertake a journey to the Land of Israel. There he seeks perfection with God:

> The invisible and spiritual *Shekhinah* [presence of God] is with every born Israelite of pure life, pure heart, and sincere devotion to the Lord of Israel. And the Land of Israel has a special relation to the Lord of Israel. Pure life can be perfectly lived only there.[15]

To this the king objects. He thought the Jew loved freedom, but the Jew finds himself in bondage by imposing duties obligatory in residing in the Land of Israel. The Jew replies that the freedom he seeks is from the ser-

vice of men and the courting of their favor. He seeks the service of one
whose favor is obtained with the smallest effort: "His service is freedom, and humility before him is true honor." He, therefore, turns to Jerusalem to seek the holy life. He closes his remarks:

> Thou shalt arise and have mercy upon Zion; for it is time to favor her, the mo-
> ment is come. For thy servants love her stones and pity her dust [Psalm
> 102:14–15]. This means, Jerusalem can only be rebuilt when Israel yearns
> for it to such an extent that we sympathize even with its stones and its
> dust.[16]

Here we find no effort to identify Judaism with rational truth, but rather the claim that the life of the pious Jew stands above—indeed constitutes the best testimony to—truth.

The source of truth is biblical revelation; it was public, complete, fully in the light of history. History, not philosophy, testifies to the truth and in the end constitutes its sole criterion. Philosophy claims reason can find the way to God. Halevi says only God can show the way to God, and he does so through revelation, and therefore in history. For the philosopher, God is the object of knowledge.[17] For Halevi, God is the subject of knowledge: "The yearning heart seeks the God of Abraham; the labor of the intellect is directed toward the God of Aristotle."[18] And Israel has a specifically religious faculty which mediates the relationship to God; so we have seen in the references to the role of Israel among the nations as similar to the role of the heart among the limbs.

Halevi seeks to explain the supernatural status of Israel. The religious faculty is its peculiar inheritance and makes it the core of humanity. He thus "predicates . . . the supernatural religious faculty."[19] That does not mean that Israel is superior in morality or intellect. But while the rest of humanity is subject to the laws of nature, Israel is subject to supernatural, divine providence, manifested in reward and punishment. The very condition of the Jews, in that God punishes them, verifies the particular and specific place of Israel in the divine plan. The teaching of prophecy thus returns in Halevi's philosophy.

These two philosophers were part of a number of important thinkers who attempted to meet the challenge of philosophy and of reason by constructing a comprehensive theological system. But the uses of reason were not exhausted by the philosophical enterprise. Reason played a central role in the study of Torah. The settings, however, were vastly different. Still, so far as reasoning power "is one of the modes of human awareness through which man constructs human experience,"[20] the classic Judaic tradition fully explored this mode.

If, in Judaic tradition, salvation was never reduced to a "confession of a creed or theological agreement," still important efforts were made, such as the one of Maimonides, to produce just such a creed. It is not, as is often asserted, that Judaism had (or has) no theology. Such a statement is obviously absurd. It is simply that the theological idiom of the Judaic tradition often diverged from that of the Christian West. In Maimonides, we meet a theological mind quite capable of addressing itself to the issues confronting any religious tradition perplexed by philosophical reason. But Judah Halevi, so much more private, subjective, and particularistic, ends up in a suprarationalist position not far divorced from neo–Platonism.

While like the Muslim and Christian intellectuals in mentality, the Jewish philosophers had more in common with the talmudic rabbis than with gentile philosophers. The rabbis accepted the Bible and the Talmud as "the whole Torah," and so did the Jewish philosophers. Both groups devoted themselves to the articulation of the role of Torah in the life of Israel, to the meaning of the fate of Israel and to the effort to form piety and shape faith. And for both, *reason* was the means of reaching into Torah—of recovering and achieving truth. For both, therefore, the "unique, personal situation in which a person is receptive to a dimension of meaning," as Streng says,[21] can indeed be exposed through linguistic and conceptual relationships. Both agreed that words could contain and convey the sacred, and, therefore, reason—the examination of the meaning and referents of words—was the golden measure. They differed only in the object of reason; the one studied law, the other, philosophy. Yet Maimonides, the complete and whole Jew, studied both and made a lasting impact upon the formation not only of both sorts of Judaic tradition, but also of the pious imagination of the ordinary Jew.

CHAPTER 17

The Mystic

Classical Judaism welcomed and placed a high value on mystical experience attained through prayer, asceticism, and devotion to godly service. It furthermore made a place within Torah for holy books of mystical doctrine. The most important of these holy books was the *Zohar*, a thirteenth-century work of immense proportions and commensurate influence. While we know that its author was Moses de Leon and that he wrote the *Zohar* in Spain between 1281 and 1286, we cannot be surprised that de Leon speaks in the name of important second-century rabbis. For the mystics before and after the *Zohar* took for granted that their doctrines were Torah and derived from the same authorities who gave them Mishnah and other parts of the Oral Torah. The intense inner life of direct encounter through prayer, doing of the commandments, and study of Torah thus strengthened the power of the rabbinic Torah-myth in the life of the Jewish people and, indeed, generated fructifying, creative forces in the way of Torah.

Especially important was the conviction that every deed of a human being on earth has its counterpart in invisible reality in heaven. The talmudic stress on practical action elevated concrete deeds into the highest mode of religious expression. What a Jew did affected the profound reality: "Thus I do this *mitzvah* for the sake of the unity of the Holy One, blessed be He," was said by a mystic before performing a commandment. This meant that the mystic was able to help effect the greater unity of the one God. The social effect was to lay stress on the performance of deeds that formed a pattern of religious living—deeds that the nonmystic performed habitually, in a more mundane spirit, and in an attitude of mere conformity. The mystic knew that one does things for a deeper, transcendent reason. The mystic therefore brought new devotion to the old, established way of life. He joined the community ever more concerned to do precisely what everyone else was doing anyhow, but for his own reason.

It is no accident that the greatest lawyers and Talmudists also were among the most profound and influential mystics. For example, the author of the code of Jewish law (*Shulhan Arukh*), Joseph Karo, believed that he received heavenly visitations from the Mishnah incarnate. A great biblical commentator, Nachmanides, introduced into his commentary on the Pentateuch important mystical considerations. The greatest genius of the talmudic tradition—Elijah, the Gaon of Vilna, who lived at the end of the eighteenth century—was a paragon of rabbinic rationality who also gave his best efforts to the study of the *Zohar* and other mystical writings. We cannot in fact locate a major legal authority who, after mystic literature became available, did not also devote himself in some measure to the study of mysticism. The reason is that the law and the inner life of the believing Jew were understood to express one and the same pattern. The former was the body and the latter, the spirit; the former was the outer capsule and the latter, the inner meaning. So when the mystics, for their part, undertook ascetic behavior, it was in the form of moral behavior. Ascetic renunciation led less to hair shirts and fasting—though there assuredly was self-torture—than to moral action—that is, giving up one's rights in favor of another. Because the Jewish mystic wanted to love God, he had also to love his neighbor.

This is how the practical expression of ascetic mysticism is described in a thirteenth-century book of mysticism, the *Book of the Pious:*

> At all times you should love your Creator with all your heart and all your soul and take counsel with your heart and a lesson from man who is but worms; if a person gives you ten gold pieces or more, how deeply engraved would his love be in your heart. And if he provides your support and the support of your children and of your household you would certainly think, "This man which I have never seen and who has extended to me such kindness I would not be able to repay for all the goodness he has shown me should I live a thousand years. I would love him with all my heart and with all my soul; he could not command me to do anything that I would not do for him, because both my wealth and my being are his." As with the love of man so with the love of the Holy One, blessed be He, raised and exalted be His fame. It is He who gives sustenance to all, how much better that we should cleave to the love of the Creator, fear Him, nor transgress His commands whether great or small. For we do not know the reward of each commandment, and the punishment for transgressions though they appear light in our eyes, as it is written, *When the iniquity of my supplanters compasseth me about* (Psalm 49:6). The transgressions to which a man becomes habituated in this world will encompass him on the Day of Judgement. If he is deserving his good deeds will bear witness for him. True and firm it is that we are not to transgress the commandments of our Creator even one of the small ones for a house full of gold and silver. If an individual says, "I will transgress a commandment and with the gold and silver they give me I will fulfill the difficult commandments. With this I will support the poor, invite wayfarers, I will do very many favors." These are all futile thoughts, for perhaps soon after the transgression he will die and not succeed to the gift. Moreover, if he should not die the money would soon be dissipated so that he dies in his sin. Come and see how much you should love your Creator

who does wonderful kindnesses with you, He creates you from a decayed drop, He gives you a soul, draws you forth from the belly, then gives you a mouth with which to speak, a heart to understand, ears to hear the pure words of His mouth, which are refined as silver and pure gold. It is He who leads you on the face of earth, who gives sustenance to all, who causes death and gives life to all. In His hand are the souls of all the living. It is He who distributes your share of bread. What is there to say? for the mouth is unable to speak, the ear unable to hear, for to Him all praise is as silence, there is no end to the length of His days, His years will have no end, He is the King of kings, the Holy One, blessed be His name and His fame. It is He who has created the heavens and earth, sea, and all that is therein. He is the provider of all, for His eyes are open upon all men's paths recompensing each according to his ways and the fruit of his deeds, whether good or bad. Behold it is He who sets forth before men two paths, the path of life and the path of death and says to you, *Choose life* (Deuteronomy 30:19). In spite of all this, we who are filled with worms do not think and do not set our hearts but to fill our appetites freely. We do not think that man's days are numbered, today he is here, tomorrow in the grave, that suddenly he dies. For no man rules over his spirit retaining it (forever). Therefore it is good for man to remove himself from all appetites and direct his heart to love and fear the Lord with all his heart at all times and revile the life of vanity. For we will not be able to humble ourselves and subdue our passion which thrusts us from the land of the living, except through subduing our heart and returning to our Maker in complete repentance, to serve Him and to do His will with a whole heart. Our sages have said, "Bread and salt shalt thou eat and water in measurement shall you drink and beware of gazing at women which drives a person from the world. Love humans and judge all people in the scale of merit." And this is what the Torah has said, *But in righteousness shalt thou judge thy neighbor* (Leviticus 19:15). Be humble before all, busy yourself with Torah, which is whole, pure and upright and do not praise yourself for it, because for this were you created.[1]

The main point of mysticism for Judaism is that God is very real, and the desire of the mystic is "to feel and to enjoy Him; not only to obey but to approach Him"; so says Abraham J. Heschel, the greatest theologian of Judaism in the twentieth century, who goes on: "They want to taste the whole wheat of spirit before it is ground by the millstones of reason. They would rather be overwhelmed by the symbols of the inconceivable than wield the definitions of the superficial."[2] What, then, is the mystic doctrine of God in Judaism? This is how Heschel answers that question:

Mystic intuition occurs at an outpost of the mind, dangerously detached from the main substance of the intellect. Operating as it were in no-mind's land, its place is hard to name, its communications with critical thinking often difficult and uncertain and the accounts of its discoveries not easy to decode. In its main representatives, the cabbala teaches that man's life can be a rallying point of the forces that tend toward God, that this world is charged with His presence and every object is a cue to His qualities. To the cabbalist, God is not a concept, a generalization, but a most specific reality; his thinking about Him full of forceful directness. But He who is "the Soul of all souls" is "the mystery of all mysteries." While the cabbalists speak of

God as if they commanded a view of the Beyond, and were in possession of knowledge about the inner life of God, they also assure us that all notions fail when applied to Him, that He is beyond the grasp of the human mind and inaccessible to meditation. He is the *En Sof*, the Infinite, "the most Hidden of all Hidden." While there is an abysmal distance between Him and the world, He is also called All. "For all things are in Him and He is in all things . . . . He is both manifest and concealed. Manifest in order to uphold the all and concealed, for He is found nowhere. When He becomes manifest He projects nine brilliant lights that throw light in all directions. So, too, does a lamp throw brilliance in all directions, but when we approach the brilliance we find there is nothing outside the lamp. So is the Holy ancient One, the Light of all Lights, the most Hidden of all Hidden. We can only find the light which He spreads and which appears and disappears. This light is called the Holy Name, and therefore All is One."

Thus, the "Most Recondite One Who is beyond cognition does reveal of Himself a tenuous and veiled brightness shining only along a narrow path which extends from Him. This is the brightness that irradiates all." The *En Sof* has granted us manifestations of His hidden life: He had descended to become the universe; He has revealed Himself to become the Lord of Israel. The ways in which the Infinite assumes the form of finite existence are called *Sefirot*. These are various aspects or forms of Divine action, spheres of Divine emanation. They are, as it were, the garments in which the Hidden God reveals Himself and acts in the universe, the channels through which His light is issued forth.[3]

Obviously, in so fresh and original a system, all the antecedent symbols and conceptions of Judaism are going to be revised and given new meanings. The single most striking revision is in the very definition of Torah. We know that for classical Judaism Torah means revelation, and revelation is contained in various documents—some of them written down and handed on from Sinai, others transmitted orally, also from Sinai. But for the mystic, Torah also becomes a "mystic reality," as Heschel explains:

The Torah is an inexhaustible esoteric reality. To enter into its deep, hidden strata is in itself a mystic goal. The Universe is an image of the Torah and the Torah is an image of God. For the Torah is "the Holy of Holies"; "it consists entirely of the name of the Holy One, blessed be He. Every letter in it is bound up with that Name."

The Torah is the main source from which man can draw the secret wisdom and power of insight into the essence of things. "It is called Torah (lit.: showing) because it shows and reveals that which is hidden and unknown; and all life from above is comprised in it and issues from it." "The Torah contains all the deepest and most recondite mysteries; all sublime doctrines both disclosed and undisclosed; all essences both of the higher and the lower grades, of this world and of the world to come are to be found there." The source of wisdom is accessible to all, yet only few resort to it. "How stupid are men that they take no pains to know the ways of the Almighty by which the world is maintained. What prevents them? Their stupidity, because they do not study the Torah; for if they were to study the Torah they would know the ways of the Holy One, blessed be He."

The Torah has a double significance: literal and symbolic. Besides their plain, literal meaning, which is important, valid and never to be overlooked, the verses of the Torah possess an esoteric significance, "comprehensible only to the wise who are familiar with the ways of the Torah." "Happy is Israel to whom was given the sublime Torah, the Torah of truth. Perdition take anyone who maintains that any narrative in the Torah comes merely to tell us a piece of history and nothing more! If that were so, the Torah would not be what it assuredly is, to wit, the supernal Law, the Law of truth. Now if it is not dignified for a king of flesh and blood to engage in common talk, much less to write it down, is it conceivable that the most high King, the Holy One, blessed be He, was short of sacred subjects with which to fill the Torah, so that He had to collect such commonplace topics as the anecdotes of Esau, and Hagar, Laban's talks to Jacob, the words of Balaam and his ass, those of Balak, and of Zimri, and such-like, and make of them a Torah? If so, why is it called the 'Law of Truth?' Why do we read *The Law of the Lord is perfect. . . . The testimony of the Lord is sure. . . . The Ordinances of the Lord are true. . . . More to be desired are they than gold, yea, than much fine gold* (Psalm 19:8–11). But assuredly each word of the Torah signifies sublime things, so that this or that narrative, besides its meaning in and for itself, throws light on the all-comprehensive Rule of the Torah."[4]

In this statement of Heschel's, we see how it was that the long and influential tradition of mysticism in Judaism was able to reinforce and vivify rabbinic Judaism in its talmudic mode. It is clear that the mystic finds in Torah meanings and dimensions not perceived in the earlier phases of talmudic Judaism. In many ways the mysterious power of the mystic is to see what lesser eyes cannot perceive. But the perception is there, and to the mystic and his audience it was very real. So Torah took on a richer meaning than it had had, even for the rabbi. Thus, Torah came to include both the literal meaning of the words and the deeper or symbolic meaning—the level of meaning far more profound than meets the eye. Torah was made to yield the meanings not solely of its sentences, but now of each and every individual letter.

The essence of the mystic way is not contained within the notion of the deeper layers of meaning to be found within Torah. Rather, the essence of mysticism is the inquiry into the very essence of God. What made mysticism a powerful force in Judaism is the vivid encounter with God made possible in mysticism as it was not in any other mode of Judaism or Judaic religiosity. This is how Gershom G. Scholem explains the mystic encounter with God:

The mystic strives to assure himself of the living presence of God, the God of the Bible, the God who is good, wise, just and merciful and the embodiment of all other positive attributes. But at the same time he is unwilling to renounce the idea of the hidden God who remains eternally unknowable in the depths of His own Self, or, to use the bold expression of the Kabbalists "in the depths of His nothingness." This hidden God may be without special attributes—the living God of whom the Revelation speaks, with whom all religion is concerned, must have attributes, which on another plane represent also the mystic's own scale of moral values: God is good, God is severe, God is merciful and just. . . . The mystic does not even recoil before the inference that in a higher sense there is a root of evil even in God. The benevolence of God is to the mystic not simply the negation of evil, but a whole sphere of divine light, in which God manifests Himself under this particular aspect of benevolence to the contemplation of the Kabbalist.[5]

In many ways, then, mysticism must be seen as the ultimate, logical conclusion of that mode of Judaism which took shape in the aftermath of the messianic disasters of the first and second century. For the encounter with God outside history and time—the direct realization of the knowledge of God, who in some measure is hidden and unknowable in the depths of His nothingness—removes the mystic from the one thing that rabbinic Judaism to begin with proposed to neutralize; namely, the vagaries of history. The essentially ahistorical quality of mystical thinking accounts for the ready home provided to mysticism by that form of Judaism which began with the Mishnah and the Talmud and, we now see, came to fruition and fulfillment—in the minds of many great Talmudists—in the mystical realization of the encounter with God's hidden self.

To what degree did the values of the rabbis of the Talmud and of the great philosophers and mystics actually influence the lives of ordinary folk? Were Jews truly the "people of Torah" that the rabbis, philosophers, and mystics wanted them to be? Next we turn to an ordinary man, and then we shall look at the spiritual traits of an ordinary woman—both of whom lived in the long centuries during which Judaism in its classical form predominated. When, at the end, we discover in the writing of a pious and traditional woman an essentially fresh aspiration, we shall know that it is time to ask what has changed in the modern period in the history of Judaism, and why that change has taken place.

CHAPTER 18

An Ordinary Man

What of the common folk who lived out their days in a community shaped by the values of the Torah? What were their ideals? One insight is to be derived from the "ethical wills" written by fathers for their children. In the ethical will, the legator would divide not his earthly property, but his highest ideals. He would ask his heirs to carry out those ideals. Such wills obviously present the father at his best, for, facing the prospect of death and judgment, the father hoped to show his best side and urge upon his children the highest and noblest ideals. But that is what makes the ethical wills interesting, for they mirror ordinary folk ideals at an extraordinary moment. The ideals of an average Jew are represented by the testament of Eleazar of Mainz, who died in 1357:

> These are the things which my sons and daughters shall do at my request. They shall go to the house of prayer morning and evening, and shall pay special regard to the Prayer and the *Shema*. So soon as the service is over, they shall occupy themselves a little with the Torah, the Psalms, or with works of charity.

> Their business must be conducted honestly, in their dealings both with Jew and gentile.

> They must be gentle in their manners, and prompt to accede to every honorable request. They must not talk more than is necessary, by this will they be saved from slander, falsehood and frivolity.

> They shall give an exact tithe of all their possessions; they shall never turn away a poor man empty-handed, but must give him what they can, be it much or little. If he beg a lodging overnight, and they know him not, let them provide him with the wherewithal to pay an innkeeper. Thus shall they satisfy the needs of the poor in every possible way.

My daughters must obey scrupulously the rules applying to women; modesty, sanctity, reverence, should mark their married lives. Marital intercourse must be modest and holy, with a spirit of restraint and delicacy, in reverence and silence. They shall be very punctilious and careful with their ritual bathing. They must respect their husbands, and must be invariably amiable to them. Husbands, on their part, must honor their wives more than themselves, and treat them with tender consideration. If they can by any means contrive it, my sons and daughters should live in communities, and not isolated from other Jews, so that their sons and daughters may learn the ways of Judaism. Even if compelled to solicit from others the money to pay a teacher, they must not let the young, of both sexes, go without instruction in the Torah. Marry your children, O my sons and daughters, as soon as their age is ripe, to members of respectable families.

Every Friday morning, they shall put themselves in careful trim for honoring the Sabbath, kindling the lamps while the day is still great, and in winter lighting the furnace before dark, to avoid desecrating the Sabbath (by kindling fire thereon). For due welcome to the Sabbath, the women must prepare beautiful candles.

In their relation to women, my sons must behave continently, avoiding mixed bathing and mixed dancing and all frivolous conversation, while my daughters ought not to speak much with strangers, nor jest nor dance with them. They ought to be always at home, and not be gadding about. They should not stand at the door, watching whatever passes. I ask, I command, that the daughters of my house be never without work to do, for idleness leads first to boredom, then to sin. But let them spin, or cook, or sew.

I earnestly beg my children to be tolerant and humble to all, as I was throughout my life. Should cause for dissension present itself, be slow to accept the quarrel; seek peace and pursue it with all the vigor at your command. Even if you suffer loss thereby, forbear and forgive, for God has many ways of feeding and sustaining His creatures. To the slanderer do not retaliate with counter-attack; and though it be proper to rebut false accusations, yet is it most desirable to set an example of reticence. You yourselves must avoid uttering any slander, for so will you win affection. In trade be true, never grasping at what belongs to another. For by avoiding these wrongs—scandal, falsehood, money-grubbing—men will surely find tranquillity and affection. And against all evils, silence is the best safeguard. . . .

Whatever happiness befall you, be it in monetary fortune or in the birth of children, be it some signal deliverances of any other of the many blessings which may come to you, be not stolidly unappreciative, like dumb cattle that utter no word of gratitude. But offer praises to the Rock who has befriended you, saying: "O give thanks unto the Lord, for He is good, for His mercy endureth for ever. Blessed art Thou, O Lord, who are good and dispensest good." Besides thanking God for His bounties at the moment they occur, also in your regular prayers let the memory of these personal favors prompt your hearts to special fervor during the utterance of the communal thanks. When words of gratitude are used in the liturgy, pause to reflect in silence on the goodness of God to you that day. And when ye make the response: "May Thy great Name be blessed," call to mind your own personal experiences of the divine favor.

Be very particular to keep your houses clean and tidy. I was always scrupulous on this point, for every injurious condition, and sickness and poverty, are to be found in foul dwellings. Be careful over the benedictions; accept no divine gift without paying back the Giver's part; and His part is man's grateful acknowledgment.

Every one of these good qualities becomes habitual with him who studies the Torah; for that study indeed leads to the formation of a noble character. Therefore, happy is he who toils in the Law! For this gracious toil fix daily times, of long or short duration, for it is the best of all works that a man can do. . . .

Be of the first ten in Synagogue, rising betimes for the purpose. Pray steadily with the congregation, giving due value to every letter and word, seeing that there are in the *Shema* 248 words, corresponding to the 248 limbs in the human body.

I beg of you, my sons and daughters, my wife and all the congregation, that no funeral oration be spoken in my honor. Do not carry my body on a bier but in a coach. Wash me clean, comb my hair, trim my nails, as I was wont to do in my life-time, so that I may go clean to my eternal rest, as I went clean to Synagogue every Sabbath day. If the ordinary officials dislike the duty, let adequate payment be made to some poor man who shall render this service carefully and not perfunctorily. At a distance of thirty cubits from the grave, they shall set my coffin on the ground, and drag me to the grave by a rope attached to the coffin. Every four cubits they shall stand and wait awhile, doing this in all seven times, so that I may find atonement for my sins. Put me in the ground at the right hand of my father, and if the space be a little narrow, I am sure that he loves me well enough to make room for me by his side. If this be altogether impossible, put me on his left, or near my grandmother, Yuta. Should this also be impractical, let me be buried by the side of my daughter.[1]

Where did the "way of Torah" lead? The human being before us clearly shapes his life and values by what Torah was supposed to mean. He stresses a life of prayer, study, and good deeds. A disciple of the sages should not bring Torah into disrepute by false dealing, and no distinction is made between Jew and Gentile. The disciple must be gentle and modest, not talk too much, and be careful to avoid slander. He must tithe and generously receive the poor man. Daughters must be modest and sons, solicitous. Jews must live with other Jews, so as to sustain one another during the long exile. Living as a nation within other nations, governed by their own laws and under their own administration, Jews had best seek one another out. Above all, one should borrow—even impoverish himself—to make certain his children study Torah. The Sabbath comes next in order of interest and then again, an appeal for modesty, sobriety, and tolerance. Life is to be lived as a gift from God. Whatever happens, one must thank God, in public and private worship, on every possible occasion. The difference between man and beast is *gratitude*. And once more, all these virtues are the habits of the student of Torah. Study leads not to learning but to nobility. As to the rites of death, they should be humble—even degrading—so that penance on earth may produce felicity in heaven.

You may well doubt that any ordinary person could live up to these high ideals. Indeed, the homely touch at the end of Eleazar's testament reminds us of his humanity: "Put me in the ground at the right hand of my father . . . he loves me well enough to make room . . . . or near my grandmother . . . . [or] by the side of my daughter." Life under Torah law was meant to produce a saint. Being men of flesh and blood, Jews cannot be thought everywhere and always to have replicated the values of the Torah; but what is important is that these values set the standard.[2] Until modern times, no others were widely adopted. Studying Torah, living in the traditional community, following the stable and serene way of life from Sabbath to Sabbath and from season to season—these were what it meant to be a Jew. It was a sweet life—sweeter than honey—full of piety, reverence, and beauty. So the pious Jew prayed—and continues to pray— day by day: "How good our lot! How pleasant our portion!"

CHAPTER 19

Two Extraordinary Women

At the end of our description of the way of Torah explored by Jews from the second to the nineteenth century, we come to the position of women. This is for two reasons. First, the matter is intrinsically important. We cannot understand a religion unless we make some sense of the role and position that religion accords to half its adherents—women—just as we must attend to the values and ideals shaped for that religion's male adherents. Second—and still more importantly—one of the principal traits of the advent of the new era in the history of Judaism will be a shift in the status and role of women on the one side, and in women's aspirations for such a shift to take place, on the other.

We may point to important roles taken by women in Israelite politics, culture, and religion in biblical times. The Hebrew Scriptures speak of women who were important political figures, such as generals, heads of state, and prophets. Women form the center of important biblical narratives from the time of Miriam, the sister of Moses, through Deborah to Ruth, Esther, Bathsheba, and others. So there is no doubt that within the complexities of a mosaic of biblical documents, one continuing trait is that women may come to the center of the stage and play a leading role. That this was so in exceptional circumstances—that men generally were the heads of state, prophets, generals, and other important political figures—is beside the point. Women could and did attain prominence.

There was one institution in ancient times in which women were afforded no role whatsoever and from which, in point of fact, women were essentially excluded. That was the Temple, and with it, the priesthood, which was no mean exclusion. The priestly law codes contained within Leviticus and Numbers take women very seriously and devote much attention to the status of women within the priesthood. But women's status was solely dependent on the priests, all of whom were males, and it was principally a vehicle for the sanctification of the priesthood. While some rites (e.g., those performed after childbirth) were defined for women, no rites could be performed by women, who were not permitted into the holier part of the Temple buildings and were kept out in a women's courtyard. We cannot now speculate on why the imagination of the priesthood should have excluded all roles for women while, by contrast, the royal house could put forward queens as well as kings, the prophetic movement could put forward a Hulda along with a Jeremiah, and the great writers could pay attention to a Ruth and an Esther as much as to a David and a Solomon. We have to recognize that exclusion from Temple and priesthood as a fact.

When, in the first and second centuries, movements took shape out of the priesthood and around the priestly ideals, the consequence of that fact became clear. Just as the priesthood excluded women, so its successor, the rabbinate, found little place for women. After the second century, we hear of few, if any women in the all-male society of the rabbinical schools (yeshivot). And for the next eighteen hundred years there is not a *single* woman associated with the writing of a commentary to the Talmud, the conduct of a rabbinical court, or the administration of the Jewish community as a rabbinical authority. The total subordination of women in the system of Judaism and their exclusion from the centers of learning and leadership does not, of course, mean that women were abused or disgraced. The contrary is the case. Every effort was made to preserve the rights, property, and dignity of women. But women could not preserve their own rights, property, or dignity. They formed a subordinated caste within the community of Judaism.

Now we must ask ourselves: Does the fact of their subordination mean women were alienated by the system? In the writings of Glückel of Hameln (1646–1724) we find that was not so. Indeed, if we now compare Glückel's letter to her children with the ethical will of Eleazar of Mainz—written three hundred years earlier!—we find pretty much the same beliefs and ethical values. Glückel's message is the same and expresses precisely the same religious world view as Eleazar's.

> In my great grief and for my heart's ease I begin this book in the year of Creation 5451—God soon rejoice us and send us His redeemer soon. Amen.
>
> . . . .
>
> With the help of God, I began writing this, my dear children, upon the death of your good father in the hope of distracting my soul from the burdens laid upon it, and the bitter thought that we have lost our faithful shepherd. In this way I have managed to live through many wakeful nights, and springing from my bed have shortened the sleepless hours.
>
> I do not intend, my dear children, to compose and write for you a book of morals. Such I could not write, and our wise men have already written many. Moreover, we have our holy Torah in which we may find and learn all that we need for our journey through this world to the world to come. Of our beloved Torah we may seize hold. . . . We sinful men are in the world as if swimming in the sea and in danger of being drowned. But our great,

merciful and kind God, in His great mercy, has thrown ropes into the sea
that we may take hold of them and be saved. These are our holy Torah where is written what are the rewards and punishments for good and evil deeds. . . .

I pray you this, my children: be patient, when the Lord, may He be praised, sends you a punishment, accept it with patience and do not cease to pray to Him; perhaps He will have mercy upon you. . . . Therefore, my dear children, whatever you lose, have patience, for nothing is our own, everything is only a loan. . . . We men have been created for nothing else but to serve God and to keep His commandments and to obey the Torah, "for that is thy life, and the length of thy days."

The kernel of the Torah is: "Thou shalt love thy neighbour as thyself." But in our days we seldom find it so, and few are they who love their fellowmen with all their heart. On the contrary, if a man can contrive to ruin his neighbour nothing pleases him more. . . .

The best thing for you, my children, is to serve God from your heart without falsehood or deception, not giving out to people that you are one thing while, God forbid, in your heart you are another. Say your prayers with awe and devotion. During the time for prayers do not stand about and talk of other things. While prayers are being offered to the Creator of the world, hold it a great sin to engage another man in talk about an entirely different matter—shall God Almighty be kept waiting until you have finished your business?

Moreover, set aside a fixed time for the study of the Torah, as best you know how. Then diligently go about your business, for providing your wife and children with a decent livelihood is likewise a mitzwah—the command of God and the duty of man. We should, I say, put ourselves to great pains for our children, for on this the world is built, yet we must bear in mind that if children did as much for their parents, the children would quickly tire of it.

A bird once set out to cross a windy sea with its three fledglings. The sea was so wide and the wind so strong that the father bird was forced to carry his young, one by one, in his claws. When he was half-way across with the first fledgling the wind turned to a gale, and he said: "My child, look how I am struggling and risking my life in your behalf. When you are grown up, will you do as much for me and provide for my old age?" The fledgling replied: "Only bring me to safety, and when you are old I shall do everything you ask of me." Whereat the father bird dropped his child into the sea, and it drowned, and he said: "So shall it be done to such a liar as you." Then the father bird returned to the shore, set forth with his second fledgling, asked the same question, and receiving the same answer, drowned the second child with the cry "You, too, are a liar!" Finally he set out with the third fledgling, and when he asked the same question, the third and last fledgling replied: "My dear father, it is true you are struggling mightily and risking your life in my behalf, and I shall be wrong not to repay you when you are old, but I cannot bind myself. This though I can promise: when I am grown up and have children of my own, I shall do as much for them as you have done for me." Whereupon the father bird said: "Well spoken, my child, and wisely; your life I will spare and I will carry you to shore in safety."

Above all, my children, be honest in money matters, with both Jews and Gentiles, lest the name of Heaven be profaned. If you have in hand money or goods belonging to other people, give more care to them than if they were your own, so that, please God, you do no one a wrong. The first question put to a man in the next world is, whether he was faithful in his business dealings. Let a man work ever so hard amassing great wealth dishonestly, let him during his lifetime provide his children fat dowries and upon his death a rich heritage—yet woe, I say, and woe again to the wicked man who for the sake of enriching his children has lost his share in the world to come! For the fleeting moment he has sold Eternity.[1]

If we look in vain for evidence that Glückel is discontented with her status as a woman, it is because, within the system, her work is as important as her husband's. She is one who shapes and transmits Judaism, as much as her husband. But she does it in a different context; she has a different job to do. And she carries out her work unself-consciously and in a thoroughly accepting spirit.

A dramatic and profound shift took place in the consciousness and culture of the Jewish people of Europe and America in the nineteenth and twentieth centuries, and an example of that shift is captured in a single document—a letter written by one woman in 1906. One symptom of the great changes of modern times is the fact that women became conscious of their subordinated and secondary role in Judaism and undertook to change that role. One of the earliest and most effective leaders in this movement was Henrietta Szold, who founded the Women's Zionist Movement (*Hadassah*) and formed it into the single most important organization in American and world Zionism. When her mother died, she insisted on saying the memorial prayer (*kaddish*) in her mother's memory and refused the offer of a well-meaning male to say it in her behalf. This is what she replied in her letter:

It is impossible for me to find words in which to tell you how deeply I was touched by your offer to act as "*Kaddish*" for my dear mother. I cannot even thank you—it is something that goes beyond thanks. It is beautiful, what you have offered to do—I shall never forget it.

You will wonder, then, that I cannot accept your offer. Perhaps it would be best form not to try to explain to you in writing, but to wait until I see you to tell you why it is so. I know well, and appreciate what you say about, the Jewish custom; and Jewish custom is very dear and sacred to me. And yet I cannot ask you to say *Kaddish* after my mother. The *Kaddish* means to me that the survivor publicly and markedly manifests his wish and intention to assume the relation to the Jewish community which his parent had, and that so the chain of tradition remains unbroken from generation to generation, each adding its own link. You can do that for the generations of your family, I must do that for the generations of my family.

I believe that the elimination of women from such duties was never intended by our law and custom—women were freed from positive duties ehn they could not perform them, but not when they could. It was never intended that, if they could perform them, their performance of them should not be considered as valuable and valid as when one of the male sex performed them. And of the *Kaddish* I feel sure this is particularly true.

My mother had eight daughters and no son; and yet never did I hear a word of regret pass the lips of either my mother or my father that one of us was not a son. When my father died, my mother would not permit others to take her daughters' place in saying the *Kaddish*, and so I am sure I am acting in her spirit when I am moved to decline your offer. But beautiful your offer remains nevertheless, and, I repeat, I know full well that it is much more in consonance with the generally accepted Jewish tradition than is my or my family's tradition. You understand me, don't you?[2]

It would not be possible to adduce a more eloquent statement of the shift toward modernity—represented for us by the change in the consciousness and aspirations of Jewish women—than this simple, deeply traditional statement. In the modern age some women would no longer accept the role—assigned to them in classical Judaism—of silent partner and member of a protected, but subordinated caste. It is time to ask: What other changes took place? And how shall we account for them?

PART FOUR

*Continuity and Change
in Modern Times*

CHAPTER 20

The Historical Setting

When the Messiah comes, he will sound a great trumpet to call the scattered people of Israel out of the four corners of creation and bring them back to Zion. In the past three hundred years the Jews have looked hopefully toward two Messiahs, and the contrast between them provides a striking symbol of how classical Judaism has changed while remaining constant in the process of modernization.

The first was Sabbetai Zevi, who with his apostle, Nathan of Gaza, proclaimed a messianic mission in 1664. Though in a crisis he renounced Judaism for Islam, his movement had already spread like wildfire throughout the entire Jewish world with the result that, in the words of G. G. Scholem: "An emotional upheaval of immense force took place among the mass of the people, and for an entire year [1665–66] men lived a new life which for many years remained their first glimpse of a deeper spiritual reality."[1] The second was Theodor Herzl, who in 1897 convened at Basel a world Zionist congress, there predicting that within fifty years a Jewish state would become a reality—as indeed it did.

What is striking about these two movements is their universal impact within Jewry: Both evoked a broad and international experience and set the issues for discussion among Jews from the Vistula to the Atlantic. Sabbateanism was the last such international movement before Zionism, and since the fulfillment of Zionism, no similarly worldwide movement has affected all Jewry. The contrast between the two is instructive. Sabbateanism was religious and mystical; it phrased its message in strictly theological, kabbalistic terms. Sabbetai Zevi was "the Messiah" and played a central role in the metaphysical drama created by tensions within the godhead itself. Zionism was worldly, practical, and spoke in political and thoroughly secular terms. It identified the Jewish problem with sociological, economic, and cultural matters—not with sin and the need to atone, believe, or adopt a new mystical Messiah. Herzl was never "the Messiah," though Zionism utilized the ancient messianic Scriptures and images of Jewish Messianism.

The contrast is, therefore, between theological and ideological Messianism. Nevertheless, it is rendered significant because the spiritual experience, apart from the verbal explanations associated with it, in each case exhibits striking features in common—an emotional, millennarian upheaval dividing friend from friend, leading some to despair and others to unworldly hope, and moving a great many to act in new ways.

What we understand by the process, or phenomenon, of modernization is illustrated in Messianism; yet we must not be bound by the limitations of our illustration. The passage from religion and theology to politics and ideology marks only one way among many leading in much the same direction. Similar contrasts of tradition and modernity may be drawn between sacred revelation and secular enlightenment; between revealed law—guiding every action from heaven and lending supernatural significance to workaday behavior—and simple rules of accepted conduct; between Torah-study and research; between the life of the corporate community of the village and that of the cold and impersonal city. One may likewise point to the internationalization of "culture," in which appeals to singular revelation carry less weight than the demands of reason, and in which parochialism, tribalism, and self-sustaining realms of discourse and meaning are set aside in favor of a single, universal language of thought and technology.

Let us first consider the two events in the modern history of the Jews that most decisively shaped the modern history of Judaism. The first was political "emancipation"—that is, the extension to Jews of the rights and privileges of full citizenship in the various countries in which they lived.[2] The first country to do so was the United States. Its Constitution extended full and equal rights to all Americans. Shortly thereafter—and of greater immediate consequence—came the emancipation of French Jewry in the aftermath of the Revolution of 1789. Later on, in the nineteenth century, British, German, and other western European Jews achieved the same rights.

What in fact had changed? Medieval society was organized by estates into a corporate society. Each estate had a specific status in law and life. As we have seen, that fact conformed to the realities of Jewish life. Jews had no reason to reject recognition as a particular class or estate among other such "corporations." If Jews as individuals were later on given "equality," they thereby lost their ethnic-religious autonomy.[3] The modern state demanded the abolition of corporate distinctions, seeking to make all men (and later, all *women*) equal under the law and therefore equally obligated to serve the state.

Emancipation in the form of the provision of equal rights, therefore, was a mixed blessing—especially so because of the universal failure fully to realize those rights and to construct a society of equal opportunity and responsibility. This meant that Jewry had lost in security and autonomy more than it had gained in liberty and freedom. Traditional religious values were undermined; new values and ideals that took their place tended to separate the Jew from the classical tradition, but to provide no certain ideals at all. Jews indeed were expected to "assimilate"—that is, to cease being Jews at all as a condition of their "acceptance" by Gentiles. It is clear that emancipation posed the most serious challenge to the Jews, as well as to their religious tradition, since the destruction of the First Temple in 586 B.C.

Second, the crisis brought on by the shaking of the sociological foundations of Judaism was greatly intensified by the growing anti–Semitism in Western countries, culminating in what Jews universally call the Holocaust. By this they refer to the destruction of approximately six million European Jews between 1933 and 1945. This historical event dominates Judaic theology today, just as it shapes the imagination of the Jewish people in many lands. To understand why, one must keep in mind the difference between the Holocaust and all former massacres, riots, expulsions, and other calamities suffered by Jewry over millennia. The first difference was quantitative: Six million Jews represented one out of every three Jews in the world in 1939. In all of human history, only the massacre of two million of the four million Armenian people by the Turks in World War I is comparable. And of all Jews alive in lands conquered by Germany after 1939, nearly 90 percent died. The second difference was the racist character of the massacres. When Christians killed Jews, they would spare those who converted to Christianity; but the Nazis spared no one, regarding as a Jew someone who had only a single Jewish grandparent. Formerly, Jews might be expelled. Now, no one was permitted to escape. As Raul Hilberg puts it: "The missionaries of Christianity had said in effect, You have no right to live among us as Jews. The secular rulers who followed had proclaimed, You have no right to live among us. The German Nazis at last decreed, You have no right to live."[4] The third and most important difference was that the Holocaust was the achievement of an efficient, modern industrial state, prepared to invest vast efforts and sums in the creation of an industry producing one thing only—dead Jews. Nothing episodic, sporadic, or occasional characterized the Holocaust. On the contrary, it was systematic, orderly, well planned and superbly carried out. Despite the need for war transport for troops, train schedules were drawn up to move hundreds of thousands—eventually millions—of human beings; despite the scarcity of men and material, great concentration camps were built and staffed; gas chambers were manufactured even in preference to war production; corpses were carefully devoted to useful ends, such as the manufacture of soap. True, Nazi special forces would also gather together Jewish communities in front of large ditches and then machine-gun the whole lot; but these special actions, carried out mainly in newly conquered territories in the east, could not in a few years have accounted for millions of people. The great bureaucracy required for this task, "operating with accelerating speed and ever-widening destructive effect, proceeded to annihilate the European Jews."[5]

To understand the impact of the Holocaust on the contemporary Jewish mind, you need only to imagine yourself a Jew and to live with the knowledge and the nightmare that had you been in Europe, you would have died on that account. There was no way out. The nations of the world did practically nothing after 1939—little enough before then. Nor did salvation come from another place.

Modern Judaism was the creation of European Jewry. And European Jewry was moving inexorably to destruction. Its creations lived on, in various ways, in America, Britain, Israel, and elsewhere; so that there is hardly an idea or an institution of contemporary Jewry whose roots do not go deep into nineteenth-century Europe. The historical foundation of modern Judaism is, therefore, deeply flawed. Raul Hilberg writes: "Jewry is faced with ultimate weapons. It has no deterrent. The Jews can live more freely now. They can also die more quickly. The summit is within sight. An abyss has opened below."[6] If what happened to the ancient Israelites bore heavy implications for the shape of Israelite religion, the same is so today. If the Exodus led to Sinai, then where does Auschwitz lead? What are its religious implications? One who broods on that perplexity has entered the contemporary Jewish situation.[7]

By way of a retrospect and prospect, let us at the end consider how Richard S. Sarason contrasts the world view of classical Judaism, which we have now examined, with the fresh perspectives of the Jews of modernity:

> The world-view of classical Judaism espouses quietism out of a fear of active messianism. The reason is that that sort of messianism leads to chaotic upheavals within the Jewish world and destruction of Jews from without. For it ignores the restraints of order and law within, and the political impotence of the context of Jewry and the ecological framework, therefore, of Judaism. Judaism preserved a cosmic optimism, that things ultimately make sense, and that God in the long run will redress the balance—for the individual, in the afterlife, and for the community, in the messianic age. Jews affected by the Enlightenment faith saw that teleological optimism truly realized in a very this-worldly European society. The primary conviction now was that the world made sense in naturalistic terms, that the human being could both comprehend and control the world.[8]

Sarason further characterizes the shifts we shall examine in these same terms:

> The early Zionist ideologues were Jews who had already bought into the secular messianism and this-worldly teleology of Europe. But they were radically disillusioned. So much the more so, then, was the quietist, long-run teleological confidence of Judaism to be rejected by Jews weaned on the promise of this world and then despairing of its fulfillment. But the Zionists too were Utopians. They merely shifted the locus of their optimism to the Jewish state. The upshot was that Jews of all persuasions did retain their faith in the ultimate reasonableness of European civilization right down to the events of 1933 to 1945.[9]

In citing Professor Sarason, we gain a perspective on past and future. But we also have gone ahead of our story. Let us now retrace some of our steps.

We shall study the history of Judaism in modern times through a con-

sideration of what we mean by "modernization" and how we may ask the
right questions about the Jews' experience of modernity. Then in Chapter 21 we shall examine the process by which the traditional community disintegrated and the internal forces that produced its destruction. Third, in Chapters 22, 23, 24, and 25, we shall review four aspects of the tradition—theology, Messianism, social ethics, and study of Torah—and how they changed in modern times. Finally, Chapter 26 is a summary.

CHAPTER 21

For Some, the End of Traditional Society

Jacob Katz, an Israeli historian, provides a comprehensive account of "traditional Judaism" on the threshold of modernization.[1] Defining "traditional society" as "a type of society which regards its existence as based upon a common body of knowledge and values handed down from the past," Katz stresses the commonalities of religion, nationhood, and messianic hope, and traces the disintegrative effect upon them of religious charisma in Hasidism and of rationalism in the Jewish Enlightenment.

To the end of the eighteenth century, when the "modern period" of the history of Judaism begins, Jewish society was corporate, segregated, and collective in emphasis. Jews in Europe spoke a common language—Yiddish—and regarded themselves as a separate nation, living within other nations and awaiting their ultimate return to their own land. The central social ideal was study of Torah, which would result in heavenly reward. The obligation to study the Torah, leading to an intense appreciation for intellectualism, prevented the sanctification of economic activity as an ultimate goal and insured effective control over the people's value structure for the tradition—study of which was the chief purpose of living. The community itself was governed by its own classical legal tradition, with the rabbi as judge and community official.

The *kehillah* (structure of community government) controlled economic activities, relations with non–Jews, family and social life, and matters of religion—including, of course, all aspects of culture and education. It was the structural embodiment of the corporate community.

How did this community disintegrate so that the focus of Judaism came to center upon the individual, and the emphasis of Jewish thought upon the individual's personal religious needs and convictions? *It was not the result of external catastrophes*. Jewish society was badly shaken by the massacres of 1648–49, but the response of the community, as Katz points out, did not deviate from the traditional pattern: "There is no record of any program of action being instituted to prevent the recurrence of such an event . . . no political or social conclusions were drawn from the historical experience. As a matter of fact, the realistic explanations were overshadowed by the traditional view of divine providence, so that the lesson that emerged from the stocktaking was a religious-moral one.² It took the form of fasting, prayer, severe sumptuary laws, and rededication to study and observance of the Torah.

During the eighteenth century it was Hasidism in eastern Europe and *Haskalah* (Enlightenment) in the West that undermined traditional society. These movements shattered the framework of the community—which had formerly been able to reconstitute itself following banishments and migrations—in the several localities.

Hasidism, a pietist movement recalling the contemporary Methodism of Britain and the Great Awakening of mid–eighteenth-century New England, weakened the fidelity of the people to the rabbinic lawyer's leadership by stressing the importance *not* of learning in the law, but of religious charisma—the capacity to say particularly effective prayers, tell evocative stories, and engage in acts of a theurgic character. Existing institutions seemed to have lost their hold on large numbers of people. The situation was ripe for new social groups to take shape among people who had lost faith in the old ones. The Hasidic rabbi, called *Tzaddik* (literally, righteous one), through the force of his personality won the loyalty of such people. He was regarded not as a mere wonder-worker, but as an intermediary between heaven and earth.

[margin note: Charisma in Hasidism]

Hasidism was more than an adjustment to new social conditions or a movement of protest. In content, value, and structure, it was a revolution that set in a new light all preceding faith. One achieved holiness through Torah or through the *Tzaddik* (by celebrating his holiness), but not through both. A movement within the community, Hasidism created sects in the traditional corporate society. Some followed the charismatic leader; others did not. The consequence of these doctrines and policies was a religious and social revolution based upon a new requirement for leadership—not learning but personality. It resulted in the formation, within the body of the old community, of new and limited societies; in consequence, the traditional *kehillah* was destroyed.

The second force for modernization of traditional society was the Enlightenment, which in France and Germany altogether revolutionized the basis of Jewish society by destroying both its legal and its philosophical foundation. External rather than internal in its impact, the Enlightenment withdrew the political basis of Jewry by extending to the Jews the rights of citizens and at the same time denying Judaism the authority over Jews it had formerly exercised. It furthermore encouraged the development within Jewry of a new type of person, the *maskil* (illumined man), who mastered areas of human erudition formerly thought to be irrelevant to Jews. So the Enlightenment's processes of dissolution reinforced one another. The *kehillah* lost its legal standing, and some of its subjects opted out of it at the same time.

[margin note: Enlightenment]

Now individual members of Jewish society began to interest themselves in the opinion of the gentile world and to seek the esteem of non–Jews on the basis of gentile values. Had Jews merely converted to Christianity, it would hardly have affected traditional society; but many left that society and *yet* chose to remain Jews. They plunged into a crisis of identity which has yet to find resolution.

As part of the Jewish community—though perhaps on its fringes—the *maskilim* held up to the tests of reason, intelligence, and nature the artifacts of the tradition which had formerly been accepted as part of the given—the revealed reality—of the world. And they did so aggressively and derisively. The values they projected were those of the neutral society, which they saw as the wave of the future. They criticized the economic structure of Jewish society, its occupational one-sidedness, the traditional organizations (whose compulsory authority they rejected), and the traditional system of education, which did nothing to prepare young people to participate in the new world then seen to be opening up.

They did not propose to abandon Jewish society, but to "modernize" it. Values formerly held to be ends in themselves now came to be evaluated in terms of their usefulness and rationality—a usefulness measured not within the Jewish framework at all. The synagogue was seen as the locus of assemblage of the faithful for prayer rather than as the focus for community life, society, and culture, as in former times. The content and language of prayer, the architecture of the synagogue and its ritual were among the earliest objects of a reformation. Most significantly, the traditional modes of social control—denunciation and excommunication—ceased to operate effectively. Deviants no longer saw themselves as sinners. They did not justify themselves by traditional values at all.

Modernization was hardly a broad, widespread phenomenon. It mattered in only a few places—and even there unevenly—to almost the present time. Though the *kehillah* in its late medieval form underwent vast changes, the traditional personality and pattern of living of Jews in many places did not. The Enlightenment's impact, even in Germany until well into the nineteenth century, was limited to the upper classes. Hasidism was a mostly regional phenomenon, and after two generations, its fervor was directed into more or less traditional channels. Today, while remaining highly sectarian, it has become a bastion of "the tradition" in its least malleable forms.

More broadly still, the Jews in Moslem countries—apart from the gallicized urban upper classes—remained deeply a part of the traditional culture, not so much affirming intellectual *reasons* for remaining so, as *practicing* the faith in its classical forms into the twentieth century. For many, arriving in the State of Israel also signified arrival in the twentieth century as we know it. The political changes we associated under the title of emancipation had hardly reached Polish, Rumanian, and Russian Jewry before the Holocaust of 1933 to 1945. Furthermore, for many Jews in Western countries, the experience of modernization was objectionable; and, as we shall see, many rejected it. If a tradition changes, it is only for some; it never disintegrates for all.

It would be impossible to offer a fully adequate delimitation of the

problems w/ term
"modernztn of Juda.

107
The
End of
Traditional
Society 2

1

3

modernization of Judaism for three reasons. First of all, substantial parts of the Jewish people never underwent such a process—not only the Jews in Moslem countries, but also very large segments of eastern European Jewry. Second, even in the great cities—to which the majority of central and western European Jews had come by 1900—significant populations of traditionalists existed to the time of the Holocaust during World War II; in the Western countries groups of traditionalists have continued to exist to the present day. Whether they are traditional in the way in which the seventeenth-century Jew was traditional is not the issue. The fact is that those qualities we have associated with traditionalism apply without qualification to large parts of Jewry and therefore to significant segments of Judaism in Israel, the United States, Great Britain, continental Europe, and elsewhere. Third, the inner dynamism of a living tradition is such that at no point may we arbitrarily arrest its development for purposes of definition and conclude that a given form is *the* tradition from which all that changes thereby deviates and therefore constitutes "modernization." Within the circles of the most traditional Jews, cultural phenomena are today accepted that a century ago would have been regarded as unacceptable; and yet, should we call such Jews modernists, the term would be deprived of any meaning whatever. In context, they think of themselves and are thought of by others as living within the classic tradition.

By this point in the discussion of the modern period in the history of Judaism, we can begin to see some of the complexity of the problem of modernity. On the one hand, we have reviewed some of the climactic moments and experiences of the life of the Jew. We have seen that the Judaic religious tradition exercises a majestic force—a power—over the imagination and feeling, the mind and the soul, of the Jew. So we must ask how it was possible for large numbers of people to break the bonds that tied them to so glorious a world as that constructed by Judaism.

On the other hand, we have examined the immense changes in political and social life that overtook Jews in western Europe and America in the nineteenth and twentieth centuries. The political status of the Jew radically changed; the Jews no longer formed a fairly closed social group, but wanted to relate to non–Jews and get to know and live with them. In Western countries—the United States, Britain, France, Holland, Belgium, Canada, and Germany—Jews were granted full civil rights and were able to exercise them in some measure. The wonder is, then, why anyone should have held to the old way of life at all. How could anyone have resisted the appeal of the new age?

This is the paradox: the power of the tradition and the force of modernity. The two spent themselves, to be sure, in the disasters of World War II. But by then the changes were pretty well in place. Western Jews (in the United States, France, Britain, and Canada, for example) clearly had found their way into the larger societies in which they were born and grew up. Few of them wanted to live on the fringes of culture and in tight little communities of the faith. On the other hand, these same Jews clearly wanted not only to remain Jewish, but to remain Jewish in a religious way. Many of them aspired to regain access to that which their grandfathers and great-grandfathers had rejected. Indeed, as the great historian of American immigration, Marcus Lee Hansen, put it: 'What the son [the first-generation American] wants to forget, the grandson [the third generation] tries to remember.'[3] To state Hansen's perception in terms of the religious history of contemporary Jews: The native-born Jew of the third and fourth and fifth generations past the immigrant times (or "emancipation") are fully acculturated—so much so that they too are in search of their roots.

The question becomes, then, whether or not the majesty of an alien world view may once more exert its reality-constructing power. To phrase the question in the language with which we began: Has the context, the natural system, of the Jewish people so vastly changed that that old, world-constructing system—Judaism—that made sense for so long can make sense no longer? Are the ecological data so new and unprecedented that a way of seeing the world that worked for so many generations of moderately skeptical, moderately optimistic people today can work no more? These are the issues of the future that is now.

But we have again moved ahead of ourselves. In stressing the paradox of modernity, we should not forget the complexity of the facts. What we shall now see is that wherever we turn, we find a very genuine question of how modern are the modern expressions of classical Judaic institutions, ideas, and ideals. Upon first glance, nothing is the same; upon second glance, nothing seems to have changed. Clearly, the problem is that there are continuities and there are changes. So we are puzzled at how to interpret what it is that we are, in fact, observing. But such puzzlement is, of course, natural to the study of religions.

In the four chapters that follow, we shall examine four significant themes within the Jewish tradition. In each instance we shall ask how the tradition has changed, and how it has preserved continuities with the past. In no instance shall we be able to locate simple or obvious examples of modernization. In each we shall see that much has changed, but much has remained the same. Nothing standing by itself is an adequate instance of pure, one-way modernization.

The four structures are not easily compared one to another. The first, *theology*, comprehends the ways in which thoughtful Jews have explained to themselves the central propositions of Judaism as a religious tradition. The modern consequences, in Reform and Orthodoxy, were superficially intellectual and are here treated as mostly so; yet the social results of changes of mind are at least as significant. Different theological affirmations produced different social, economic, and cultural ideals, and thus, different styles of life.

The second theme, *Messianism*, produced the Zionist movement—a chief formative factor in creating the State of Israel—so the direct consequence of the new Messianism lay in political, rather than in religious or cultural life. Yet here, too, we shall see important theological and cultural results.

The third theme, *social ethics*, produced the most "secular" of all movements in modern Judaism—Jewish Socialism in eastern Europe and the United States. Jewish Socialism was a movement of workers committed both to socialist ideology and ideals and to the improvement of the condi-

tion of Jews as part of the working classes. In Europe the movement took
the shape of the General Jewish Workers Bund (alliance) in Poland; this title was a contradiction in terms, for a party calling itself Marxist could
hardly propose to solve a particular nationality problem and to limit its
constituency to a single persecuted national minority. In the United States
the movement created labor unions, supported social legislation, and
joined in the struggle to achieve a decent standard of living for the vast
majority of Jews and others who lived by their own labor. The Jewish
Socialists held classic Marxist views on religion, especially Judaism; but
that most secular movement seems to have preserved the most profoundly
religious theme of Jewish tradition—the primacy of morality—and hence to
have revealed the most ambiguous result.

The fourth theme, *scholarship*, is peculiarly Jewish, for the traditional
impulse, which so dominated Jewish life, was to study the Torah. The
highest virtues were those of the master of the Torah, and no value more
deeply informed Jewish culture. Yet traditional learning and modern
scholarship are by no means congruent with one another.

These four facets of the Jewish tradition reveal changes in religious,
political, historical, social, and intellectual ways of being Jewish. In the
past century and a half, the Jews have endured a lingering crisis of identity, for they have not agreed since the eighteenth century upon the most
basic propositions of self-definition, as we saw at the outset. Some Jews
have found it possible to exhaust the meaning of Jewishness in religion,
narrowly construed as the West defines "religion"—that is, faith and cult—
while some expressed it in nationalism, equally narrowly defined in terms
of sovereignty, state, and flag. Some expressed their Jewishness in socialism, the new homeland for an international folk; and some few in scholarship, understood in the university way as the detached and open-minded,
nonprotagonistic study of a past long dead and gone.

These have not been the only options. Vast numbers of Jews have found
a satisfying expression of their Judaism through philanthropic, nonsec-
tarian enterprises; others through clinging close to an ethnic group, in
ghettos of the assimilated in all but name; and still others in intense
participation—largely with other Jews for company—in the most advanced
cultural enterprises of the day. And of course, we cannot ignore the fact
that for many Jews, modernization signified the end of Jewishness
altogether. In the nineteenth and twentieth centuries, as the changes of
modernity affected Jews of the first generation of the new age, many converted to the dominant religion of their own society, by becoming
Anglican, Lutheran, Roman Catholic, Greek Orthodox—or, in the Soviet
bloc, by joining the Communist party. Other Jews lapsed into a curious
situation in which they were not practitioners of Judaism, but also did not
become "something else." Of these, some simply walked out of the Jewish
world. Others abandoned Judaism but developed a mode of life deemed, in
their setting, to be distinctively Jewish. So modernization not only ended
"Jewishness"; more interestingly, it vastly complicated the modes by
which people who were Jewish interpreted for themselves and in the contexts of their own lives just what—if anything—that fact was supposed to
mean.

CHAPTER 22

Theology: Reform and Orthodoxy

Since the nineteenth century, the efforts of Judaic theologians have been devoted to formulating a "modern" statement of the faith, congruous to contemporary philosophy. The theological enterprise itself is the most striking exemplification of modernization. One chief issue faced by these thinkers has been this: Having abandoned what I conceive to be "the traditional faith," do I thereby cease to be a Jew?

It is a very slight step from such a question to a sociological, rather than a theological, reply. Many have not hesitated to take that step: Your "Jewish identity" remains valid. Each of us may supply whatever reasons we choose, but none of us is likely to conceive of a more striking transformation of theological into ideological language than the very question with which such discourse begins. The issue of "identity," then, is sociological, not theological. Nor are the concomitant issues less secular: survival, consensus, commitment. Central issues of the Judaic tradition have, therefore, taken on a secular character in the hands of modern Judaic theologians.

The two most interesting cases of theological modernization are Reform Judaism and Orthodox Judaism. We shall concentrate on these groups, even though numerous individual thinkers would well have supplied interesting examples.

Reform Judaism, as its name implies, began as an effort to effect a reformation of the classical tradition. The "Judaic Reformation" proceeded on two levels: that of the virtuosi and that of the masses.

Large numbers of Jews in the great cities of Germany—and, later on, in France, Britain, and the United States—responded to the new situation of emancipation by acculturation. They thereby sought to meet the requirements of the world to which they supposed they were invited. Accepted as citizens, they abandoned any pretense of separate nationality. Granted full economic equality, they shaped their own economic ideals to conform to those of the majority. They were desperately eager to deserve the promises of cultural emancipation. Like the *maskilim* (enlightened ones) a generation or two earlier, they examined their cult to discover those practices that were alien to the now interested world and determined to do away with them.

These were *not* Jews who would choose the road of assimilation through conversion—perfunctory or otherwise. They chose to remain Jews and retain Judaism. One might say they wanted to be Jews but not too "Jewish"—not so "Jewish" that they could not be ordinary people achieving a place in the undifferentiated society. This they wanted so badly that they saw and eagerly seized upon a welcome that few Gentiles, if any, really proffered.

The religious virtuosi—those who had a better European education, a richer family experience, a deeper involvement in the tradition to begin with—had the task of mediating between "the tradition" and the changes they saw about them and enthusiastically approved. For them, change became *reform*. The direction of the people proved to be providential. As Solomon Freehof wrote: "It was the Reformers who hailed the process and believed in it."[1] They founded their reformation upon the concept that "essential Judaism" in its pure form required none of the measures that separated the Jew from other enlightened people, but consisted rather of beliefs and ethics—beliefs that were rational and destined in time to convince all mankind, and ethics that were universal and far in advance of any available from other sources. Freehof commented: "Reform Judaism is the first flaming up of direct world-idealism in Judaism since the days of Second Isaiah."

Isolating the prophets as the true exponents of Judaism, they chose within the messages of the prophets those texts that best served as useful pretexts for the liberalism of the age. The reformers looked back upon the "golden age" when Judaism spoke to all mankind of the obligations of justice and mercy. It was that message they saw to be essential. All else was expendable. So the social ideals of the masses, who yearned for a liberal society in which even Jews would find acceptance, and those of "essential Judaism" were identical. The necessary changes would indeed constitute a reformation and return *to that time* of the true and unadorned faith.

But more than this, the reformers turned not only back to a golden age of "uncorrupted Judaism," but also forward to a golden age in the future, that time when bigotry and injustice would cease. They exhibited an idealism—an almost otherworldly confidence in mankind—that suggests a radical disjuncture between their fantasies on the one hand and reality on the other. The Jews were Europe's blacks, and Germany was their Mississippi or New York. They were excluded from the universities, ridiculed in the pulpits, libeled in the newspapers, insulted in private life. Yet they saw humanity as God's partners in the rebuilding of creation. They had the effrontery even to see themselves as bearers of a mission to mankind: God's dominion would be realized only through Judaism, "that most rational and ethical of all religions." The Jews had, they believed, an inherited, innate ability to give the world an ethical consciousness. In the symphony of the nations—so common a metaphor in these decades—Jews would play the ethical melody.

Orthodoxy is a creation of the reformation of Judaism, for only in response to the reformers did traditionalists self-consciously formulate what they regarded as orthodox *about* Judaism.

Orthodox organizations were founded a half-century after the Reform movement took shape—not only in Germany, but in the United States. Orthodoxy, too, accepted the premises of the reformation—that the Jews were going not only to live *among* Gentiles, but *with* them, and that therefore they had better learn the languages and adopt the culture, in its broadest form, of the West. But Orthodoxy determined on a different interpretation of what living with Gentiles must mean—a different ideal for modern Judaism. Orthodoxy stood for the tradition first, last, and always; it accepted—but only grudgingly affirmed—the conditions of modern life. Modernism was to be judged by the criterion of Torah, not the contrary. What was up-to-date was, standing by itself, no source of truth, let alone revelation.

Underlying this presupposition, nonetheless, is a vast reformation in traditional attitudes. Before the Jews could conceive themselves in such a new situation, they had to accept living with Gentiles as a good thing. They had to affirm it as the will of heaven, in a way in which they never had accepted or affirmed the high cultures of medieval and ancient times. Modernization long antedated both the modernist movement *and its opposition.* But the opposition at first was at a deep disadvantage, for it had to debate the issues already set by the reformation and to take a negative view where, in a more congenial situation, it might have found the grounds for affirming natural change as within the spirit of the Torah.

Favoring the Orthodox party were four factors. First was the natural conservatism of religious men who, within Judaism, followed not only the path of their fathers, but the ways of the *Father* himself. These ways were set by traditional parents, who lent powerful psychic support to the Orthodox viewpoint.

Second, the Orthodox claimed that they represented the true and authentic Judaism. This claim was strengthened by the fact that the Orthodox were more like the preceding generations than were the reformers. The reformers' claim that they were "the true Judaism" had to be based upon a highly sophisticated, historicistic argument that if the prophets or the Pharisees were alive in the nineteenth century, they would have been Reform Jews; therefore Reform Judaism was authentic and Orthodox Judaism was not. But that argument persuaded only those who believed in it to begin with. For the rest, the claim of Orthodoxy to historical authenticity seemed reasonable, for it conformed to their own observations of religious life.

Third, the virtuosi of Reform Judaism were concerned for authenticity, but the Reform laity were not. The Orthodox continued to attract those Jews most serious about Judaism. Orthodoxy therefore benefited from the high level of commitment of its lay men and women—people prepared to make every sacrifice for the faith. In a measure, reform was attractive not only to reformers, but also to assimilationists. That is to say, whatever the virtuosi's intent, for the lay followers the Reform movement was a vehicle of their own convenience, used by the passengers to reach a point quite outside the itinerary of the driver. Two sorts of Jews participated in the creation of the Reform movement. One was the virtuoso—the Jew who not only was raised in a traditional environment, but took seriously the propositions of the tradition, and therefore made changes on the basis of commitment and reflection. The other was the ordinary person who, while intending to remain a faithful Jew, could see no reason to preserve what he thought were outdated, "medieval," or simply outlandish habits of dress, nourishment, speech, prayer, and the like. For such people the Reform movement offered a satisfactory way to continue within the Judaic faith; they felt not the slightest interest in the rationalizations for that way. Thus, for example, praying in the manner of Protestant Christians—that is, in the vernacular, in decorous manner, with organ music and choirs, with men and women sitting together—that sort of public worship had great appeal to German Jews eager to find acceptance among Gentiles not only for themselves as individuals but also for their faith. But those responsible for such changes needed to persuade themselves that greater, more solemn truths than merely aping the Gentile were expressed through the reform of the liturgy.

The fourth factor favoring Orthodox Judaism was that, as the Orthodox claim to constitute the one legitimate form of Judaism and to measure by itself the "authenticity" of all "deviant" forms developed, Orthodoxy came to offer a security and a certainty unavailable elsewhere. Its concept of a direct relationship between the individual's conformity to the tradition and the will of the Creator of the universe bore a powerful attraction for those seeking a safe way in the world and feeling less concerned with the golden age to come, though still hoping for it.

Just as not all Europeans were liberals, but preferred another way, so too not all Jews—not even most Jews in many places—responded to the liberal message of the reformation. And many who did were in time won back to the "tradition"—in its central European "cultured" form to be sure—when Orthodoxy addressed itself to them in good German rather than in good Yiddish. What some wanted was merely to dress like Gentiles and speak like them—but to live, nonetheless, by patterns they believed were revealed at Sinai. The achievement of the Orthodox thinkers was to offer reassurance that certain parts of life were truly neutral; in so saying, they accomplished the grandest reformation of all.

Samson Raphael Hirsch (1808–1888), the chief spokesman for western European Orthodoxy, was raised in Germany. His knowledge of the traditional learning was acquired mainly through his own efforts. The chief influence on his thought about contemporary Judaism was Jacob Ettlinger, who stated: "Let not him who is engaged in the war of the Lord against the heretics be held back by the false argument that great is peace and that it is better to maintain the unity of all designated as Jews than to bring about disruption."[2] Such an affirmation of the sectarian option represents a strange attitude indeed among those who would lay claim to "sole legitimacy."

Hirsch, by contrast, in his *Nineteen Letters*,[3] issued no threats of excommunication, but stressed the affirmative requirement to study the Torah, with the rationalistic, perhaps ironic, certainty that knowledge would yield assent—an optimism different in form but not in substance from that of the reformers. When he settled in Frankfurt, he found a community dominated by the reformation. At his death, he left in it a bastion of Orthodoxy, originally established in separation from the "community"— that is, the government-recognized *Gemeinde*—which was Reform.

Hirsch accomplished this radical change chiefly by founding a school. He designed the curriculum so that the next generation would conform to the ideal by which he lived: "Torah and *Derekh Eretz*"—that is, traditional science combined with general secular enlightenment. Judaism, he held,

> . . . encompasses all of life, in the synagogue and in the kitchen. . . . To be a Jew—in a life which in its totality is borne on the world of the Lord and is perfected in harmony with the will of God—this is the scope and goal of Judaism. . . . In so far as a Jew is a Jew, his views and objectives become universal. He will not be a stranger to anything which is good, true, and beautiful in art and in science, in civilization and in learning. . . . He will hold firmly to this breadth of view in order to fulfill his mission as a Jew and to live up to the function of his Judaism in areas never imagined by his father.[4]

Hirsch therefore proposed a model of "the Jewish-man," who fears God, keeps the commandments, and looks at the "wonders of the Lord in nature and the mighty deeds of the Lord in history." He added, however, that "Jewish-man" brings about not only the redemption of Israel, but also the redemption of all mankind. No less than the reformers', Hirsch's reformation spoke of a "mission of Israel," and aimed at the "redemption of mankind"—both the hallmarks of the liberal, enlightened German of the day.

Both Reform and Orthodox Judaism represent, therefore, modes of response to modernization. For both, the constants were Scriptures, concern for the religious dimension of existence, concentration upon the historical traditional sciences—though in different ways—and concern for the community of Jews. These persisted, but in new forms. Hirsch's "Torah and *Derekh Eretz*," no less than the "science of Judaism" (*Wissenschaft des Judentums*) produced within the Reform movement, constituted a strikingly new approach to the study of the Torah. The rhetoric of Israel's mission, now focusing in both movements upon the private person, reflected the new social datum of Jewish living—no longer as a nation but as individuals—and concealed, in both instances, the utter decay of the traditional social context. For both, concentration upon the community and its structures, policies, and future involved considerable use of sociological language. For neither were the traditional categories of covenant and sacred community any longer characteristic of a broad and catholic concern for *all* Jews in a given place. Both addressed themselves, because the times required it, to German- or French- or English-speaking Jews.

Neither could conceive of a parochial and self-sustaining language of

Jewish discourse. Both spoke of a mission of Israel to the world and conceived of redemption in terms at least relevant to the Gentile. This is not to
suggest that the tradition in its earlier formulations was here misrepresented; but both Orthodox and Reform Judaism were very different from
contemporary, premodern, archaic Judaism in eastern Europe, North
Africa, and elsewhere. Both were far more sophisticated, intellectual, ar-
ticulate, and self-conscious than traditional Judaisms outside western
Europe.

The religious virtuosi of Reform and Orthodoxy were already prepared
for a new formulation of the tradition long before either Reform or
Orthodoxy made an appearance. Indeed, in significant ways, both represent a very considerable lag. The rigidity of Orthodoxy, moreover, is
peculiarly modern and was called forth by changes in the quality of the
Jews' way of living. We can hardly locate, in earlier times, an equivalent
rejection of contemporary learning. We can find only a few premodern examples of such paralysis in the face of need to update legal doctrines.
Quite obviously, it was a fearful inability to cope with changes that
produced the claim that change was, for the most part, undesirable and
even impossible. Change not only was *not* reform; it was the work of the
devil. Similarly, the sectarianism of both Reform and Orthodox groups—
their abandonment of the ambition to struggle with all Jews for the
achievement of universal goals within a single, united community—
constitutes a failure of nerve in the face of the diversities and inconstancies
of the modern situation.

Modernization called forth many changes indeed, but those were
produced by a tradition already much in flux and by men and women who
had come a long way toward the modern situation before the challenges of
modernization in political, cultural, and religious matters had to be faced
consciously. Nor is it a consistent matter, for modernization ought to have
produced one response only—that is, the Reform one. Yet in Germany the
responses were in significant measure reaffirmations of what men conceived to be the tradition. Modern culture acted upon traditional religion,
but the contrary proved also to be the case; the modern Jew was surely as
much shaped by his inherited culture as that culture was shaped by
modernization. And that modern Jew had a significant impact indeed upon
the formation of what subsequent generations understood to be modernity. This becomes self-evident when we consider the modernization of
Messianism.

CHAPTER 23

Nationality and Peoplehood: Messianism and Zionism

Unlike the Bombay Parsees, the Jews sustained the hope of returning to the homeland, and the very heart of their messianic belief—its symbols and fantasies—was shaped by that hope. Some Jews always remained in the Land of Israel, but all Jews until the nineteenth century expected to assemble to witness the resurrection of the dead there. Judaic Messianism was, as Professor Joseph L. Blau emphasizes, invariably supposed to be a political phenomenon by contrast to the restorationism of non–Jews, in which Zion was in heaven, not on earth.[1] William Blake's "Jerusalem" could perhaps be built in England; the Zion of Jewish piety could *only* be the earthly, specific place. For this reason the early reformers found Messianism an embarrassment.

When Napoleon asked the French Rabbinical Sanhedrin of 1807 whether those Jews born in France regarded France as their native country, the answer of the rabbis could only have been in the affirmative. Yet such an answer could not possibly have been a true one, except during the reformation. Ludwig Philippson wrote: "Formerly the Jews had striven to create a nation . . . but now their goal was to join other nations. . . . It was the task of the new age to form a general human society which would encompass all peoples organically. In the same way, it was the task of the Jews not to create their own nation . . . but rather to obtain from the other nations full acceptance into their society."[2] Similarly, the West London Synagogue of British Jews heard from its first rabbi in 1845: "To this land [England] we attach ourselves with a patriotism as glowing, with a devotion as fervent, and with a love as ardent and sincere as any class of our British non–Jewish fellow citizens."[3] One could duplicate that statement—and with it, its excessive protest—many times.

The reformation emphasized that Judaism could eliminate the residue of its nationalistic phase that survived in traditional doctrine and liturgy. The reformers saw Messianism not as Zionist doctrine, but as a call to the golden age in which a union of nations into one peaceful realm to serve their one true God would take place. The happy optimism that underlay these hopes and affirmations survived among some even after Auschwitz.

Universalist world union

But for the assimilated Western Jews of Paris, Vienna, and London, the rise of virulent scientific and political anti–Semitism during the last third of the nineteenth century raised significant doubts. Nor did the political situation of eastern Europe Jewry that was characterized by pogroms, repression, and outright murder provide reassurance. Mankind did not seem to be progressing very quickly toward that golden day.

Modern Zionism—the movement to establish a Jewish state in Palestine—represented a peculiar marriage of Western romantic nationalism and Eastern Jewish piety. The virtuosi of the movement were mostly Western, but the masses of followers were in the East. Fustel de Coulanges' saying, "True patriotism is not love of the soil, but love of the past, reverence for the generations which have preceded us," in his book, *The Ancient City*, at once excluded Jews (who were newcomers to French culture and could hardly share love for a French past that included banishment of their ancestors) and invited some of them to rediscover their own patriotism—that is, Zionism. The Jews could not share the "collective being" and could not be absorbed into a nation whose national past they did not share. The Dreyfus trial of 1893–94 involved one of the handful of Jewish officers in the French army; he was falsely accused of selling military secrets to Germany. Because of widespread anti–Semitism, Dreyfus was represented as an example of the bigoted notion that Jews were not loyal citizens. When he was publicly disgraced, the crowds shouted—not, "Down with the traitor!"—but, "Down with the Jews!" That fact forced upon the Viennese reporter, Theodor Herzl, a clear apprehension that the "Jewish problem" could be solved only by complete assimilation or complete evacuation. It occurred to no one in the West that extermination was an option, though the czarist Russians thought of it.

In response to the Dreyfus trial, Herzl published *Der Judenstaat (The Jewish State)*, from whose appearance in 1896 is conventionally dated the foundation of modern Zionism. One can hardly overemphasize the secularity of Herzl's vision. He did not appeal to religious sentiments, but to modern secular nationalism. His view of anti–Semitism ignores the religious dimension altogether, and stresses only economic and social causes. Modern anti–Semitism grows out of the emancipation of the Jews and their entry into competition with the middle classes. The Jews cannot cease to exist as Jews, for affliction increases their cohesiveness.

Herzl's solution was wholly practical: Choose a country to which Jews could go—perhaps Argentina or Uganda, which was made available by the British government a few years later. What was important was a rational plan: The poor would go first and build the infrastructure of an economy; the middle class would follow to create trade, markets, and new opportunity. The first Zionist Congress was not a gathering of Messianists, but of sober men. Herzl's statement, "At Basel I founded the Jewish state," was not, however, a sober statement; nor was his following one: "The State is already found in essence, in the will of the people of the State." All that remained were mere practicalities.

Herzl's disciple, Max Nordau, held that Zionism resulted from nationalism and anti–Semitism. Had Zionism led to Uganda, one could have believed it. When Herzl proposed Uganda, he was defeated. The masses in the East had been heard from. They bitterly opposed any "Zion" but Jerusalem. To them, Zionism could mean only Zion; Jerusalem was in one place alone. The classical messianic language—much of which was already associated with Zion in the messianic era—was taken over by the Zionist movement, and it evoked a much more than political response in the Jewish hearts. Zionism swept the field, and in the twentieth century even the Reform movement affirmed it and contributed some of its major leaders. Only small groups within Reform and Orthodoxy resisted—the latter because they saw Zionism as an act of pride, contravening the hope in supernatural Messianism.

Calling a land-colonization fund—known in English as the Jewish National Fund—by the Hebrew words *Keren Kayemet Le-Yisrael*, (the Eternal Fund of Israel) was a deliberate effort to evoke the talmudic *Keren Kayemet le-Olam HaBa* (Eternal Fund for the World to Come), which consisted of acts of merit, piety, or charity destined to produce a heavenly reward. To the doggedly religious ear, such a title was nothing less than blasphemy, for it made use of sacred language in a secular sense. But that represents the very ambiguity of Zionism: a strange marriage between Western, assimilated leaders, on the one hand, and Eastern traditionalists on the other.

The history of Zionism has not here been adumbrated, let alone exhausted; but for our purposes, its peculiarity has become clear. As Rabbi Arthur Hertzberg stated: "Zionism cannot be typed, and therefore easily explained as a 'normal' kind of national risorgimento [reorganization]. . . . From the Jewish perspective, messianism, and not nationalism, is the primary element in Zionism. . . . Writers too numerous to mention here have characterized the modern movement as 'secular messianism,' to indicate at once what is classical in Zionism—its eschatological purpose; and what is modern—the necessarily contemporary tools of political effort." Hertzberg rejects this characterization as too simple. Rather, he sees as the crucial problem of Zionist ideology "the tension between the inherited messianic concept and the radically new meaning that Zionism, at its most modern, was proposing to give it."[4]

Hertzberg's analysis is very searching, but it seems to be precisely this tension that is acknowledged by those who have seen Zionism as a modernized, if not wholly secularized, Messianism. Hertzberg greatly deepens the discussion when he says that the crisis is "not solely in the means but in the essential meaning of Jewish messianism . . . it is the most radical attempt in Jewish history to break out of the parochial molds of Jewish life in order to become part of the general history of man in the modern world. Hence we are face to face with a paradoxical truth: for the general historian finds it hard to define because it is too general."[5]

But so far as Zionism aspired to create a state like other states and to normalize the existence of the Jews, it represented a massive movement toward assimilation. Its goal was to end the particular and peculiar Judaic way of living and to substitute for it the commonplace and universal modern mode of life. And it succeeded. So while Zionism was expressive of the unique and special aspects of Judaic Messianism and bound up with the most private hopes of Jewry, it served, in a paradoxical way, as the means for ending the unique and making public what had been private. In creating the largest Jewish neighborhood in the world, where Jews lose a sense of being different, it refocused the center of Judaic existence out of its parochial mold and placed the Jews within the mainstream of international life.

CHAPTER 24

Law and Ethics

Among the most influential ideologies in late nineteenth- and twentieth-century Jewry in eastern Europe and the United States, and in the Zionist movement in both places, was Jewish Socialism. If Reform and Orthodoxy are heirs to the traditional theology and Zionism to the traditional eschatology, then one must see Jewish Socialism—a deeply secular movement by conviction and orientation—as the heir of the ethical and moral idealism that in traditional society had found expression in the vast legal enterprise of *halakhah* that lay at the heart of Jewish existence.

No less than Zionism, Jewish Socialism exhibited the many ambiguities and eccentricities of a modernized tradition: the psychic and emotional continuities and the formal differences. Zionism chose to restore the Hebrew language; Jewish Socialism chose to use Yiddish. Zionism turned to the ancient land; Jewish Socialism saw all lands as equally sacred in the struggle for humanity. Zionism's impact proved significant mainly in the Middle East. Jewish Socialism left its mark on the vast American Jewish community—a product far more directly the heir of Jewish Socialism than of any other single force in modern Judaism—as well as on the State of Israel, with its socialist orientation over the past thirty years.

Nowadays most people, Jews and non-Jews, regard Judaism as the foundation of American Jewish life. "We are Americans by nationality, and Jews by religion" is frequently said. But though today American Jews explain their difference from other Americans in terms of religious convictions, the earlier generations of Jews in this country did not. They regarded themselves as an ethnic group, and what was important about that ethnic group was not uniquely religion, but culture, language, and, especially, social ideals. The immigrant generation, to be sure, founded synagogues; but what excited them was the formation of trade unions, political movements, social welfare agencies—instrumentalities to create a better world. Their social idealism was perhaps born in the classical tradition, particularly in the prophetic teachings about the centrality of ethics and morality, but the Jewish Socialists of the day did not regard themselves as within that tradition or as religious.

American Jewry now looks back upon the supposed orthodoxy of its grandfathers, but the life of the ghettos, which the current generation would like either to idealize or forget, was not orthodox, but socialist. Charles S. Liebman makes this quite clear.[1] The immigrants, he says, simply did not give their children a religious education. In 1908, only 28 percent of the Jewish children in New York City received any Jewish education at all. "The immigrants flocked instead to the public schools, to night classes, and to adult-education courses—not only for vocational purposes but for general cultural advancement."

It was only in the 1920s, after the wave of emigration from eastern Europe spent itself, that traditional Judaism revived in eastern Europe. Those who migrated before then were the least religious. Liebman calls their piety "situational or environmental," rather than personal, theological, or traditional. It was a matter of habit and culture, not faith. They had been told America was simply not *kosher;* yet they came. One can hardly turn back now and praise their piety. Renowned rabbis warned against emigration. If the immigrant generations were not Orthodox, nor, quite evidently, Reform, then what were they? The obvious answer is that they were, in the mass, residually pious, but actively socialist. The synagogue meant less—even to those who attended it—than did the union hall, the Socialist party centers, the cultural clubs.

For many, socialism replaced Judaism. The radicals—seeing in "religion" the opiate of the masses, and in its exponents, agents of reaction—could not but conceive of themselves as more truly heirs of prophecy and ethical rabbinism than others who made more vociferous claim to the legacy. What is it, then, that they affirmed, and how shall we assess it by "the tradition"? A poem by J. L. Kantor provides a testament to the radicals' faith:

> We believe
> —that misdeeds, injustice, falsehood, and murders will not reign forever, and a bright day will come when the sun will appear
> —men will not die of hunger and wealth not created by its own labor will disappear like smoke
> —people will be enlightened and will not differentiate between man and man; will no longer say, "Christian, Moslem, Jew," but will call each other "Brother, friend, comrade"
> —the secrets of nature will be revealed and people will dominate nature instead of nature dominating them
> —man will no longer work with the sweat of his brow; the forces of nature will serve him as hands.[2]

Many of them marginal Jews, the radicals harbored sentiments that bore so strong an affinity to the eschatological visions of Isaiah and other prophets that one hardly knows how to intrepret them. Obviously, they did not set out to paraphrase prophetic vision and did not do so. Yet how far away have they strayed from a tradition that both saw in a starving child an affront to heaven, and contained a grand variety of proof texts for precisely the kind of social revolution espoused by the radicals?

It is here that the complexity of our problem poses the severest challenges. It would be inviting to identify the new social idealism with the elements within Jewish tradition that seem so obviously similar to it—for example, the ethical will of Eleazar of Mainz (see Chapter 18). The radicals never offered a Jewish equivalent to Christian Socialism. The radicals delighted in conducting dances on the evening of the Day of Atonement. They aroused consternation precisely among those who were held to be "religious."

Our problem is not simplified, moreover, by the Jewish secularist ideologists, who offer a statement of the "secularity" of the Jewish Socialists that is hardly irreligious. The secularists to whom I refer are the so-called Yiddishists—that is, those who seek to preserve and enhance the Yiddish language as a major vehicle for Jewish creativity. In "Who Needs Yiddish? A Study in Language and Ethics,"[3] Joseph C. Landis describes the Yiddish language as the embodiment of the ethic of European Jewry: "Jewish value and Jewish sense of life are embodied in the the repatterned sentence style and structure, in the altered pronunciation and word order, in the reshaped inflectional forms, and their derivatives, in the enlarged vocabulary, in the created folk expressions and sayings, in the metaphors and allusions."

Its capacity—to express man's obligation to be his brother's keeper, to convey human relatedness, to express tenderness, endearment, sentimentality, and more than that, morality—renders a language (surely the most secular of all phenomena) into the instrument, as Landis says, "in which Jewish *mentschlekhkayt* (humanity) expresses its religious *yidishkayt* (Jewishness, Judaism)."

Yiddish, he adds, "is . . . the voice of Jewish ethic, the voice of Judaism as a religiously centered pattern of life . . . the voice of Jewish loyalty and self-acceptance, the voice of Jewish rejoicing in Jewishness." Even addressing himself to the secular Jewish values of a language, therefore, an exponent of the secular viewpoint returns very unashamedly to the religious core of Jewish existence. Religious ethics and morality become embedded in a language. The secular proponents of that language—even as they firmly oppose piety and religion in the commonplace forms—cannot for one instant truly divorce themselves from the religious tradition, and in the end do not really want to.

It is this fact that renders our inquiry so delicate and tentative. On the one hand, Judaic theologians have been willing to argue that religion has functional value because it contributes to the survival of the Jewish people, or is the bearer of certain values or ideas. On the other hand, secularists affirm values and ideas that in any other context would mark them as deeply pious Jews.

In modern times, the classical tradition evolved into an exceptionally complex phenomenon, so that an ethnic religion, dividing like an amoeba, became an ethnicism and a religion in the Western sense. The "religious" part of the tradition, narrowly construed, focused upon the theological component. The "ethnic" part centered upon the messianic and ethical component, if our understanding of Zionism and Jewish Socialism makes sense.

As a concept, Judaism, understood to mean the Jewish religion (a datum to be studied by reference to creed, cult, liturgy, and even law), thus appears as the most modern phenomenon of all. The disintegration of Jewish tradition into Judaism, on the one hand, and Jewishness or culture, on the other, is the direct consequence of the modern experience. It is not, however, that the tradition thus revealed the impact of modernization. Rather, the tradition grew and changed in a growing and changing context.

What has happened to the religiousness of men who either do not express their religiousness formally at all, or, if they do, express it in new, untraditional ways? In so stating the question, we evoke a clear response for Judaism. The tradition persisted in the very same patterns of the past. Its emphasis upon learning was secularized, so that the Jews, who at the end of the nineteenth century were believed to be unable to produce mathematicians and physicists, by the middle of the twentieth century had produced at least a few significant names. More broadly, the intellectual devotion was still present, but it had entered new channels. Study remained central, but *Torah* became a narrow corpus of books rather than a way of life. Intellectualism applied everywhere else.

The messianic hopefulness persisted, but in new ways. The strong stress upon ethical and moral conduct of society received renewed emphasis. The theological suppleness continued; the traditional hesitation to spell out in great and rigid detail what, precisely, it had to say about God characterized modern religious thought as well. Theology, Messianism, and ethics—the three pillars of Jewish tradition in earlier ages—continued strong and firm. But with substantial differences! In Jewish Socialism, the ethical and messianic impulses were divorced from theology. In Reform and Orthodoxy alike, theology parted company from Messianism by so reconstituting the messianic hope as to render it something entirely different from what it had been. Now ancient, supernatural Messianism was transformed into a rather secular nineteenth-century optimistic affirmation of the progress of *this* world and its infinite perfectibility. In Zionism, as Hertzberg so trenchantly argued, the name remained the same, but all else changed. So, depending on how we read it, we see the persistence of forms with changed content and of attitudes with a drastically reshaped rationale and, even, focus. If from one perspective nothing seems to have changed, from another, nothing is the same.

CHAPTER 25

Study of Torah and Modern Scholarship: Yeshiva, Seminary, and University

The fourth case proves the most subtle. In the earlier ones, what was really modern and what was traditional seemed fairly clear. We could isolate the classical forms and the modern substance. In the realm of Jewish intellectualism, by contrast, the powerful impetus of the tradition—which laid tremendous stress upon the study and transmission of sacred texts as an act of religious consequence—and the equally powerful influence of modern Western culture never ceased to play one upon the other.

Had we stood at the threshold of the nineteenth century with a prevision of what was to come, we should have felt some confidence in predicting that the Jews would remain literate in their own holy books. Learning was so important in their lives and values that whatever would happen, they would continue to place the highest value upon the educated person. So it would surely have seemed likely to any observer that whatever else would change, Jewish learning would remain a vital enterprise.

We could not have foreseen what actually happened: The Jews remained as a group deeply devoted to all forms of learning, *except to Jewish learning*. They entered each field of modern science and scholarship as it opened to them—from natural and social science to classics, Romance languages, and finally, English. Their children and grandchildren attended universities and entered the professions if they

125
*Study
of Torah
and
Modern
Scholarship*

were able. Their great-grandchildren became professors in the very universities that fifty years earlier had excluded Jews.

At the same time, the traditional devotion to learning so changed that the one thing Jews ceased to study was the Jewish tradition. In the history of Judaism, we cannot locate a comparable situation in which the Jews so resolutely studied everything but their own sacred texts. The great Jewish physicians of the Middle Ages were also noted doctors of the law. The Jewish astronomers of Babylonia were also—and mainly—teachers of Torah. The masses of every age could read the Hebrew Bible in the original language; recite their prayers and understand the meaning of the Hebrew and Aramaic original; read a book of Jewish thought, broadly construed; and look respectfully upon those who wrote it.

In the Jewish communities of the West today, "the people of the book" has long since forgotten the language in which it is written. In the libraries of "the people of the book" are represented the great literatures of the world, but—if at all—only the most banal and philistine examples of Jewish writing. The expansion of taste came to everything but the Jewish tradition, which was rendered trivial and bourgeois. Experts in many subjects hardly even comprehended the profundity of their ignorance of Judaism in its historical forms. So one may suppose that the tradition of scholarship exhibits, in the end, the most striking phenomenon: the perfect and continuing viability of the intellectual tradition, along with its absolute de-Judaization.

But that is not the whole story of what has happened to Jewish learning. If among the masses the tradition of learning directed itself away from the holy books of Judaism, among the virtuosi a more interesting change took place in the development of the "science of Judaism."

Modern Jewish scholarship emerged, first of all, in Germany where the nascent Reform movement, for essentially theological reasons, committed itself to *Wissenschaft* (science, learning). The motive of the reformers was originally to substantiate their claim that if one could discover the "essence" of Judaism—if one could reach back to the golden time in which the faith was pure and unembellished—then one might find the true *authority* for a reformation; namely, historical precedent. Against the legal precedent of the Orthodox, it was a powerful argument. It motivated the adoption of German science and its methodologies in the service of Jewish theology. Leopold Zunz, an early reformer, made this point quite clear in a letter to M. A. Stern, 8 December, 1857: "I have discovered the one correct method which will both pave the way for historical insight and truly initiate a continued development based on firm foundations."[1]

A second motive was the eagerness of the reformers for gentile acceptance, so powerful a concern of their followers. That acceptance seemed to them more likely in the universities, which were, supposedly, centers of reason and enlightenment. Hence the adoption of university methods of study was important. Zunz never complained that the Orthodox did not read his books. But he did write to Theodor Nöldeke, a great professor of Semitics, that it was strange that the Christian scholars of Germany did not cite his works—that the *Zeitschrift* he edited was not even received by

[margin handwriting:] WISSENSCHAFT LOOKS BACK FOR PRECEDENTS FOR REFORM

the University of Göttingen library. Zunz rightly saw this as "startling evidences of the narrowest kind of prejudice."[2] Whatever tension characterized the early generations of Reform scholars, however, had resolved itself by the end of the nineteenth century, to be replaced by a phenomenon persisting even to this day: the transit from classical *yeshiva*, where Torah is studied as revelation, to university.

That transit, at first characteristic of the Reform movement alone, persisted through the whole era of modernization, and became *the* shaping force in modern Jewish learning from about 1880 to the end of World War II. One generation after another of *yeshiva*-trained students went through the spiritual crisis of deciding that the Talmud did not encompass all worthwhile learning. There were other things worth knowing and doing and better ways to do them.

Of course, many who made such a decision went into other areas of learning entirely; but some—and these are most interesting for our purposes—sought to add to their *yeshiva* training the methods and sciences of the "West," and to achieve a synthesis between the tradition and the "modern world" as they understood it. These came to dominate modern Jewish scholarship in the United States, Israel, and Central Europe before World War II. The absence of traditional training, combined with the presence of spiritual initiation provided by a crisis of faith and conscience in abandoning the *yeshiva*, therefore, were regarded as insuperable obstacles in the path of a Jewish scholar.

We have so far concentrated upon broad social structures, movements, and ideal types. We may consider, finally, how a significant individual exemplified the process of modernization—and suffered from it. He was Louis Ginzberg, professor of Talmud at the Jewish Theological Seminary of America for the first half of the twentieth century, a highly regarded *yeshiva* student in his youth and later, a doctor of philosophy in Semitic philology in a German university. Ginzberg's magnum opus, his commentary on the Palestinian Talmud, was both modern and traditional—that is, modern in its choice of text, for the traditional academies neglected the Palestinian Talmud in favor of the Babylonian one, but modern in little else.

While, to be sure, Ginzberg's extensive philological training led to a new range of questions and interests, the commentary remained just that—*a commentary*—mostly exegetical but always compendious, in which texts were brought to contrast with one another, not in order to make the traditional *hiddush* (new point), but to make something much like it in a modern mode. Stress was laid on finding the right "reading," but traditional doctors of the law were not indifferent to variant readings. The texts were read, by and large, in a fundamentalist spirit. That is, if the text stated that a certain rabbi had issued a decree, it was assumed not only that such a decree was issued, but that it was therefore carried out; stories were not subjected to the kind of higher criticism commonplace in biblical studies, classics, and history.

As in traditional literature, no serious effort was made to organize the data or to spell out in a clear and abstract language the consequences of the

127
*Study
of Torah
and
Modern
Scholarship*

author's research. The only framework of organization was the text itself, just as it was in the traditional schools. No index was provided; nor was any very substantial introduction prepared to explain what the author had contributed, though an elaborate statement about the Palestinian Talmud—in English, unlike the commentary itself—was included. It was paradigmatic, exemplifying the divisions between the traditional and the modern modes in Ginzberg's mind.

Nor should it be thought that the man himself exhibited a more soundly integrated personality. As reported by his son,[3] Ginzberg never fully achieved a separation from the attitudes and affirmations of the *yeshivot* of eastern Europe, by the best of whose products he was trained—and fathered. He is quoted as believing that a Jew should eat *kosher* and think *tref* (i.e., not *kosher*); he should conform to the traditional laws, but preserve the freedom to think in new ways. Orthopraxy is not new in Judaism. What is new is the suspension of intellectual endeavor to unite traditional practice with a new way of understanding the tradition—that is, the effort to integrate faith and practice.

Ginzberg's failure to find some sort of an integrated perception of the faith is most dramatically illustrated by two facts. First of all, toward the end of his life he grew increasingly concerned about the breach his approach and method had caused between his father and his father's father and himself. His son, Eli Ginzberg, reports: "He told me regretfully that he could never have published his *Commentary* during his father's lifetime."[4]

Second, his reaction to a poison-pen letter accusing him of heresy was so utterly out of proportion that a deep-seated ambivalence, resulting in psychosomatic manifestations, became revealed. Within twenty-four hours after reading a perfectly routine piece of vitriol, Ginzberg fell ill with an acute nervous disease, and, his son says: "Although the acute infection subsided after a time, he was left with an aggravated neuralgia which plagued him every day and night until he died."[5]

The despair he felt at the death of his father four decades earlier seems an appropriate foil: "My father was the embodiment of all the noble and great Rabbinical Judaism has produced and his death takes away from me the concreteness of my 'Weltanschauung,' " he wrote.[6] He later said: "I know my poor father did not die peacefully on account of my becoming a scholar instead of a gaon [talmudical sage] and on account of my bachelorship."[7] Shortly afterward he married, but he was never able to retrace the path that had led him from the East.

Louis Ginzberg wrote: "The vitality of an organism is shown in its power of adaptation. Judaism in modern times . . . was confronted with the almost insurmountable difficulty of adapting itself to modern thought. . . . Judaism passed from the fifteenth century into the nineteenth, and this could not take place without a formidable shock. That it withstood this shock is the best proof of the power and energy inherent in Judaism."[8]

Ginzberg himself—making the transition from the scholarly modes of one world to those of another, required by the facts of psychology and the affirmations of theology not to give up the one in the acquisition of the other—more nearly absorbed that shock in his person than others of his day. He seemed more aware of it, suffered more deeply from its effects, and in the end proved unable to preserve health within the tensions it imposed. Those who preceded him, like those who followed, accepted the given as normal. It was he who had to make his way across the abyss between traditional and modern scholarship.

CHAPTER 26

The Unbroken Myth

How are we to interpret the situation of modern Jews? I have suggested that archaic Judaism constituted a rich, mythic structure, realized in important elements in every sort of experience. The issue of modern Judaism is not: Do Jews still *believe* in the old myths? It is, rather: <u>How have the old myths been transformed?</u> Which of them have vanished—that is, ceased to shape the consciousness, the view of reality, of ordinary Jews? And which ones persist into modern times and continue to shape the Jewish interpretation of ordinary events?

What we referred to as "the Jewish tradition" has become, in the felicitous phrase of Professor Ben Halpern "the Jewish consensus." Halpern says:

> If certain laws, rituals, linguistic and literary traditions, together with the myth of Exile and Redemption, were the universal values that bound Jews together, then with their loss the Jewish people should have disintegrated. But these values *were* lost and the Jews did *not* fall apart. In the nineteenth century, values which have been universal among traditional Jewry still continued to be shared—but only by part of the Jews. There were some who no longer shared them, yet these dissenters continued to be regarded as Jews by the remainder who preserved the old values. . . . <u>Apparently there must have been a different "consensus" binding them together—that is, a set of values that were *universally* shared among all the Jews.</u>[1]

<u>What were these values</u>? Halpern denies that it is necessary to define them, for, he points out: "What was the most striking thing . . . about the cohesion and the survival . . . of traditional Jewry? It was the fact that they were united and survived without many of the shared values that are generally believed to hold a normal people together and constitute essential parts of the consensus of comparable groups." Judaism had few dogmas, and the Jewish law and courts were backed by little power or hierarchial authority.

The Jewish concensus was not what it seemed (that they survived ?

*fate
rather
than
faith*

What constituted this inchoate consensus? Halpern sees it in a "community of fate," rather than of "faith." He writes: "Only because they are constantly involved in the consequences of each other's acts need each care what the other wants." It was a consensus, too, of shared sensitivity. The Jews remained what they had been in earlier times: a singular people, not quite like any other; and Judaism, instead of positing a providence receptive to the prayers and responsive to the deeds of Jewry, became instead the repository of those experiences Jews could share in common, however much they differed.

It seems to me, however, that the fundamental mythic structure in important ways is unbroken. Highly secular Jews continue not only to recognize the sociological facts of their group life, but to interpret them as important—that is, worth maintaining and transmitting to their children. Difference is still destiny, still normative and meaningful. And the vast majority of Jews, secular and religious, still continue to respond to this-worldly events through the pattern of the classical Judaic myth.

By way of illustration, let me cite a guidebook—published by the American Jewish Congress, a secular organization—to the monuments and memorials in Europe and Israel in memory of the victims of the Holocaust. The booklet states:

> Why should the vacationer go out of his way to visit the places where European Jewry suffered its catastrophe? Not a vow of hate toward the murderers. Not a feeling of shame that a crime of such enormity should have taken place in our time. Not even the renewed pledge to be a "good Jew" in the future. We want only that the visitor standing at the gate of Dachau or the grave of Bergen Belsen recognize that he too was behind barbed wire; that his own children were led into the gas chamber.[2]

We have here not merely an echo of the Passover liturgy, but rather an authentic example of participation in its existence, in the mythic being that sees people as themselves redeemed from Egyptian bondage, though they live in a free land many centuries later.

Another telling example is the view, held almost universally by Jews, that the events of Europe from 1933 to 1945 and of the Middle East from 1948 to 1969 (and beyond) are interrelated and meaningful in a more than commonplace way. It was not just the killing of millions of people that happened in Europe; not merely the creation of another state in the Middle East. It was a holocaust and a rebirth, the fulfillment of prophecy, interpreted by prophetic teachings about dry bones, the suffering servant, and the return to Zion.

And, as we saw, these same supposedly secular people see *themselves* as having been asphyxiated at Auschwitz and reborn in the State of Israel. They understand their group life in the most recent times as conforming to the paradigm of ancient prophecy. The state is not merely another nation, but the State of *Israel*. Events of the day remain highly charged and full of meaning.

Israelis and European and American Jews alike respond to ordinary happenings in an extraordinary way, and this response, it seems to me, is the very essence of mythic being. Whether we call the myth "religious" or not depends upon our definition of religion; but the phenomenon of contemporary Jewish responses to, and Jewish shaping of, reality constitutes a striking continuation of archaic mythical structures—an exemplification of what it means to live in and by myth.

Let me confess at the end that I have never read the vision of the valley of the dry bones without tears. We Jews were the dry bones in 1945, without hope. We Jews were given sinews, flesh and the breath of life in 1948 and afterward; until, in 1967, we returned to the old Temple wall. And all of this bore immense meaning not only for the religious sector within Jewry, but for millions of secular, assimilated individuals who long had supposed they were part of no particular group, least of all the Jewish one into which they were born.

The myths of old live because no one thinks they are other than accurate and ordinary descriptions of what is true about what happens. What people claim they *know* to be true, not what they profess to *believe*, constitutes the testimony that myth continues to shape their view of reality. That events have meaning, that the only kid yet lives, that the dry bones have risen—these affirmations profoundly shape the contemporary Jewish imagination. As to creation, revelation, and redemption—the complex symbolism that embodies them, and the action-symbols that express them—these too remain, if in subtle ways, central categories by which the world is understood and interpreted. Much has changed, but the people—who began at Sinai to interpret reality *as a people*—that people endures. In the study of the history of religions in postarchaic times, Judaism must occupy a special place, for without the perspective of the history of religions, no one would imagine that today such a phenomenon as Judaism continues at all.

Still, perhaps Judaism does not endure. One might argue that what seems to be a continuity of myth—an abiding effort to interpret events in the light of ancient archetypes of suffering and atonement, disaster and salvation—is really sentimentality. How are we to know whether seeing oneself as saved from Auschwitz is merely practical wisdom or whether it is, as I have argued, to be interpreted as continuing participation in archaic mythical structures? Where does mythic being end and bourgeois nostalgia begin? Perhaps we have dignified the secular and profane artifacts of American–Jewish middle class life by our effort to understand them as something more profound than they really are. We have established no sound, theoretical criterion by which we may separate spurious and cheap emotionalism from exacting and penetrating spirituality.

If archaic piety is the only true piety, then the classic tradition of Judaism endures only within the circles of the archaic orthodox in the State of Israel, Great Britain, the United States, and elsewhere. The larger part of world Jewry, then, cannot be said to constitute a religious group at all, and its cultural and imaginative life supplies no data for the study of religion in modern times. But if that is so, then one must admit modernity excludes the possibility of true religiosity. And such an admission denies the self-understanding of modern people, aware of the abyss between themselves and the classic formulation of their ancient religious traditions, yet nonetheless certain of the authenticity and reality of their religious experience. Are we to take modern people at their word? Then religiosity endures, and with it, the modern modes of Judaic religiosity described here. Perhaps it is too soon to tell, for modernity has been a brief experience, and its full meaning has yet to be deeply and completely apprehended. Meanwhile, we are left with ambiguity and perplexity. God alone knows the truth from fraud.

Notes

CHAPTER 1

1. *Midrash on Psalms* to Ps. 90:3, Louis Ginzberg, *The Legends of the Jews*, trans. by Henrietta Szold (Philadelphia: Jewish Publication Society, 1947), vol. I, p. 3.

2. Gerhard Lenski, *The Religious Factor* (New York: Doubleday, Anchor, 1963), p. 36: "In the case of Judaism we are confronted with a group in which the religious associations have been seriously weakened . . . [but] while the *associational* bond is weak in the Jewish group, the *communal* bond is extremely strong . . . while the ties binding individual Jews to their religious associations have been seriously weakened in modern times, the ties of communalism remain strong."

CHAPTER 2

1. Morton Smith, *Palestinian Parties and Politics That Shaped the Old Testament* (New York: Columbia University Press, 1971), pp. 10–11.

2. Yehezkel Kaufmann, "The Biblical Age," in *Great Ages and Ideas of the Jewish People*, ed. by Leo W. Schwarz (New York: Random House, 1956), pp. 3–93, provides the best brief account of biblical religion.

3. Ibid., p. 15.

4. Ibid., pp. 77*ff.*

5. Gerson D. Cohen, "The Talmudic Age," in *Great Ages and Ideas of the Jewish People*, pp. 143–214, is a helpful introduction.

6. Ibid., p. 154.

7. Wilfred Cantwell Smith, "Traditional Religions and Modern Culture," address at the Eleventh Congress of the International Association for the History of Religions, Claremont, Calif., 9 September 1965. This entire analysis follows Smith's paper, and all quotations are drawn from it. The lecture has now been published in *Proceedings of the XIth International Congress of the International Association for the History of Religions* (Leiden: E. J. Brill, 1968), vol. I, *The Impact of Modern Culture on Traditional Religions*, pp. 55–72.

CHAPTER 3

1.   See Nahum N. Glatzer, *Hillel the Elder: The Emergence of Classical Judaism* (Washington, D.C.: Bnai Brith Hillel Foundations, 1959), pp. 74*ff.*

2.   Judah Goldin, *The Living Talmud: The Wisdom of the Fathers* (New York: Mentor, 1957), p. 95.

3.   Wilfred Cantwell Smith, *The Meaning and End of Religion* (New York: Mentor, 1964), p. 108.

4.   Raphael Loewe, "Defining Judaism: Some Ground-Clearing," *Jewish Journal of Sociology* (London) 7, no. 2 (December 1965):153–75.

5.   Ibid., p. 166.

6.   Ibid., p. 166.

7.   Ibid., p 171.

CHAPTER 4

1.   Frederick J. Streng, *Understanding Religious Man* (Belmont, Calif.: Dickenson Publishing Co., 1968), p. 56.

2.   Ibid., p. 57.

3.   E. P. Sanders, *Paul and Palestinian Judaism* (Philadelphia: Fortress, 1977).

CHAPTER 5

1.   *Weekday Prayer Book*, ed. by the Rabbinical Assembly of America Prayerbook Committee, Rabbi Jules Harlow, Secretary (New York: Rabbinical Assembly, 1962), p. 42.

2.   Ibid., p. 141.

3.   Ibid., pp. 45–56.

4.   Ibid., pp. 50*ff.*

5.   Frederick J. Streng, *Understanding Religious Man* (Belmont, Calif.: Dickenson Publishing Co., 1968), p. 57.

CHAPTER 6

1.   *A Rabbi's Manual*, ed. by Jules Harlow (New York: The Rabbinical Assembly, 1965), p. 45. The "seven blessings" said at a wedding are printed in traditional Jewish prayer books.

2.   I must stress that in classical times the marriage ceremony included provision for bride and groom to consummate their marriage with sexual intercourse while left in private for an appropriate period. Nowadays the privacy is brief and symbolic, to be sure.

1.   Maurice Samuel trans., *Haggadah of Passover* (New York: Hebrew Publishing Co., 1942), p. 9.

2.   Ibid., p. 26.

3.   Ibid., p. 13.

4.   Ibid., p. 27.

5.   *Weekday Prayer Book*, ed. by the Rabbinical Assembly of America Prayerbook Committee, Rabbi Jules Harlow, Secretary (New York: Rabbinical Assembly, 1962), pp. 97–98.

CHAPTER 8

1.   Maurice Samuel, trans., *Haggadah of Passover* (New York: Hebrew Publishing Co., 1942), p. 80. Translation is mine.

2.   *Weekday Prayer Book*, ed. by the Rabbinical Assembly of America Prayerbook Committee, Rabbi Jules Harlow, Secretary (New York: Rabbinical Assembly, 1962), pp. 58–60.

3.   Ibid., pp. 58–60.

CHAPTER 9

1.   Judah Goldin, trans., *The Grace After Meals* (New York: The Jewish Theological Seminary of America, 1955), pp. 9, 15*ff*.

CHAPTER 11

1.   *Weekday Prayer Book*, ed. by the Prayer Book Commission of the Rabinical Assembly of America, Gershon Hadas, Chairman, and Jules Harlow, Secretary (New York: Rabbinical Assembly, 1961), pp. 56–67.

CHAPTER 12

1.   Traditional prayer; author's translation from the Hebrew.

2.   Abraham J. Heschel, *The Sabbath: Its Meaning for Modern Man* (New York: Farrar, Strauss & Young, 1951), p. 8.

3.   Ibid., p. 10.

4.   Hayyim Schauss, *The Jewish Festivals from their Beginnings to Our Own Day* (New York: Union of American Hebrew Congregations, 1938), pp. 40*ff*.

5.   Ibid., pp. 86*ff*.

6.   Traditional prayer; author's translation from the Hebrew.

CHAPTER 13

1. Abraham Z. Idelsohn, *The Ceremonies of Judaism* (New York: National Federation of Temple Brotherhoods, 1930), p. 120.

2. *A Rabbi's Manual*, ed. by Jules Harlow (New York: The Rabbinical Assembly, 1965), p. 96.

3. Idelsohn, *The Ceremonies of Judaism*, p. 133.

CHAPTER 16

1. Abraham S. Halkin, "The Judeo-Islamic Age," in *Great Ages and Ideas of the Jewish People*, ed. by Leo W. Schwarz (New York: Random House, 1956), p. 235.

2. Ibid., pp. 238–39.

3. Ibid., p. 245.

4. Julius Guttmann, *Philosophies of Judaism: The History of Jewish Philosophy from Biblical Times to Franz Rosenzweig*, trans. by David Silverman (New York: Holt, Rinehart & Winston, 1964), p. 158.

5. Ibid., p. 158.

6. Halkin, "The Judeo-Islamic Age," p. 251.

7. Ibid., p. 251.

8. Ibid., pp. 251–52.

9. Alice Lucas, trans., quoted in Bernard Martin, *Prayer in Judaism* (New York & London: Basic Books, 1968), pp. 84–85.

10. Halkin, "The Judeo-Islamic Age," p. 253.

11. Ibid., p. 253.

12. Cited from Isaak Heinemann, "Judah Halevi, Kuzari," in *Three Jewish Philosophers*, ed. by Isaak Heinemann, Alexander Altmann, and Hans Lewy, (Philadelphia: Jewish Publication Society, 1960), p. 33.

13. Ibid., p. 72.

14. Ibid., p. 75.

15. Ibid., p. 75.

16. Ibid., pp. 126–29.

17. Guttmann, *Philosophies of Judaism*, p. 125.

18. Ibid., p. 125.

19. Ibid., p. 126.

20. Frederick J. Streng, *Understanding Religious Man* (Belmont, Calif.: Dickenson Publishing Co., 1968), p. 92.

21. Ibid.

CHAPTER 17

1. Scholom Alchanan Singer, trans., *Medieval Jewish Mysticism: The Book of the Pious* (Northbrook, Ill.: Whitehall Company, 1971), pp. 37–38.

2. Abraham J. Heschel, "The Mystical Element of Judaism," in *The Jews: Their History, Culture, and Religion*, ed. by Louis Finkelstein (New York: Harper & Row, 1971).

4. Ibid., pp. 292–93.

5. Gershom G. Scholem, "Major Trends in Jewish Mysticism," in *Understanding Rabbinic Judaism*, pp. 253–54.

CHAPTER 18

1. Israel Abrahams, *Hebrew Ethical Wills* (Philadelphia: Jewish Publication Society of America, 1948), vol. 2, pp. 207–18.

2. For an excellent account of medieval Jewish life, see Cecil Roth, "The European Age," in *Great Ages and Ideas of the Jewish People*, ed. by Leo W. Schwarz (New York: Random House, 1956), pp. 267–314.

CHAPTER 19

1. Cited from Franz Kobler, *A Treasury of Jewish Letters* (Philadelphia: Jewish Publication Society of America, 1954), vol. 2, pp. 565–67.

2. Cited from "The Jewish Woman, An Anthology," *Response: A Contemporary Jewish Review*, no. 18 (Summer 1973): 76.

CHAPTER 20

1. G. G. Scholem, *Major Trends in Jewish Mysticism* (New York: Shocken, 1961), p. 288.

2. Salo W. Baron, "The Modern Age," in *Great Ages and Ideas of the Jewish People*, ed. by Leo W. Schwarz (New York: Random House, 1956), pp. 313–484.

3. Ibid., p. 317.

4. Raul Hilberg, *The Destruction of the European Jews* (Chicago: Quadrangle, 1961), p. 3.

5. Ibid., p. 17.

6. Ibid., p. 765.

7. The works by Emil Fackenheim, Leo Baeck, A. J. Heschel, and Richard Rubenstein, listed in Suggestions for Further Reading, exemplify theological responses to the Holocaust.

8. Original essay by Richard S. Sarason prepared especially for this book.

9. Ibid.

CHAPTER 21

1. Jacob Katz, *Tradition and Crisis* (New York: The Free Press, 1961.)

2. Ibid., pp. 214–15.

3. Marcus Lee Hansen, "The Problem of the Third Generation Immigrant," *Commentary* 14 (1952): 492–500.

CHAPTER 22

1. Solomon Freehof in his preface to W. Gunther Plaut, *The Rise of Reform Judaism* (New York: World Union for Progressive Judaism, 1963), p. viii.
2. Quoted in Samuel Raphael Hirsch, *Nineteen Letters* (New York: P. Feldheim, 1960).
3. Ibid.
4. Ibid.

CHAPTER 23

1. Joseph L. Blau, *Modern Varieties of Judaism* (New York: Columbia University Press, 1966), p. 121.
2. Ibid., p. 124.
3. Ibid., p. 140.
4. Arthur Hertzberg, *The Zionist Idea* (New York: Doubleday, 1959), pp. 14*ff.*
5. Ibid., p. 20.

CHAPTER 24

1. Charles S. Liebman, "Orthodoxy in American Jewish Life," *American Jewish Yearbook 1966* (Philadelphia: Jewish Publication Society, 1966), pp. 27*ff.*
2. Quoted in Melech Epstein, *Profiles of Eleven* (Detroit: Wayne State University Press, 1965), p. 17.
3. Joseph C. Landis, "Who Needs Yiddish? A Study in Language and Ethics," *Judaism* 13, no. 4 (1964): 1–16.

CHAPTER 25

1. Letter from Zunz to Stern, 8 December 1857, in Max Wiener, *Abraham Geiger and Liberal Judaism: The Challenge of the Nineteenth Century* (Philadelphia: Jewish Publication Society, 1962), p. 121.
2. Ibid., letter from Zunz to Nöldeke, 28 December 1865, p. 127.
3. Eli Ginzberg, *Keeper of the Law: Louis Ginzberg* (Philadelphia: Jewish Publication Society, 1966).
4. Ibid., p. 265.
5. Ibid., p. 266.
6. Ibid., p. 121.
7. Ibid., p. 121.
8. Louis Ginzberg, *Students, Scholars, and Saints* (Philadelphia: Jewish Publication Society, 1928), p. x.

CHAPTER 26

1. Ben Halpern, "The Jewish Consensus," *Jewish Frontier*, September 1962.
2. *In Everlasting Remembrance: A Guide to Memorials and Monuments Honoring the Six Million* (New York: American Jewish Congress, 1969), p. 2.

Glossary

Adon Olam: Lord of the World, hymn containing dogmas of divine unity, timelessness, providence.

aggadah: lit.: telling, narration; generally: lore, theology, fable, biblical exegesis, ethics.

ahavah: love; *Ahavah rabbah*: great love; first words of prayer preceding *Shema.*

Alenu: It is incumbent on us: first word of prayer cited, pp. 19–20.

aliyah: going up; migration to the Land of Israel.

Am HaAres: lit.: people of the land; rabbinic usage: boor, unlearned, not a disciple of the sages.

Amidah: lit.: standing. The main section of obligatory prayers morning, afternoon, and evening, containing eighteen benedictions: (1) God of the fathers; (2) praise of God's power; (3) holiness; (4) prayer for knowledge; (5) prayer for repentance; (6) prayer for forgiveness; (7) prayer for redemption; (8) prayer for healing the sick; (9) blessing of agricultural produce; (10) prayer for ingathering of dispersed Israel; (11) prayer for righteous judgment; (12) prayer for punishment of wicked and heretics; (13) prayer for reward of pious; (14) prayer for rebuilding Jerusalem; (15) prayer for restoration of house of David; (16) prayer for acceptance of prayers; (17) prayer of thanks; (18) prayer for restoration of Temple service; (19) prayer for peace.

amora: rabbinical teacher in Palestine and Babylonia in talmudic times (ca. A.D. 200–500).

Apikoros: Hebrew for Epicurus; generally: belief in hedonism.

Ashkenaz *(im)*: European Jews, those who follow the customs originating in medieval German Judaism.

Ashré: "Happy are they," Psalm 145; read in morning and afternoon worship.

Av, Ninth of: Day of Mourning for destruction of Jerusalem Temple in 586 B.C. and A.D. 70.

Baal Shem Tov (ca. 1700–1760): Master of the Good Name, Founder of Hasidism.

bar mitzvah: ceremony at which thirteen-year-old boy becomes adult member of Jewish community; an adult male Jew who is obligated to carry out the commandments (*mitzvah/mitzvot*).

bat mitzvah: adult female Jew who is obligated to carry out commandments; marked by ceremony as for *bar mitzvah.*

R. J. Zwi Werblowsky and Geoffrey Wigoder, eds., *The Encyclopedia of the Jewish Religion* (New York: Holt, Rinehart & Wilston, 1966) has been consulted throughout.

B.C.E.: before the common era; used in place of B.C.

Berakhah: benediction, blessing or praise.

Bet Am: house of people; early word for synagogue.

Bet Din: court of law judging civil, criminal, religious cases according to *halakhah.*

Bet Midrash: house of study.

Bimah: place from which worship is led in synagogue.

Birkat HaMazon: blessing for food; Grace after Meals.

brit milah: covenant of circumcision; removal of foreskin of penis on eighth day after birth.

C.E.: common era; used instead of A.D.

Central Conference of American Rabbis: association of Reform rabbis.

cohen/kohen: priest.

Conservative Judaism: religious movement, reacting against early Reform; attempts to adapt Jewish law to modern life on the basis of principles of change inherent in traditional laws.

dayyan: judge in Jewish court.

Decalogue: Ten Words; the Ten Commandments (Hebrew: *'Aseret HaDibrot*).

Derekh Eretz: lit.: the way of the land; normal custom, correct conduct; good manners, etiquette.

diaspora: dispersion, exile of Jews from the Land of Israel.

dietary laws: pertaining to animal food; pious Jews may eat only fish that have fins and scales, animals that part the hoof and chew the cud (e.g., sheep, cows, but not camels, pigs). Animals must be ritually slaughtered (Hebrew: *shehitah*), humane method of slaughter accompanied by blessing of thanks. Jews may not eat shellfish, worms, snails, flesh torn from a living animal, etc. Any mixture of meat and milk is forbidden; after eating meat, one may not eat dairy products for a period of time (one to six hours, depending on custom). Fish are neutral (*pareve*). See *kosher.*

El, Elohim: God, divinity.

erev: evening, sunset, beginning of a holy day.

Etrog: citron, one of four species carried in synagogue on *Sukkot,* from Leviticus 23:40, *fruit of a goodly tree.*

exilarch: head of the exile; Aramaic: *Resh Galuta;* head of the Jewish community in Babylonia in talmudic and medieval times.

gaon: eminence, excellency; title of head of Babylonian academies; later on, distinguished talmudic scholar.

Gedaliah, fast of: third day of autumn month of *Tishri,* commemorating assassination of Gedaliah (II Kings 25, Jeremiah 40:1).

Geiger, Abraham (1810–1874): early reformer in Germany; produced modern prayer book; wanted Judaism to become a world religion.

Gemara: completion; comments and discussions of Mishnah. Mishnah + *Gemara* = Talmud.

get: bill of divorce, required to dissolve Jewish marriage.

golus: Ashkenazic pronunciation of *galut:* exile; life in *diaspora;* discrimination, humiliation.

Hadassah: U.S. women's Zionist organization.

Halakhah: "the way things are done," from *halakh:* go; more broadly, the prescriptive, legal tradition.

Haskalah: Jewish Enlightenment, eighteenth-century movement of rationalists.

Hebrew Union College–Jewish Institute of Religion: founded in Cincinnati in 1875; center for training Reform rabbis, teachers; campuses in Los Angeles, Cincinnati, New York City, and Jerusalem.

heder: room; elementary school for early education.

hiddush: novella; new point, insight, given as a comment on classical text. Often ingenious; sometimes hairsplitting.

Hillel: first-century Pharisaic leader; taught, "Do not unto others what you would not have them do unto you."

Hillul HaShem: profanation of God's

name; doing something to bring disrepute on Jews, Judaism—particularly among non–Jews.

Hillul Shabbat: profanation of the Sabbath.

Hol HaMoed: intermediate days of festivals of Passover, *Sukkot.*

huppah: marriage canopy, under which ceremony takes place.

Jehovah: transliteration of Divine name, based on misunderstanding of Hebrew letters YHWH. Jews did not pronounce name of God; referred to the name as *Adonai,* Lord. Translators took vowels of *Adonai* and added them to consonants *JHVH;* hence JeHoVaH.

Jewish Theological Seminary: founded 1888; center for training conservative rabbis, teachers; in New York City, Los Angeles, Jerusalem.

Judah the Prince: head of Palestinian Jewish community, A.D. 200; promulgated Mishnah.

kabbalah: lit.: tradition; later, the mystical Jewish tradition.

kaddish: doxology said at end of principal sections of Jewish service; praise of God with congregational response, "May his great name be praised eternally." Eschatological emphasis; hope for speedy advent of Messiah. Also recited by mourners.

Karaites: eighth- to twelfth-century Middle Eastern Jewish sect; rejected Oral Torah; lived by written one alone.

kehillah: Jewish community.

Keneset Israel: assembly of Israel; Jewish people as a whole.

Keriat Shema: recital of *Shema.*

ketuvah: marriage contract specifying obligations of husband to bride.

Ketuvim: writings; biblical books of Psalms, Proverbs, etc.

kibbutz: collective settlement in State of Israel where property is held in common.

kibbutz galuyyot: gathering together of the exiles; eschatological hope that all Israel will be restored to land; now applied to migration of Jewish communities to State of Israel.

Kiddush: sanctification, generally of wine, in proclamation of Sabbath, festival.

Kiddush HaShem: sanctification of the name of God; applies to conduct of Jews among non–Jews that brings esteem on Jews, Judaism; in medieval times: martyrdom.

Kol Nidré: all vows; prayer opening *Yom Kippur* eve service, declaring that all vows made rashly during the year and not carried out are null and void.

kosher: lit.: fit, proper; applies to anything suitable for use according to Jewish law.

Lag BeOmer: thirty-third day in seven-week period of counting the *Omer,* from second day of Passover to Pentecost (Leviticus 23:15); day of celebration for scholars.

Lamed Vav: thirty-six men of humble vocation not recognized, but by whose merit the world exists; they bring salvation in crisis.

lulav: palm branch used on *Sukkot.*

Maariv: Evening Service.

Magen David: Shield of David; six-pointed star; distinctive Jewish symbol after the seventeenth century.

Mah Nishtannah: "Wherein is this night different from all others," opening words of four questions asked by child at Passover *seder.*

Mahzor: prayer book for New Year and Day of Atonement.

Malkhuyyot: sovereignties, section of New Year Additional Service devoted to theme of God's sovereignty.

Maoz Tsur: "Fortress, Rock of My Salvation"; Hanukkah hymn.

maror: bitter herbs, consumed at Passover *seder* in remembrance of bitter life of slaves.

mashgiah: supervisor of rituals, particularly ritual slaughter; must be expert in laws, pious and God-fearing. Ignorant man, motivated by financial gain, cannot supervise religious rites.

maskil: enlightened man, follower of *Haskalah* (Enlightenment).

masorah: tradition.

matzah: unleavened bread, used for Passover.

mazzal: lit.: constellation, star.

mazzal tov: good luck.

Megillah: scroll; usually, scroll of Esther, read at Purim.

Melavveh Malkah: accompanying the Queen; the Sabbath meal held at end of holy day to prolong Sabbath celebration.

menorah: candelabrum; nine-branched *menorah* is used at *Hanukkah;* seven-branched *menorah* was used in ancient Temple.

Messiah: eschatological king to rule in end of time.

Mezuzah: parchment containing first two paragraphs of *Shema*, rolled tightly and placed in case, attached to doorposts of home.

Midrash: exegesis of Scripture; also applied to collection of such exegeses.

mikveh: ritual bath for immersion to wash away impurity; baptism.

minhah: afternoon prayers.

minyan: number needed for quorum for worship; ten.

Mishnah: code of law promulgated by Judah the Prince (ca. A.D. 200); in six parts, concerning agricultural laws, festival and Sabbath law, family and personal status, torts, damages, and civil law, laws pertaining to the sanctuary and to rules of ritual cleanness.

mitnaged: opponent; opposition to Hasidism on the part of rationalists, talmudists.

mitzvah: commandments; technical sense: scriptural or rabbinical injunctions; later on, also used in sense of good deed; every human activity may represent an act of obedience to divine will.

moed: festival.

mohel: ritual circumciser.

Musaf: additional service on Sabbath and festivals, commemorating additional offering in Temple times.

musar: lit.: chastisement; instruction in right behavior; movement in modern Judaism emphasizing study and practice of ethical traditions, founded by Israel Salanter (1810–1883).

nasi: prince.

navi: prophet.

neder: vow.

Neilah: closing service at end of *Yom Kippur*, at nightfall when fast ends.

niggun: melody, traditional tune for prayer.

Olam Hazeh, Olam Haba: this world, the world to come.

omer: sheaf cut in barley harvest.

Oneg Shabbat: Sabbath delight.

Orthodoxy: traditional Judaism; belief in historical event of revelation at Sinai of Oral and written Torah, in binding character of Torah, and in authority of Torah sages to interpret Torah.

Passover: (Hebrew: *Pesah*) festival commemorating Exodus from Egypt, in spring month of *Nisan* (April).

peot: corners; Leviticus 19:27 forbids removing hair at corners of head, meaning not to cut earlocks.

peshat: literal meaning of Scripture; distinct from *derash*, or homily.

Pharisee: (from Hebrew, *Parush*) separatist; party in ancient Judaism teaching Oral Torah revealed at Sinai along with written one, preserved among prophets and sages down to the Pharisaic party; espoused prophetic ideals and translated them to everyday life of Jewry through legislation. Distinctive beliefs according to Josephus: (1) immortality of the soul; (2) existence of angels; (3) divine providence; (4) freedom of will; (5) resurrection of the dead; (6) Oral Torah.

pilpul: dialectical reasoning in study of oral law.

piyyut: synagogue poetry.

Purim: festival commemorating deliverance of Persian Jews from extermination in fifth century B.C., as related in Scroll of Esther; on 14th of *Adar*, generally in March.

Rava: fourth-century talmudic master, head of Babylonian school at Mahoza.

rabbi: my master; title for teacher of Oral Torah.

Rabbinical Assembly: association of conservative rabbis.

Rabbinical Council: association of Orthodox rabbis in United States.

Rashi: a name for R. Solomon Isaac (1040–1105), composed of *R*abbi *SH*lomo *Y*izhak: *RSHY*; hence, *Rashi.* He was the writer of the most widely consulted of all commentaries on the Bible and Talmud.

Reconstructionism: movement to develop modern, naturalist theology for Judaism; founded by Mordecai M. Kaplan (b. 1881); emphasizes Jewish peoplehood, sees Judaism as natural outgrowth of Jewish people's efforts to insure survival and answer basic human questions.

Reform: religious movement advocating change of tradition to conform to conditions of modern life. Holds *halakhah* to be human creation, subject to judgment of man; sees Judaism as historical religious experience of Jewish people.

Rosh Hashanah: New Year, first day of Tishri (September).

Rosh Yeshivah: head of talmudical academy.

Sabbateanism: Movement of followers of Sabbetai Zevi (1626–1676), messianic leader who became an apostate. Followers believed this apostasy was part of divine plan.

Sabbetai Zevi (1626–1676): Messiah, kabbalist; made mystical revelations; announced himself as Messiah in Smyrna (Turkey) synagogue, 1665; went to Constantinople to claim his kingdom from sultan; was imprisoned; converted to Islam.

Sadducees: sect of Temple priests and sympathizers; stressed written Torah and the right of the priesthood to interpret it against Pharisaic claim that oral tradition held by Pharisees was means of interpretation; rejected belief in resurrection of the dead, immortality of soul, angels, divine providence.

Sanhedrin: Jewish legislative-administrative agency in Temple times.

seder: order; Passover home service.

sefer Torah: Scroll of Torah.

Selihot: penitential prayers, recited before New Year.

semikhah: laying on of hands; ordination.

Sephardi(m): descendants of Spanish Jewry, generally in Mediterranean countries.

shaharit: morning service; dawn.

shalom: peace.

Shammai: colleague of Hillel, first-century Pharisaic sage.

Shavuot: feast of weeks; Pentecost; commemorates giving of Torah at Mt. Sinai.

shehitah: ritual slaughter; consists in cutting through both windpipe and gullet by means of sharp knife, examining to see both have been cut through.

Shekhinah: presence of God in world.

Shema: proclamation of unity of God: Deuteronomy 6:4–9, 11:13–21, Numbers 15:37–41.

Shemini Atzeret: eighth day of solemn assembly (Numbers 30:35); last day of *Sukkot.* This is a holy day in itself.

Sheva Berakhot: Seven Blessings recited at wedding ceremony.

Shiva: seven days of mourning following burial of close relative.

shohet: ritual slaughterer.

shofar: ram's horn, sounded during high holy day period, from a month before New Year until end of *Yom Kippur.*

Shoferot: *Shofar*-verses, concerning revelation, read in New Year Additional Service.

Shulhan Arukh: prepared table; code of Jewish law by Joseph Karo, published 1565; authoritative for orthodox Jewry.

Siddur: Jewish prayer book for all days except holy days.

simhah: celebration.

Simhat Torah: rejoicing of law; second day of *Shemini Atzeret,* on which the Torah-reading cycle is completed; celebrated with song and dance.

sukkah: booth, tabernacle.

Sukkot: autumn harvest festival, ending high holy day season.

synagogue: Greek translation of Hebrew *bet hakeneset* (house of assembly). Place of Jewish prayer, study, assembly.

takkanah: decree, ordinance issued by rabbinical authority.

tallit: prayer shawl, four cornered cloth with fringes (Numbers 15:38) worn by adult males in morning service.

Talmid Hakham: disciple of the wise.

Talmud: Mishnah (above) plus commentary on the Mishnah produced in rabbinical academies from ca. A.D. 200 to 500 (called *Gemara*) form the Talmud. Two Talmuds were produced—one in Palestine, the other in Babylonia. From A.D. 500 onward, Babylonian Talmud was the primary source for Judaic law and theology.

Talmud Torah: study of Torah; education.

Tanakh: Hebrew Bible; formed of Torah, Nevi'im, Ketuvim, Pentateuch, Prophets, Writings; hence, TaNaKh.

tanna: one who studies and teaches; a rabbinical master mentioned in Mishnah is called a *tanna*.

Tehillim: psalms.

tefillin: phylacteries worn by adult males in morning service, based on Exodus 13:1, 11, Deuteronomy 6:4–9, 11:13–21. These passages are written on parchment, placed in leather cases, and worn on left arm and forehead.

tekiah: sounding of *shofar* on New Year.

Teref, terefa: lit.: torn; generally: unkosher food.

Torah: lit.: revelation. At first, the Five Books of Moses; then Scriptures as a whole; then the whole corpus of revelation, both written and oral, taught by Pharisaic Judaism. Talmud Torah: study of Torah. Standing by itself, Torah can mean "study," the act of learning and discussion of the tradition.

Tosafot: novellae on the Talmud, additions generally to the commentary of *Rashi*. The *Tosafists*, authorities who produced *Tosafot*, flourished during the twelfth and thirteenth centuries in northern France.

Tosefta: supplements to the Mishnah.

tzaddik: righteous man; in Hasidism, intermediary, master of Hasidic circle.

tzedakah: righteousness; used for charity, philanthropy.

Tzidduk HaDin: justification of the judgment; prayer of dying man.

tzitzit: fringes of *tallit*.

Wissenschaft des Judentums: science of Judaism; scientific study using scholarly methods of philology, history, and philosophy of Jewish religion, literature, and history; founded in nineteenth-century Germany.

yahrzeit: anniversary of death of relative.

Yahveh: see Jehovah.

Yamim Noraim: Days of Awe; *Rosh Hashanah*, intervening days, and *Yom Kippur*; ten in all.

yeshiva: session; talmudic academy.

Yetzer HaRa, Yetzer Tov: evil inclination, good inclination.

Yiddish: Jewish language of eastern Europe, now used in the United States, Israel, Argentina, and Mexico, in addition to vernacular; originally a Judeo–German dialect, with large number of Hebrew and Slavic words.

Yom Kippur: Day of Atonement; fast day for penitence.

Zikhronot: remembrances, prayers on theme of God's remembering his mercy, covenant, in New Year Additional Service.

Zionism: movement to secure Jewish state in Palestine, founded 1897 by Theodor Herzl.

Zohar: medieval kabbalistic (mystical) book, completed by fourteenth century in Spain; mystical commentary on biblical passages; stories of mystical life of the *tanna*, Simeon b. Yohai.

Suggestions for Further Reading

If you have time to read only one more book, and want to know what is meant to be a Jew in the classical tradition, read Mark Zborowski and Elizabeth Herzog, *Life Is with People* (New York: International Universities Press, 1952). Taking the approach of anthropologists, the authors lead you through the daily life of the traditional villager.

If you can read still a second book, then add an account of classical Judaic theology. Written with love and immense learning, Abraham J. Heschel, *God in Search of Man: A Philosophy of Judaism* (Philadelphia: Jewish Publication Society, 1956) is the single best introduction to the intellectual heritage of Judaism.

My beginning students greatly enjoy James Michener, *The Source* (New York: Random House, 1965), a practically painless way to learn about the whole history of the Jews; and Herman Wouk, *This is My God* (New York: Doubleday, 1959), a warmhearted and enthusiastic account of Judaism by a faithful Orthodox Jew. Despite the fact that both books were best sellers, they remain interesting, generally reliable, and good reading—classics in their own way.

Do not ignore novels about the Jews. Many represent spiritual documents of absolutely fundamental importance for studying Judaism, for they tell, better than historians of religion, theologians, and anthropologists, what "being Jewish" means to sensitive men and women. The book lists that follow do not include novels, for literary critics with interests in the relationship between theology and literature are alone qualified to distinguish among the many novels on Jews and Judaism and to suggest the ones that convey an authentic human truth. By the same token, works by Jewish artists pertaining to Jewish themes require attention; likewise, compositions by Jewish composers for both liturgical and secular situations should be studied with care. Without claiming much knowledge, I should mention the names of the novelists Elie Wiesel and Isaac Bashevis Singer. Ludwig Lewisohn's *The Island Within* (Philadelphia: Jewish Publication Society, 1968) exemplifies how novels serve as profound testimonies to the nature and meaning of Jewish existence. The artists Marc Chagall and Ben Shahn, and the composers Ernest Bloch, Darius Milhaud, and Arnold Schoenberg are among many who have

created art and music out of the datum of, or in response to, "being Jewish."
Sculpture, dance, drama, poetry, cinema, Broadway musicals, operas, and other creative arts—there is no medium of human creativity in which Jews have not expressed themselves *as Jews.*

Books pertinent to the several units and chapters of the present book follow. For reference works, I recommend R. J. Zwi Werblowsky and Geoffrey Wigoder, eds., *The Encyclopedia of the Jewish Religion* (New York: Holt, Rinehart, & Winston, 1966), and the *Jewish Encyclopedia* (repr. New York: KTAV Publishing House, 1965).

PART I: THE HISTORY AND DEFINITION OF JUDAISM

CHAPTERS 1–3

Many one-volume histories of the Jews have been written. Among them Max Margolis and Alexander Marx, *History of the Jewish People* (Philadelphia: Jewish Publication Society, 1953) is most reliable. For modern times, Howard Morley Sachar, *The Course of Modern Jewish History* (New York: Delta, 1963) is both readable and comprehensive. Cecil Roth, *Short History of the Jewish People* (London: East and West Library, 1953), is highly recommended.

Excellent collections of essays have been assembled by Haim H. Ben-Sasson and Leo Schwarz; exceptionally inclusive and of the highest scholarly order is the collection edited by Louis Finkelstein.

For any particular problem from biblical times to the present, Salo W. Baron's works are the starting point: text and notes. Baron has written the greatest comprehensive history of the Jews.

Baron, Salo W. *The Jewish Community.* Philadelphia: Jewish Publication Society, 1942.

——. *Social and Religious History of the Jews,* 16 vols. New York: Columbia University Press, 1952 et seq.

Bridger, David, and Samuel Wolk, eds. *The New Jewish Encyclopaedia,* rev. ed. New York: Behrman House, 1976.

Ben-Sasson, Haim H., et al. *Social Life and Social Values of the Jewish People. Journal of World History,* vol. II. New York: UNESCO, 1968.

Finkelstein, Louis, ed. *The Jews: Their History, Culture, and Religion,* 3rd ed. Philadelphia: Jewish Publication Society, 1960.

Goldin, Judah, ed. *The Jewish Expression: Three Thousand Years of the Jewish Tradition Examined and Interpreted by the Leading Modern Scholars.* New York: Bantam Books, 1970.

Kedourie, Elie, ed. *The Jewish World.* London: Thames and Hudson, 1979.

Schwarz, Leo, ed. *Great Ages and Ideas of the Jewish People.* New York: Random House, 1956.

Waxman, Meyer. *History of Jewish Literature,* 4 vols. New York: Bloch, 1936.

Weiss-Rosmarin, Trude. *Jewish Survival.* New York: KTAV Publishing House, 1978.

Zinberg, Israel. *A History of Jewish Literature,* 12 vols., trans. and ed. by Bernard Martin. New York: KTAV Publishing House, 1972 et seq.

PART II: THE MYTHIC STRUCTURE OF CLASSICAL JUDAISM

CHAPTERS 4–9

Judaic liturgy and the life of piety are to be studied in two ways. First, the classical prayers and ceremonies should be considered, with satisfactory commentaries, in the works of Agnon, Arzt, Birnbaum, Garfiel, Gaster, Idelsohn, Martin, and Schauss. Second, the way in which classical piety shaped the everyday life of ordinary Jews is best described by Zborowski and Herzog, and Dawidowicz. Both books pertain to eastern European Jewry, the primary source of American and Israeli Judaism. Dawidowicz provides a remarkable anthology of the rich and immensely varied life of eastern European Jewry. As I said, Zborowski and Herzog give an integrated, anthropological account of how that life was lived. Heschel writes its obituary.

Agnon, S. Y. *Days of Awe.* New York: Schocken, 1948.

Arzt, Max. *Justice and Mercy.* New York: Holt, Rinehart & Winston, 1967.

Birnbaum, Philip, ed. and trans. *Daily Prayer Book.* New York: Hebrew Publishing Co., 1949.

Dawidowicz, Lucy. *The Golden Tradition.* New York: Holt, Rinehart & Winston, 1968.

Freehof, S. *The Responsa Literature.* Philadelphia: Jewish Publication Society, 1955.

Garfiel, Evelyn. *The Service of the Heart: A Guide to the Jewish Prayerbook.* New York: Yoseloff, 1948.

Gaster, Theodor. *Festivals of the Jewish Year: A Modern Interpretation.* New York: Sloane, 1955.

Gutmann, Joseph. *The Synagogue: Studies in its Origins, Archaeology and Architecture.* New York: KTAV Publishing House, 1975.

Heinmann, Joseph, and Jakob J. Petuchowski, eds. *Literature of the Synagogue.* New York: Behrman, 1976.

Heschel, Abraham J. *The Earth Is the Lord's.* New York: Henry Schuman, 1950.

———. *The Sabbath: Its Meaning for Modern Man.* New York: Farrar, Straus, and Young, 1951.

Idelsohn, Abraham Z. *The Ceremonies of Judaism.* New York: National Federation of Temple Brotherhoods, 1930.

Martin, Bernard. *Prayer in Judaism.* New York: Basic Books, 1968.

Neusner, Jacob. *Between Time and Eternity: The Essentials of Judaism.* Encino, Calif.: Dickenson, 1976.

Samuel, Maurice. *I, the Jew.* New York: Harcourt, Brace, 1927.

Schauss, Hayyim. *The Jewish Festivals.* New York: Union of American Hebrew Congregations, 1938.

———. *The Lifetime of the Jew.* New York: Union of American Hebrew Congregations, 1950.

Scholem, Gershom. *The Messianic Idea in Judaism and Other Essays on Jewish Spirituality.* New York: Schocken Books, 1971.

Siegel, Richard, Michael Strassfeld, and Sharon Strassfeld. *The Jewish Catalog,* 2 vols. Philadelphia: Jewish Publication Society, 1975.

Werblowsky, R. J. Zwi. "Judaism." *Historia Religionum: Handbook for the History of Religions,* ed. by C. Jouco Bleeker and Geo. Widengren. *Religions of the Present,* vol 2. Leiden: E. J. Brill, 1971.

Zborowski, Mark, and Elizabeth Herzog. *Life Is with People.* New York: International Universities Press, 1952.

PART III: THE WAY OF TORAH: A WAY OF LIVING

149
*Suggestions
for
Further
Reading*

The Rabbi and Study of Torah

CHAPTERS 14 AND 15

For the history of the Jews in talmudic times, in addition to the essays in Finkelstein, *The Jews*, and Schwarz, *Great Ages*, by Judah Goldin and Gerson D. Cohen, respectively, these more detailed accounts are of interest: for Palestine, Bickerman and Schürer; for the Hellenistic world, Tcherikover; for Babylonia and Mesopotamia, Neusner.

Bickerman, Elias. *The Maccabees.* New York: Schocken, 1947.

Neusner, Jacob. *History of the Jews in Babylonia,* 5 vols. Leiden: E. J. Brill, 1965–1970.

Schürer, E. *The Jewish People in the Time of Jesus Christ.* Edinburgh: T. & T. Clark, 1898.

Tcherikover, Victor. *Hellenistic Civilization and the Jews.* Philadelphia: Jewish Publication Society, 1959.

The religious life and ideals of the talmudic rabbis are best described by Belkin, Finkelstein (*Pharisees*), Ginzberg, Kadushin, Moore, and Schechter. Particular rabbis' lives are related by Finkelstein (*Akiba*), Glatzer, and Neusner. Rabbinical literature is a vast corpus. Good accounts of the whole are Mielziner and Strack. Montefiore and Loewe provide the best anthology available. Goldin is recommended as a fine example of accurate and elegant translation. Ginzberg's *Legends*, Samuel, and Spiegel give excellent studies of the contents of rabbinic *midrash*, or scriptural study. For Hellenistic Judaism, Wolfson and Goodenough present the greatest Hellenistic Jewish thinker, Philo, and the art and artifacts of Hellenistic Judaism, respectively. Kadushin's *Worship and Ethics* is an exceptional account of the relationship between rabbinic liturgy and rabbinic theology.

The best way to begin is a novel; Milton Steinberg, *As a Driven Leaf* (New York: Behrman House, 1939) has given several generations of readers their first glimpse into the life and mind of the great first- and second-century rabbis. For scholarly purposes, the complex theology is best approached, first of all, in Moore, more simply still in Schechter. For instances of the way in which the abstractions of rabbinic Judaism became concrete in the lives of great masters, the biographies mentioned above should come next. Studies of the literature in translation are best begun in Montefiore and Loewe, a neat and comprehensive arrangement. Translations of the Babylonian Talmud and of the Midrash Rabbah, both published by Soncino Press, London, may also be consulted.

Alon, Gedalyahu. *Jews, Judaism, and the Classical World.* Jerusalem: Magnes, 1977.

Avi-Yonah, M. *The Jews of Palestine: A Political History from the Bar Kokhba War to the Arab Conquest.* Oxford: Blackwell, 1976.

Baeck, Leo. *The Pharisees.* New York: Schocken, 1947.

Belkin, Samuel. *In His Image: The Jewish Philosophy of Man as Expressed in Rabbinic Tradition.* New York: Abelard-Schuman, 1960.

Bickerman, Elias, and Morton Smith. *The Ancient History of Western Civilization.* New York: Harper & Row, 1976.

Buechler, A. *Studies in Sin and Atonement in the Rabbinic Literature of the First Century.* New York: KTAV Publishing House, 1967.

Davies, W. D., ed. *The Cambridge History of Judaism,* 4 vols. Cambridge: Cambridge University Press, 1979.

Finkelstein, Louis. *Akiba: Scholar, Saint, and Martyr.* Philadelphia: Jewish Publication Society, 1962.

——. *The Pharisees,* 2 vols., 3rd ed. Philadelphia: Jewish Publication Society, 1962.

Ginzberg, Louis. *Students, Scholars, and Saints.* Philadelphia: Jewish Publication Society, 1928.

——. *The Legends of the Jews,* 7 vols. Philadelphia: Jewish Publication Society, 1962.

Glatzer, Nahum N. *Hillel the Elder: The Emergence of Classical Judaism.* Washington: Bnai Brith Hillel Foundations, 1959.

Goldin, Judah. *The Living Talmud: The Wisdom of the Fathers.* New York: Mentor, 1957.

Goodblatt, David M. *Rabbinic Instruction in Sasanian Babylonia.* Leiden: E. J. Brill, 1975.

Goodenough, Erwin R. *Jewish Symbols in the Greco–Roman Period,* 13 vols. New York: Pantheon, 1953 et seq.

Green, William Scott, ed. *Approaches to Ancient Judaism.* Missoula, Montana: Scholars Press/Brown Judaic Studies, 1978.

Kadushin, Max. *Worship and Ethics.* Evanston, Ill.: Northwestern University Press, 1964.

Klausner, Joseph. *The Messianic Idea in Israel.* New York: Macmillan, 1955.

Marmorstein, A. *Doctrine of Merits in Old Rabbinical Literature.* New York: KTAV Publishing House, 1969.

Mielziner, Moses. *Introduction to the Talmud.* New York: Bloch, 1969.

Montefiore, C. G., and H. Loewe. *A Rabbinic Anthology.* Philadelphia: Jewish Publication Society, 1963.

Moore, George Foot. *Judaism in the First Centuries of the Christian Era.* Cambridge, Mass.: Harvard University Press, 1954.

Neusner, Jacob. *Early Rabbinic Judaism: Historical Studies in Religion, Literature, and Art.* Leiden: E. J. Brill, 1975.

——. *First-Century Judaism in Crisis: Yohanan ben Zakkai and the Renaissance of Torah.* Nashville: Abingdon Press, 1975.

——. *A History of the Mishnaic Law of Purities,* 22 vols. Leiden: E. J. Brill, 1974–1977.

——. *A History of the Mishnaic Law of Holy Things,* 6 vols. Leiden: E. J. Brill, 1979.

——. *A History of the Mishnaic Law of Women,* 5 vols. Leiden: E. J. Brill, 1980.

——. *A Life of Yohanan ben Zakkai.* Leiden: E. J. Brill, 1962, 1970.

——. *Development of a Legend: Studies on the Traditions Concerning Yohanan ben Zakkai.* Leiden: E. J. Brill, 1970.

——, ed. *The Formation of the Babylonian Talmud.* Leiden: E. J. Brill, 1970.

——. *From Politics to Piety: The Emergence of Pharisaic Judaism.* Englewood Cliffs, N.J.: Prentice-Hall, 1973. KTAV, 1979.

——. *Invitation to the Talmud.* New York: Harper & Row, 1973.

——, ed. *The Modern Study of the Mishnah.* Leiden: E. J. Brill, 1972.

——. *The Rabbinic Traditions about the Pharisees before 70,* 3 vols. Leiden: E. J. Brill, 1971.

——. *Talmudic Judaism in Sasanian Babylonia.* Leiden: E. J. Brill, 1976.

———. *There We Sat Down: The Story of Classical Judaism in the Period in Which It Was Taking Shape.* Nashville: Abingdon Press, 1972. KTAV, 1977.

Samuel, Maurice. *Certain People of the Book.* New York: Knopf, 1955.

Sanders, E. P. *Paul and Palestinian Judaism.* Philadelphia: Fortress, 1977.

Sanders, James A. *Torah and Canon.* Philadelphia: Fortress, 1972.

Schechter, Solomon. *Some Aspects of Rabbinic Theology.* New York: Behrman House, 1936.

Schürer, Emil. *The History of the Jewish People in the Age of Jesus Christ. A New English Edition,* revised and edited by Geza Vermes, Fergus Millar, and Pamela Vermes. Edinburgh: T. & T. Clark, 1973.

Spiegel, Shalom. *The Last Trial.* New York: Pantheon, 1968.

Strack, Herman L. *Introduction to the Talmud and Midrash.* Philadelphia: Jewish Publication Society, 1931.

Urbach, Ephraim E. *The Sages: Their Concepts and Beliefs.* Jerusalem: Magnus Press, 1975.

Vermes, Geza. *The Dead Sea Scrolls: Qumran in Perspective.* Cleveland, Ohio: World, 1978.

Wolfson, Harry. *Philo.* Cambridge, Mass.: Harvard University Press, 1947.

The Philosopher and Mystic: The Ordinary Jew in Medieval Times

CHAPTERS 16–19

For the history of medieval Jewish philosophy, both Husik and Guttmann are thoroughly reliable. Philosophical texts may be consulted in Altmann. For important medieval rabbinical lawyers (and, in the case of the latter, mystics), Twersky and Werblowsky are of the highest scholarly order. The cultural, social, and economic life of ordinary Jews is revealed in Abrahams, Goitein, and Trachtenberg. The history of Spanish and German Jewry is found in Baer and Lowenthal. The rabbinic interpretation of Jewish history is illustrated in the text edited and brilliantly expounded by Gerson D. Cohen. Other figures of historical interest are described in Netanyahu and Stern. Mysticism, ending in Hasidism, is discussed in Scholem and Buber; see Mintz and Newman for stories of the Hasidim; and, for the *taddik,* Dresner. The life of the community is to be studied in Baron, cited above, and Jacob Katz.

Abrahams, Israel. *Hebrew Ethical Wills.* Philadelphia: Jewish Publication Society, 1948.

———. *Jewish Life in the Middle Ages.* Philadelphia: Jewish Publication Society, 1958.

Altmann, Alexander et al., eds. *Three Jewish Philosophers.* Philadelphia: Jewish Publication Society, 1960.

Baer, Yizhak. *History of the Jews in Christian Spain,* 2 vols. Philadelphia: Jewish Publication Society, 1961.

Blumenthal, David. *Understanding Jewish Mysticism.* New York: KTAV Publishing House, 1978.

Buber, Martin. *Tales of the Hasidim.* New York: Schocken, 1966.

Chazan, Robert, ed. *Church, State, and Jew in the Middle Ages.* New York: Behrman, 1976.

———, ed. *Medieval Jewish Life: Studies from the Proceedings of the American Academy of Jewish Research.* New York: KTAV Publishing House, 1976.

Cohen, Gerson D., trans. *The Book of Tradition.* Philadelphia: Jewish Publication Society, 1968.

Cohen, Seymour J., trans. *The Ways of the Righteous*. New York: Feldheim, 1969.

Dan, Joseph, ed. *Readings in Hasidism*. New York: Behrman, 1979.

Dresner, Samuel H. *The Zaddik*. New York: Abelard-Schuman, 1960.

Goitein, S. D. *Jews and Arabs: The Contacts through the Ages*. New York: Schocken, 1955.

——. *A Mediterranean Society*, 2 vols. Berkeley and Los Angeles: University of California Press, 1967, 1970.

Guttmann, Julius. *Philosophies of Judaism*. New York: Holt, Rinehart & Winston, 1964.

Heinemann, Benno. *The Maggid of Dubno and his Parables*. New York: Feldheim, 1967.

Husik, Isaac. *History of Mediaeval Jewish Philosophy*. Philadelphia: Jewish Publication Society, 1948.

Hyamson, Moses., trans. *Duties of the Heart by R. Bachya ibn Paquda*. New York: Feldheim, 1968.

Jacobs, Louis. *Hasidic Prayer*. New York: Schocken, 1973.

Katz, Jacob. *Tradition and Crisis*. Glencoe, Ill.: Free Press, 1961.

Lampel, Zvi L., trans. *Maimonides: Introduction to the Talmud*. New York: Judaica Press, 1975.

Langer, Jiri. *Nine Gates to the Chassidic Mysteries*. New York: Behrman, 1976.

Lowenthal, Marvin. *The Jews of Germany*. New York: Harper, 1936.

Mann, Jacob. *The Jews in Egypt and in Palestine under the Fatimid Caliphs*, with Preface and Reader's Guide by Shelomo D. Goitein. New York: KTAV Publishing House, 1970.

Mintz, Jerome R. *Legends of the Hasidim*. Chicago: University of Chicago Press, 1968.

Netanyahu, B. Z. *Don Isaac Abravanel*. Philadelphia: Jewish Publication Society, 1968.

Neusner, Jacob. *Understanding Rabbinic Judaism*. New York: KTAV, 1974.

Newman, Louis I. *The Hasidic Anthology*. New York: Schocken, 1963.

Oschry, Leonard, trans. *Ahavath Chessed by the Chofetz Chaim*. New York: Feldheim, 1966.

Rabinowitz, A. H., trans. *Menorath HaMaor by Rabbi Isaac Aboah*. New York: Feldheim, 1965.

Scholem, Gershom G. *Major Trends in Jewish Mysticism*. New York: Schocken, 1961.

——. *On the Kabbalah and Its Symbolism*. New York: Schocken, 1965.

Silverstein, Shraga, trans. *The Gates of Repentence by R. Jonah ben Avraham of Gerona*. New York: Feldheim, 1967.

——, trans. *The Path of the Just by R. Moshe Chayim Luzzatto*. New York: Feldheim, 1967.

Stern, Selma. *Josel of Rosheim: Commander of Jewry in the Holy Roman Empire of the German Nation*. Philadelphia: Jewish Publication Society, 1965.

Trachtenberg, Joshua. *Jewish Magic and Superstition*. Philadelphia: Jewish Publication Society, 1961.

Twersky, Isidore. *Rabad of Posquieres*. Cambridge, Mass.: Harvard University Press, 1962.

——. *A Maimonides Reader*. New York: Behrman House, 1972.

Weinbach, Mendel, ed. *Who Wants to Live: 101 Mesholim of the Chofetz Chaim*. Jerusalem: Nachat Publications, 1968.

Werblowsky, R. J. Z. *Joseph Karo, Lawyer and Mystic*. Oxford: Oxford University Press, 1962.

Wigoder, Geoffrey, trans. *The Meditation of the Sad Soul by Abraham Bar Hayya.* New York: Schocken Books, 1969.

153
*Suggestions
for
Further
Reading*

PART IV: CONTINUITY AND CHANGE IN MODERN TIMES

History of the Jews in Modern Times

CHAPTERS 20 AND 26

The general history of Sachar may be supplemented by Hertzberg for modern France to the French Revolution; Glazer (below) and Learsi and Karp for the United States; Halkin and Spiegel for the rebirth of the Hebrew language in Europe and Israel. Steinberg gives the best account of the impact of anti–Semitism on modern Jews. Rotenstreich and Meyer offer solid historical accounts of German Judaism; these are to be supplemented by the items listed below in the section on Judaic theology.

Albert, Phyllis Cohen. *The Modernization of French Jewry: Consistory and Community in the Nineteenth Century.* Hanover, N.H.: Brandeis University Press, 1977.

Elazar, Daniel J. *Community and Polity: The Organizational Dynamics of American Jewry.* Philadelphia: Jewish Publication Society, 1976.

Feingold, Henry L. *Zion in America: The Jewish Experience From Colonial Times to the Present.* New York: Hippocrene, 1974.

Halkin, Simon. *Modern Hebrew Literature.* New York: Schocken, 1950.

Hertzberg, Arthur. *The French Enlightenment and the Jews.* Philadelphia: Jewish Publication Society, 1967.

Karp, Abraham J., ed. *The Jewish Experience in America,* 5 vols. New York: KTAV Publishing House, 1969.

Learsi, Rufus. *The Jews in America.* Cleveland: World, 1954.

Liebman, Charles S. *The Ambivalent American Jew.* Philadelphia: Jewish Publication Society, 1973.

Mahler, Raphael. *A History of Modern Jewry.* New York: Schocken Books, 1971.

Meyer, Michael A. *The Origins of the Modern Jew.* Detroit: Wayne State University Press, 1967.

Rotenstreich, Nathan. *Jewish Philosophy in Modern Times.* New York: Holt, Rinehart & Winston, 1968.

Sachar, Howard. *The Course of Modern Jewish History.* New York: World Publishing Co., 1958.

Spiegel, Shalom. *Hebrew Reborn.* New York: Macmillan, 1930.

Steinberg, Milton. *Partisan Guide to the Jewish Problem.* Indianapolis: Bobbs-Merrill, 1945.

Yerushalmi, Yosef Hayim. *From Spanish Court to Italian Ghetto. Isaac Cardoso: A Study in Seventeenth-Century Marranism and Jewish Apologetics.* New York: Columbia University Press, 1971.

Anti-Semitism and the Holocaust; Christianity

CHAPTERS 20 AND 21

Hannah Arendt's account of anti–Semitism is sophisticated, generalized. Flannery, Hilberg, Poliakov, Reitlinger, and Trachtenberg give more specific data on anti–Semitism through the ages, the facts of the destruction of European Jewry and related matters. Glatstein's anthology provides texts on the Holocaust.

For relationships between Judaism and Christianity, see Baeck and Schoeps and again Flannery and Poliakov. Baeck is highly polemical in the German philosophical context. Schoeps gives a detailed historical account. These should be supplemented by Malcolm Hay, *Europe and the Jews* (also published as *The Foot of Pride* [Boston: Beacon, 1960]).

Abel, Ernest L. *The Roots of Anti-Semitism.* New Jersey: Association of University Presses, 1945.

Arendt, Hannah. *Origins of Totalitarianism.* New York: Meridian, 1958.

Baeck, Leo. *Judaism and Christianity.* Philadelphia: Jewish Publication Society, 1958.

Brod, Max. *Paganism-Christianity-Judaism: A Confession of Faith.* University: University of Alabama Press, 1970.

Cohen, Arthur A. *The Myth of the Judeo-Christian Tradition.* New York: Harper & Row, 1970.

Dawidowicz, Lucy S., ed. *A Holocaust Reader.* New York: Behrman House, 1975.

————. *The War Against the Jews, 1933–1945.* New York: Holt, Rinehart & Winston, 1975.

Flannery, Edward. *The Anguish of the Jews.* New York: Macmillan, 1965.

Forster, Arnold, and Benjamin Epstein. *The New Anti-Semitism.* New York: McGraw-Hill, 1974.

Glatstein, Jacob, Israel Knox, and Samuel Margoshes. *Anthology of Holocaust Literature.* Philadelphia: Jewish Publication Society, 1969.

Higham, John. *Send These To Me: Jews and Other Immigrants in Urban America.* New York: Atheneum, 1975.

Hilberg, Raul. *The Destruction of the European Jews.* Chicago: Quadrangle, 1961.

Mocatta, Moses, trans. *Faith Strengthened by Isaac ben Abrahm of Troki.* Introduction by Trude Weiss-Rosmarin. New York: KTAV Publishing House, 1970.

Morse, Arthur D. *While Six Million Died: A Chronicle of American Apathy.* New York: Ace Books, 1968.

Neusner, Jacob. *Aphrahat and Judaism: The Christian-Jewish Argument in Fourth-Century Iran.* Leiden: E. J. Brill, 1970.

Oesterley, W. O. E. et al. *Judaism and Christianity.* New York: KTAV Publishing House, 1969.

Poliakov, Leon. *Harvest of Hate: The Program for the Destruction of the Jews of Europe.* New York: Vanguard, 1965.

Reinharz, Jehuda, *Fatherland or Promised Land.* Ann Arbor, Mich.: University of Michigan Press, 1975.

Reitlinger, Gerald. *The Final Solution.* New York: Beechhurst, 1953.

Rosenstock-Huessy, Eugen, ed. *Judaism Despite Christianity: The 'Letters on Christianity and Judaism' between Eugen Rosenstock-Huessy and Franz Rosenzweig.* University: University of Alabama Press, 1969.

Rotenstreich, Nathan. *The Recurring Pattern.* London: Weidenfeld and Nicholson, 1963.

Schoeps, Hans Joachim. *The Jewish-Christian Argument: A History of Theologies in Conflict.* New York: Holt, Rinehart & Winston, 1963.

Steiner, Jean-Francois. *Treblinka.* New York: New American Library, Signet Books, 1967.

Trachtenberg, Joshua. *The Devil and the Jews: The Medieval Conception of the Jew and Its Relation to Modern Anti-Semitism.* Philadelphia: Jewish Publication Society, 1943.

CHAPTER 22

General introductions to modern Judaic theology include those of Rotenstreich and Meyer, cited above, as well as Agus (*Evolution*), Blau, and Cohen. Blau is easiest; Cohen the most sophisticated. For an anthology of writings, Glatzer gives substantial readings in ancient, medieval, as well as modern Judaism; it is certainly the best single anthology.

Agus (*Banner*) and Herbert Wiener (*Wild Goats*, cited below) give some insight into modern Israeli Orthodoxy; for Germany, see Glenn and Hirsch; and for the United States, Liebman on the sociology of American Orthodoxy, and the excellent essays in Stitskin for theology and law. Conservative Jewish writings are represented by Schechter and Ginzberg, anthologized by Waxman; the conservative movement is described by Sklare; Kaplan, Miller, and Steinberg give the reconstructionist viewpoint. The Reform movement is studied by Meyer, (cited above) and, for modern Germany, Albert Friedlander on Leo Baeck; for Reform's nineteeth-century beginnings, see Petuchowski, Plaut, Max Wiener, and Philipson. On contemporary mysticism, Herbert Weiner is reliable and engaging.

Contemporary Judaic theology by Reform rabbis includes Baeck, Borowitz, Fackenheim, Petuchowski, and the writers in the anthology by Wolf. Jewish existentialism begins with Glatzer on Rosenzweig, proceeds to Baeck, Buber, Herberg, and Heschel. But Heschel should be read as a masterful expositor of traditional theology, starting with Rothschild. Psychoanalytically oriented theology is found in Rubenstein, who stands alone and apart. Bakan offers an interesting hypothesis. The secular viewpoint occurs in Greenberg and Kallen. American Jewish life is described in Sklare's anthology, and shown in all its vitality in Elliot Cohen's collection of essays.

Each of these writers has produced more than the items listed here. Extensive bibliographies are given in most of the books listed.

The beginner should start with Blau's brief and lucid account, and then proceed, according to the themes he or she finds of greatest interest, with both descriptive accounts of movements in modern Judaism and the writings of individual theologians and ideologists.

Journals: Contemporary Judaic theologians frequently write in the following journals: *Dimensions, Judaism, Journal of the Central Conference of American Rabbis, Jewish Observer, Tradition, Reconstructionist, Jewish Spectator, Moment,* and *Conservative Judaism.* Zionist thought (below) appears in *Midstream, American Zionist,* and *Jewish Frontier. Congress BiWeekly* and *Commentary* print studies of contemporary Jewish thought and life and review books on modern Jewish themes, particularly literature, politics, and sociology. Scholarship in Judaica will be found in *Hebrew Union College Annual, Proceedings of the American Academy of Jewish Research, American Jewish History Quarterly, Jewish Quarterly Review, Jewish Social Studies, American Jewish Archives, Journal of Jewish Studies* as well as in journals in Oriental studies, religion and theology, and Bible. Most Jewish communities are served by local English–Jewish weeklies. The better ones are the *Boston Jewish Advocate, Chicago Jewish Sentinel, Heritage* (Los Angeles), *Jewish News* (Newark), *Philadelphia Jewish Exponent, Jewish Week* (New York) and, best of all in the United States, *Baltimore Jewish Times.* The viewpoint of more traditional Orthodoxy is in the *Jewish Observer.* The best Jewish newspaper in English is The *Jewish Chronicle* (London).

Agus, Jacob. *Banner of Jerusalem: The Life, Times, and Thought of Abraham Isaac Kuk.* New York: Bloch, 1946.

——. *The Evolution of Jewish Thought.* New York: Abelard-Schuman, 1959.

Alter, Robert. *After the Tradition.* New York: Dutton, 1968.

Baeck, Leo. *The Essence of Judaism.* New York: Schocken, 1948.

——. *This People Israel.* New York: Holt, Rinehart & Winston, 1964.

Bakan, David. *Sigmund Freud and the Jewish Mystical Tradition.* New York: Van Nostrand, 1958.

Bermant, Chaim. *Troubled Eden: An Anatomy of British Jewry.* New York: Basic Books, 1970.

Blau, Joseph L. *Judaism in America.* Chicago: University of Chicago Press, 1976.

——. *Modern Varieties of Judaism.* New York: Columbia University Press, 1966.

Borowitz, Eugene B. *A New Jewish Theology in the Making.* Philadelphia: Westminster, 1968.

——. *Reform Judaism Today,* 3 vols. New York: Behrman, 1978.

Buber, Martin. *On Judaism.* New York: Schocken, 1968.

Cohen, Arthur A. *The Natural and Supernatural Jew: An Historical and Theological Introduction.* New York: McGraw-Hill, 1962.

——, ed. *Arguments and Doctrines: A Reader of Jewish Thinking in the Aftermath of the Holocaust.* Philadelphia: Jewish Publication Society, 1970.

——. *In the Days of Simon Stern.* New York: Random House, 1973.

Cohen, Elliot E., ed. *Commentary on the American Scene.* New York: Knopf, 1953.

Diamond, Malcolm L. *Martin Buber: Jewish Existentialist.* New York: Oxford, 1960.

Fackenheim, Emil L. *God's Presence in History: Jewish Affirmations and Philosophical Reflections.* New York: New York University Press, 1970.

——. *Quest for Past and Future.* Bloomington: University of Indiana Press, 1968.

Friedlander, Albert. *Leo Baeck: Teacher of Theresienstadt.* New York: Holt, Rinehart & Winston, 1968.

Gay, Peter. *Freud, Jews and Other Germans: Masters and Victims in Modernist Culture.* New York: Oxford, 1978.

Ginzberg, Eli. *Keeper of the Law: Louis Ginzberg.* Philadelphia: Jewish Publication Society, 1966.

Glatzer, Nahum N. *Franz Rosenzweig: His Life and Thought.* Philadelphia: Jewish Publication Society, 1962.

——. *The Judaic Tradition.* Boston: Beacon, 1965.

Glazer, Nathan. *American Judaism.* Chicago: University of Chicago Press, 1957.

Glenn, Menahem G. *Israel Salanter: The Story of a Religious-Ethical Current in Nineteenth-Century Judaism.* New York: Bloch, 1953.

Goodman, Saul L. *The Faith of Secular Jews.* New York: KTAV Publishing House, 1976.

Greenberg, Gershon, ed. *Modern Jewish Philosophies.* New York: Behrman, 1979.

Greenberg, Hayim. *The Inner Eye.* New York: Jewish Frontier, 1953.

Hadas, Moses, ed. *Solomon Maimon: An Autobiography.* New York: Schocken Books, Inc., 1967.

Herberg, Will. *Judaism and Modern Man.* Philadelphia: Jewish Publication Society, 1951.

Heschel, Abraham J. *God in Search of Man: A Philosophy of Judaism.* Philadelphia: Jewish Publication Society, 1955.

——. *A Passion for Truth.* New York: Farrar, Straus, and Giroux, 1973.

Hirsch, Samson R. *The Nineteen Letters.* New York: Feldheim, 1960.

Isaacs, Harold R. *Idols of the Tribe: Group Identity and Political Change.* New York: Harper & Row, 1975.

Janowsky, Oscar I., ed. *The American Jew: A Reappraisal.* Philadelphia: Jewish Publication Society, 1964.

Jospe, Alfred, ed. *Jerusalem and Other Jewish Writings by Moses Mendelssohn.* New York: Schocken, 1969.

———, ed. *Tradition and Contemporary Experience.* New York: Schocken Books, 1970.

Jospe, Eva, ed. and trans. *Reason and Hope: Selections from the Jewish Writings of Hermann Cohen.* New York: W. W. Norton & Co., 1971.

Kahn, Lothar. *Mirrors of the Jewish Mind: A Gallery of Portraits of European Jewish Writers of Our Time.* New York: Thomas Yoseloff, 1968.

Kallen, Horace M. *The Liberal Spirit.* Ithaca, N.Y.: Cornell University Press, 1948.

Kaplan, Mordecai. *The Future of the American Jew.* New York: Reconstructionist, 1948.

———. *A New Zionism.* New York: Herzl, 1955.

———. *The Purpose and Meaning of Jewish Existence* [an epitome and commentary on Hermann Cohen's *Rational Religion in the Life of the Source-Material of Judaism*]. Philadelphia: Jewish Publication Society, 1964.

Kaufman, William E. *Contemporary Jewish Philosophies.* New York: Behrman, 1976.

Leiman, Six Z., ed. *Jewish Moral Philosophy.* New York: Behrman, 1979.

Lewisohn, Ludwig. *What Is This Jewish Heritage?* New York: Bnai Brith Hillel Foundations, 1954.

Liebman, Charles S. "Orthodoxy in American Jewish Life." *American Jewish Year Book 1966.* Philadelphia: Jewish Publication Society, 1966.

———. "Reconstructionism in American Jewish Life." *American Jewish Year Book 1970.* New York: American Jewish Committee, 1971.

———. "The Training of American Rabbis." *American Jewish Year Book 1968.* New York: American Jewish Committee, 1968.

Martin, Bernard, ed. *Contemporary Reform Jewish Thought.* Chicago: Quadrangle, 1968.

———, trans. *Lev Shestov: Athens and Jerusalem.* New York: Simon and Schuster, 1968.

Memmi, Albert. *The Liberation of the Jew.* New York: Orion Press, 1966.

Meyer, Michael A., ed. *Ideas of Jewish History.* New York: Behrman, 1974.

Miller, Alan W. *God of Daniel S.* New York: Macmillan, 1968.

Neusner, Jacob. *The Academic Study of Judaism,* 2 vols. New York: KTAV Publishing House, 1975, 1977.

———. *American Judaism: Adventure in Modernity.* Englewood Cliffs, N.J.: Prentice Hall, 1972. KTAV, 1972.

———. *Contemporary Judaic Fellowship.* New York: KTAV Publishing House, 1972.

———. *History and Torah: Essays on Jewish Learning.* New York: Schocken, 1965.

———. *Judaism in the Secular Age.* New York: KTAV, 1969.

———, ed. *Understanding American Judaism: Toward the Description of a Modern Religion.* (*The Synagogue and the Rabbi,* vol. I, and *The Sectors of American Judaism: Reform, Orthodoxy, Conservatism, Resontructionism,* vol. II). New York: KTAV Publishing House, 1975.

———. *Understanding Jewish Theology.* New York: KTAV Publishing House, 1973.

———.Petuchowski, Jacob J. *Ever Since Sinai*. New York: Scribe, 1961.

———. *Heirs of the Pharisees*. New York: Basic Books, 1970.

———. *Prayerbook Reform in Europe*. New York: World Union for Progressive Judaism, 1969.

Philipson, David. *The Reform Movement in Judaism*. New York: KTAV Publishing House, 1969.

Plaut, W. Gunther. *The Rise of Reform Judaism*. New York: World Union for Progressive Judaism, 1963.

Raphael, M. L., ed. *Understanding American Judaism*. (*Jewish Philanthropy in America*, vol. 3.) New York: KTAV Publishing House, 1979.

Rawidowicz, Simon. *Studies in Jewish Thought*, ed. by N. Glatzer. Philadelphia: Jewish Publication Society, 1974.

Raz, Simcha. *A Tzaddik in Our Time: The Life of R. Aryeh Levin*. Jerusalem: Feldheim, 1976.

Rischin, Moses. *The Promised City: New York's Jews, 1870–1914*. New York: Harper Torchbooks, 1970.

Rosenberg, Stuart E. *The Search for Jewish Identity in America*. New York: Anchor Books, 1965.

Rosenbloom, Noah H. *Tradition in an Age of Reform: The Religious Philosophy of Samson Raphael Hirsch*. Philadelphia: Jewish Publication Society, 1976.

Rosenthal, Gilbert. *Four Paths to One God: Today's Jew and His Religion*. New York: Bloch, 1973.

Roth, Leon. *Judaism: A Portrait*. New York: Viking, 1961.

Rothschild, Fritz A. *Between God and Man: An Interpretation of Judaism from the Writings of Abraham J. Heschel*. New York: Harper, 1959.

Rubenstein, Richard A. *After Auschwitz*. Indianapolis: Bobbs-Merrill, 1966.

———. *The Religious Imagination: A Study in Psychoanalysis and Jewish Theology*. Indianapolis: Bobbs-Merrill, 1969.

Sandmel, Samuel. *The Several Israels, And an Essay: Religion and Modern Man*. New York: KTAV Publishing House, 1971.

Schechter, Solomon. *Studies in Judaism*. Philadelphia: Jewish Publication Society, 1958.

Schorsch, Ismar, ed. *Heinrich Graetz: The Structure of Jewish History and Other Essays*. New York: KTAV Publishing House, 1975.

Schwab, Hermann. *The History of Orthodox Jewry in Germany*. London, 1950.

Sigal, Philip. *The Emergence of Contemporary Judaism*. Pittsburgh: Pickwick Press, 1977.

Sklare, Marshall. *America's Jews*. New York: Random House, 1971.

———. *Conservative Judaism*. Glencoe, Ill.: Free Press, 1955.

——— and Joseph Greenblum. *Jewish Identity on the Suburban Frontier: A Study of Group Survival in the Open Society*. New York: Basic Books, 1967.

———, ed. *The Jews: Social Patterns of an American Group*. Glencoe, Ill.: Free Press, 1958.

———, ed. *The Sociology of the American Jew*, 2 vols. New York: Behrman, 1976.

Sleeper, James A., and Alan L. Mintz, eds. *The New Jews*. New York: Vintage Books, 1971.

Steinberg, Milton. *The Making of the Modern Jew*. Indianapolis: Bobbs-Merrill, 1934.

———. *Basic Judaism*. New York: Harcourt, Brace, 1947.

Stitskin, Leon, ed. *Studies in Torah Judaism*. New York: KTAV Publishing House, 1969.

Van den Haag, Ernest. *The Jewish Mystique*. New York: Dell, 1969.

Waxman, Mordecai. *Tradition and Change*. New York: Burning Bush Press, 1958.

Weiner, Herbert. *9½ Mystics: The Kabbala Today*. New York: Holt, Rinehart & Winston, 1969.

Weiner, Max. *Abraham Geiger and Liberal Judaism*. Philadelphia: Jewish Publication Society, 1962.

Wolf, Arnold Jacob, ed. *Rediscovering Judaism: Reflections on a New Theology*. Chicago: Quadrangle, 1965.

Zionism and the State of Israel

CHAPTER 23
Hertzberg's anthology gives substantial selections from all important Zionist ideologists. Fein describes the State of Israel. Weiner's account of religious life in Israel today, comprehending Christians, various sorts of Jews, and Moslems, is not only reliable and informative, but also a beautiful spiritual document in its own right. Spiro on the *kibbutz* is a masterful study. Buber's Zionism cannot be neglected. Sachar is the best history.

Alter, Robert, ed. *Modern Hebrew Literature*. New York: Behrman, 1975.

Buber, Martin. *Israel and Palestine*. London: East and West, 1952.

——. *Israel and the World*. New York: Schocken, 1963.

Dubnow, Simon. *Nationalism and History*, ed. by K. S. Pinson. Philadelphia: Jewish Publication Society, 1958.

Elon, Amos. *Herzl*. New York: Holt, Rinehart & Winston, 1975.

——. *The Israelis: Founders and Sons*. New York: Holt, Rinehart & Winston, 1971.

Fein, Leonard J. *Israel: Politics and People*. Boston: Beacon, 1967.

Halkin, Hillel. *Letters to an American Jewish Friend: A Zionist's Polemic*. Philadelphia: Jewish Publication Society, 1977.

Halpern, Ben. *The American Jew: A Zionist Analysis*. New York: Herzl Press, 1956.

——. *The Idea of the Jewish State*. Cambridge, Mass.: Harvard University Press, 1970. Second edition.

Hertzberg, Arthur. *The Zionist Idea*. New York: Herzl Press, 1959.

Kahler, Erich. *The Jews among the Nations*. New York: Frederick Ungar Publishing Co., 1967.

Laqueur, Walter. *A History of Zionism*. New York: Holt, Rinehart & Winston, 1972.

Naamani, Israel T., David Rudavsky, and Abraham I. Katsch. *Israel: Its Politics and Philosophy*. New York: Behrman, 1977.

Sachar, Howard. *A History of Israel*. New York: Knopf, 1977.

Singer, Howard. *Bring Forth the Mighty Men: On Violence and the Jewish Character*. New York: Funk and Wagnalls, 1969.

Spiro, Melford E. *Kibbutz: Adventure in Utopia*. New York: Schocken, 1963.

Weiner, Herbert. *The Wild Goats of Ein Gedi*. New York: Doubleday, 1961.

Jewish Socialism

CHAPTER 24
The Jewish labor movement in the United States is described by Epstein; in Poland, by Johnpoll. For a secular Jewish viewpoint, see the essays by Deutscher. Liebman gives the best account of Jews and political liberalism.

Deutscher, Isaac. *The Non–Jewish Jew and Other Essays.* New York: Oxford, 1968.

Epstein, Melech. *Jewish Labor in USA: An Industrial, Political, and Cultural History of the Jewish Labor Movement, 1882–1914.* New York: Trade Union Sponsoring Committee, 1950.

Goodman, Saul L., ed. *The Faith of Secular Jews.* New York: KTAV Publishing House, 1977.

Johnpoll, Bernard K. *The Politics of Futility: The General Jewish Workers Bund of Poland, 1917–1943.* Ithaca, N.Y.: Cornell University Press, 1967.

Levin, Nora. *While Messiah Tarried: Jewish Socialist Movements, 1871–1917.* New York: Schocken, 1977.

Liebman, Charles S. "Toward a Theory of Jewish Liberalism." *The Religious Situation 1969,* ed. by Donald R. Cutler. Boston: Beacon, 1969.

Portnoy, Samuel A. *Vladimir Medem: The Life and Soul of a Legendary Jewish Socialist.* New York: KTAV Publishing House, 1977.

Study of Torah and Modern Scholarship

CHAPTER 25

There is little literature at this time on modern Jewish intellectual history as done by Jewish intellectuals. Gay's essay on Freud shows the Jew in the non–Jewish intellectual world; Schorsch's on Graetz shows the Jew speaking to Jews. The only studies of Jewish learning in diverse settings are mine.

Gay, Peter. *Freud, Jews, and Other Germans.* New York: Oxford, 1977.

Neusner, Jacob. *The Academic Study of Judaism.* New York: KTAV Publishing House, 1975.

——. *The Academic Study of Judaism: Second Series.* New York: KTAV Publishing House, 1977.

Schorsch, Ismar. *Heinrich Graetz: The Structure of Jewish History and Other Essays.* New York: KTAV Publishing House, 1975.

Index

Acculturation. *See* Assimilation
Agricultural festivals: 60–61
Amemar: 69
Anti-Semitism: 19, 24; political emancipation, 101–02; Zionism, 117–18
Ashi, R.: 72
Assimilation: 5; civil rights for Jews, 100–01; modernization of Judaism, 110–15

Bar Kokhba: 11
Bar mitzvah: 64–65
Bathsheba: 91
Benedictions: 53–57
Ben Sira: 13
Biblical period, Judaic history: 7–12
Birth, circumcision: 64–65
Blake, William: 116
Blau, Joseph L.: 116

Circumcision: 64–65
Civil rights, emancipation of Jews: 100–02
Classical Judaism: creation account, 3–4, 7; festivals, mythic structure of Judaism, 39–45; Judaism, defined, 23; law, adherence to, 51–52; mythic structure of, 29–48; mystics, 81–86; Passover, mythic structure of Judaism, 39–45; philosophy, 72–80; redemption and Passover, 39–45; Sabbaths and festivals, 58–63; Torah study, center of life, 66–69
Classical period, rabbinic Judaism: 7, 12–16, 18–19
Confession, onset of death: 65

Coulanges, Fustel de: 117
Creation account: 3–4, 7; mythic structure of Judaism, 30–35; Sabbath observance, 58–63; *Shema,* 32–35

David, King of Israel: 8
Day of Atonement: 61–62
Days of Awe: 61–62
Death, confession and onset of death: 65
Deborah: 91
Dreyfus, Alfred: 117

Eighteen Benedictions: 53–57
Eleazar of Mainz: 87; ethical wills, 92, 122
Elijah, the Gaon of Vilna: 82
Emancipation, civil rights: 100–02
Enlightenment: Jewish Enlightenment, 104–06; secular, 100
Esther: 91–92
Eternal Fund of Israel: 118
Eternal Fund for the World to Come: 118
Ethical wills: 87–90, 122; women, 88–89, 92–94
Ettlinger, Jacob: 113
Exile: effect of, 16; prayer for gathering exiles, 54
Exodus from Egypt: 8; messianic hope, 42–45; Passover, 35, 39–45
Ezekiel, vision of: 43–44
Ezra: 10

Feast of Weeks: 60–61
Festivals: agricultural festivals, 60–61;

Day of Atonement, 61–62; Days of
Awe, 61–62; Eighteen Benedictions,
53–57; Feast of Tabernacles, 61;
Feast of Weeks, 60–61; mythic struc-
ture of Judaism, 39–45; New Year,
61–62; Passover, 60; Pentecost,
60–61; rejoicing, 58–63; *Rosh
Hashanah*, 61–62; *Shavuot*, 60–61;
Sukkot; 61; *Yom Kippur*, 61–62
Forgiveness, prayer of: 54
Freehof, Solomon: 111

General Jewish Workers Bund: 109
Ginzberg, Eli: 127
Ginzberg, Louis: 126–28
Glückel of Hameln: 92
Great Awakening: 105

Habakkuk, Judaism defined: 22
Hadassah: 94
Halakhah, adherence to law: 51–52
Halevi, Judah: 77–80
Halpern, Ben: 129–30
Hansen, Marcus Lee: 108
Hasidism: 16, 105–06
Hebrew scriptures: 7–20; historic
periods, 7–12; Judaism defined, 23
Hertzberg, Arthur: 118, 123
Herzl, Theodor: 18; Zionism and
Messianism, 99–100, 117–18
Heschel, Abraham J.: 59–60, 83–85
Hilberg, Raul: 101–02
Hillel: 21–22
Hirsch, Samson Raphael: 113–14
Holocaust: mythic structure transfor-
mations, 130–31; political emancipa-
tion, 101–02
Humility, prayer of: 55

Isaiah, Judaism defined: 22
Israel, State of: 18–20; Judaism
defined, 24; mythic structure transformations, 130–31

Jerusalem: destruction of, 8–9; redemp-
tion, 46–48; Second Temple, 10
Jew, Jewishness, defined: 21–26
Jewish Enlightenment: 16, 19, 104–06
Jewish National Fund: 118
Jewish socialism: 108–09; Judaism
replaced by, 121; law and ethics, 108,
120–23

Judaism: biblical period, 7–12; classical
Judaism, mythical structure, 29–48;
classical period, 7, 12–16; defined,
21–26; development of, 3–6; Jewish
socialism replacing, 121; modernization of Judaism, 99–132; modern
period, 7, 16–20; scholarship and
Torah study, 109, 124–28; talmudic,
classical period, 12–18
Judaist, defined: 21–26

Kantor, J. L.: 121
Karen Kayemet le-Olam HaBa: 118
Karen Kayemet Le-Yisrael: 118
Karo, Joseph: 82
Katz, Jacob: 104–05

Labor: Jewish socialism, 109, 120–23
Landis, Joseph C.: 122
Law, adherence to: 51–52
Leon, Moses de: 81
Liebman, Charles S.: 121
Loewe, Raphael: 24–25

Maimonides, Moses: 75–77, 79
Marriage blessings: 36–38
Mar Zutra: 68–69
Maturity, *bar mitzvah:* 64–65
Mesharsheya, R.: 69
Messianism: Judaic development,
11–12, 14–15, 18–20; messianic
hope, 42–45; modernization of
Judaism, 98, 108; Sabbetai Zevi,
99–103; Theodor Herzl, 99–100;
Zionism, 99–103; Zionism and
nationality, 108, 116–19
Micah, Judaism defined: 22
Miriam: 91
Mishnah, rabbinic Judaism: 13–14
Modernization of Judaism: 99–132
Modern period: tradition and culture,
16–17
Myth: classical Judaism and mythic
structure, 29–48; *Shema*, mythic
structure of Judaism, 32–35
Mythic structure of Judaism: creation
32–35; marriage blessings, 36–38;
Passover, 39–45; redemption, 34–35;
revelation, 33–35; transformations,
129–32
Mysticism, rabbinic Judaism: 12–13,
15–16, 18

Mystics: 81–86; Abraham J. Herschel, 83–85; Judah Halevi, 77–80

Nachmanides: 82
Nathan of Gaza: 99
New Year festival: 61–62
Nöldeke, Theodor: 125
Nordau, Max: 118

Oral Torah: 13–14; study, center of life, 66–69
Orthodox Judaism: American, 20; Israeli, 20; modernization of Judaism, 108, 110–15; Zionism, 118

Passover: festival, rejoicing, 60; mythic structure of Judaism, 39–45
Pentecost: 60–61
Philippson, Ludwig: 116
Philosophy: classical Judaism, 72–80; Judah Halevi, 77–80; rabbinic Judaism, 12–13, 16
Political emancipation: 100–02
Prayer, Eighteen Benedictions: 53–57
Priesthood, Judaic development: 11–15
Procreation of life: 52
Puberty, *bar mitzvah:* 64–65

Rabbinic Judaism: classical period, 7, 12–16, 18–19; salvation, 67
Rabbinical academies: 70–72; women in, 92
Rabina: 69
Rava: 51–52, 72
Redemption: land and Jerusalem, 46–48; mythic structure of Judaism, 30–31, 34–35; Passover, 39–45; Sabbath observance, 58–63
Reform Judaism: modernization of Judaism, 108, 110–15; scholarship and Torah study, 125; Zionism, 118
Repentence, prayer of: 54
Revelation: Sabbath observance, 58–63; law, adherence to, 51–52; mythic structure of Judaism, 30–31, 33–35
Rosh Hashanah: 61–62
Ruth: 91–92

Sabbetai Zevi: 18; Messianism, 99–103
Sabbath observance: 58–63
Salvation: 67

Sanders, E. P.: 30
Sarason, Richard S.: 102
Scholarship: modernization of Judaism and Torah study, 100, 109, 124–28
Scholem, Gershom G.: 85–86, 99
Schools and rabbis: 70–72
Scribes: Judaic development, 11–15; rabbinic Judaism, 13–15
Secular enlightenment: 100
Shavuot: 60–61
Shema: 32–35
Shulhan Arukh: 82
Simlai, R.: 22
Smith, Morton: 7
Smith, Wilfred Cantwell: 16–17, 23
Social ethics: Jewish socialism, 108–09, 120–23
Socialism, Jewish socialism: 108–09
Stern, M. A.: 125–26
Streng, Frederick J.: 29–30, 80
Sukkot: 61
Szold, Henrietta: 94

Theology: modernization of Judaism, 108, 110–15
Torah study, modernization of Judaism: 109, 124–28
Tradition: and culture, 16–17; mythic structure of classical Judaism, 29–48; *Shema,* 32–35
Traditional Judaism: modernization of Judaism, 99–132; mythic structure transformations, 129–32; scholarship and Torah study, 109, 124–28

Wills: ethical wills, 87–90, 122; women and ethical wills, 92–94
Women: 91–92; ethical wills, 88–89, 92–94; Henrietta Szold, 94–95; rabbinical schools, 92; role of, 69; Zionism, 94
Women's Zionist Movement: 94
Written Torah: 13–14; study, center of life, 66–69

Yeshiva and rabbis: 70–72; women in, 92
Yohanan ben Zakkai: 8, 10, 22
Yom Kippur: 61–62

Zionism: anti-Semitism, 117–18; Henrietta Szold, 94; Jewish socialism,

120–23; land and Jerusalem, 46–48;
Messianism, 99–103, 108, 116–19;
modern Judaism, 18–20, 108;
Orthodox Judaism, 118; Reform
Judaism, 118; Theodor Herzl,
99–100; women's movement, 94
Zohar: 81–82
Zunz, Leopold: 125

Biblical References:
Deuteronomy 6:5–9, 34; 11:13–21, 34;
30:19, 83
Ezekiel 37, 43;
Genesis 1:1–4, 3; 1:26, 15
Habakkuk 2:4*ff*, 22
Hosea 6:6*ff*, 10
Isaiah 9:1–6, 44; 11:1–10, 44; 14:5, 69;
30:20*ff*, 69; 32:1–5, 44; 33:6, 52;

33:25–26*ff*, 22; 56:1*ff*, 22
Jeremiah 33:10–11, 38
I Kings 19:10–14, 64
Leviticus 19:15, 83; 19:18, 21
Micah 6:8*ff*, 22
Numbers 15:37–41, 34
Psalms 15*ff*, 22; 19:8–11, 85; 49:6, 82;
90:12*ff*, 69; 102:14–15*ff*, 79; 126,
47; 137, 37

Babylonian Talmudic References:
Bava Batra 12(*a*), 69
Eruvin 53(*a*), 72
Keritot 6(*a*), 69
Makkot 24(*a*), 22
Shabbat 31(*a*), 21, 52; 139(*a*), 69
Sotah 22(*a*), 71